Expert Android Programming

Master skills to build enterprise grade Android applications

Prajyot Mainkar

BIRMINGHAM - MUMBAI

Expert Android Programming

First published: September 2017

Production reference: 1270917

Published by Packt Publishing Ltd.
Livery Place
35 Livery Street
Birmingham
B3 2PB, UK.

ISBN 978-1-78646-895-6

www.packtpub.com

Credits

Author
Prajyot Mainkar

Reviewer
Nanik Tolaram

Commissioning Editor
Smeet Thakkar

Acquisition Editor
Shweta Pant

Content Development Editor
Aditi Gour

Technical Editor
Ralph Rosario

Copy Editor
Dhanya Baburaj

Project Coordinator
Ritika Manoj

Proofreader
Safis Editing

Indexer
Rekha Nair

Graphics
Jason Monteiro

Production Coordinator
Shantanu Zagade

About the Author

Prajyot Mainkar is the Founder-Director of Androcid, a mobile app development company based out of Goa, India. He is an android developer with experience of working on Android development since Android's Froyo edition. Prajyot is also the chairman of Goa Chamber of Commerce & Industry's IT committee. Androcid was one of the winners of Goa CM's Startup Award for the year 2017.

Prajyot is one of the few Intel Innovators in the country and has been a speaker at more than 300 Android developer conferences across the globe, some of the prominent ones being Droidcon Greece and Android Developer Days In Turkey.

Prajyot has always been passionate about teaching and was instrumental in building the Android ecosystem in India during the early stage of Android penetration in India by forming one of the premier Android communities in India--The Goa Android User's Group under the Google Developer community. He is passionate about teaching Android development and has been one of the drivers of introducing Android as curriculum at the Goa University, which became one of the earliest Indian-based universities to have the curriculum for Android development.

Recently, Prajyot was awarded as the young entrepreneur of the year by Business Goa and one of the leading portals in India marked him as one of the top techies in India. He has been a mentor to more than 100 companies, and he is part of India's one of the leading start up incubation centers--Startup Village--as a tech mentor of mobile development.

Popularly known as *Android Man of Goa*, Prajyot is a professional technology blogger and a columnist on several portals and print media specially focusing on Smartphone trends.

He considers exploring new places as one of his passions and loves watching tennis. He loves to play chess and tennis.

Specialties:Android Developer,Android Consultancy,Android Programming, Mobile Startups, and Mobile app Development.

Firstly, I would like to thank my parents, Mr. Prakash V Mainkar and Mrs. Shital P. Mainkar for inspiring me to write this book. Their constant motivation and support has always been the key in this book journey. I would also like to thank the Androcid Team (Mr. Laximan Chodankar and Mr. Vishal Vernekar) for always being there to support me, and without whom this book would quite possibly not have happened. The team brings out the best in you, and this book is just one such result.

I would also like to thank all the mentors and teachers who have been part of my life. Their teachings have always been the key DNA for what I am today.

About the Reviewer

Nanik Tolaram works as senior Android platform engineer for BlocksGlobal in Australia, where he is responsible for developing Screener (screener.digital) and Lumin (`mylumin.org`). He is passionate about Android and is very active within both the local and international Android developer community--from talks and teaching, to writing articles for ODROID open source magazine (`magazine.odroid.com`). In his spare time, he loves tinkering with electronics and studying human psychology and behavior. He lives in Sydney, Australia, with his lovely wife and two beautiful boys.

www.PacktPub.com

For support files and downloads related to your book, please visit www.PacktPub.com.

Did you know that Packt offers eBook versions of every book published, with PDF and ePub files available? You can upgrade to the eBook version at www.PacktPub.com and as a print book customer, you are entitled to a discount on the eBook copy. Get in touch with us at service@packtpub.com for more details.

At www.PacktPub.com, you can also read a collection of free technical articles, sign up for a range of free newsletters and receive exclusive discounts and offers on Packt books and eBooks.

https://www.packtpub.com/mapt

Get the most in-demand software skills with Mapt. Mapt gives you full access to all Packt books and video courses, as well as industry-leading tools to help you plan your personal development and advance your career.

Why subscribe?

- Fully searchable across every book published by Packt
- Copy and paste, print, and bookmark content
- On demand and accessible via a web browser

Customer Feedback

Thanks for purchasing this Packt book. At Packt, quality is at the heart of our editorial process. To help us improve, please leave us an honest review on this book's Amazon page at https://www.amazon.com/dp/1786468956.

If you'd like to join our team of regular reviewers, you can e-mail us at customerreviews@packtpub.com. We award our regular reviewers with free eBooks and videos in exchange for their valuable feedback. Help us be relentless in improving our products!

Table of Contents

Preface

Introduction

The book deep dives into understanding the design, develop, and distribute mechanism of building restaurant discovery app features that can be served "hot" to the end users. The book highlights key elements of building the app using Google's Material Design guidelines. Building for performance is one of the aspects of a good app, and we have it covered in this book. We will wrap up the book with how to publish to the Google Play Store.

What this book covers

Chapter 1, *Understanding Gradle*, teaches developers how to prepare Android Studio and its components for development. The developers will use Android Nougat 7.0 Edition for development.

Chapter 2, *Exploring Android Studio Developer Tools*, explains that over the years, Android Studio has received a lot of productivity updates. This chapter highlights how in-house tools will get the best of productivity while building restaurant discovery app features.

Chapter 3, *Leap into Android Support Library*, focuses on Android N. Understanding support library will offer a number of features that are not built into the framework. Using support libraries will provide backward compatibility with the previous versions, providing some useful UI element support.

Chapter 4, *Google Play Services*, enables developers to harness the latest APIs for Google services used in food discovery apps such as Google Maps and Google Login.

Chapter 5, *Material Design*, explains that material design is almost over two years old now. Understanding design principles and implementing them in the key features of the restaurant discovery app are covered in this chapter.

Chapter 6, *SOLID Android Development and its Design Principles*, informs the readers that Android apps often have complex interactions among application logic, UI views, data models and controllers, and networking. This calls for a strong architecture planout. In this chapter, there are more insights into SOLID Android architecture patterns.

Chapter 7, *Understanding MVC, MVP, MVVM, and Clean Arch pattern,* covers building a clean architectural pattern while building the app.

Chapter 8, *Decision making,* focuses on which is the development architecture followed while developing food discovery app and reasoning for the same.

Chapter 9, *Performance Matters,* we will discussed how performance, impacts the app quality, followed by in ways by which we can target different elements of app performance such as UI, and resources such as the battery. We also discussed the tools that we can use to improve the app performance.

Chapter 10, *Building Restaurant finder,* in this we will understand the core techniques of coding the different components and screens of the Zomato app by yourself. After reading these topics, you understood what are the components required to develop certain sections on a screen. Once you get a hold of these components, they can be reused in other screens with similar requirements.

Chapter 11, *Backend Service,* looks at the development life cycle as having three different phases: development, testing, and distribution. The first of these is building an app and having the stuff you need to develop and support the app, which we have done in the earlier chapters. The firebase will allow us to have the backend in place. It also sports Cloud Messaging, which lets you deliver messages and notifications reliably at no cost.

Chapter 12, *App Quality Service,* helps developers understand how Firebase's services can assist developers improve app quality. Firebase Test Lab for Android enables developers to catch bugs before ship. The apps can be tested on physical devices hosted in Google's data centers.

Chapter 13, *Grow Up,* says that Admob supports a number of engaging formats, including video, natics, and interstitial ads. This chapter will help developers understand ads, Firebase dynamic links, and app indexing.

Chapter 14, *Testing,* assists developers in testing the entire app flow and improving the tests of the app. It will also highlight the best practices for testing and supported tools.

Chapter 15, *Preparing for Google Play,* focuses on how to prepare the store listing for the app.

Chapter 16, *Understanding App Store Analytics for Optimization,* helps understand industry-followed best practices for App Store optimization.

What you need for this book

Developers will be required to work with some of the following software:

- Java
- Android Studio IDE
- Firebase

Who this book is for

This book is for mobile developers having some expertise in building android apps and who wish to now take a leap into building app features that are part of restaurant spotting app using the Android Nougat of Google.

Conventions

In this book, you will find a number of text styles that distinguish between different kinds of information. Here are some examples of these styles and an explanation of their meaning.

Code words in text, database table names, folder names, filenames, file extensions, pathnames, dummy URLs, user input, and Twitter handles are shown as follows: Here, `jsouza` is the user John Souza's uid. So, to fetch his details the path would be `;/users/jsouza`.

A block of code is set as follows:

```
A block of code is set as follows:
[default]
exten => s,1,Dial(Zap/1|30)
exten => s,2,Voicemail(u100)
exten => s,102,Voicemail(b100)
exten => i,1,Voicemail(s0)
```

When we wish to draw your attention to a particular part of a code block, the relevant lines or items are set in bold:

```
[default]
exten => s,1,Dial(Zap/1|30)
exten => s,2,Voicemail(u100)
exten => s,102,Voicemail(b100)
exten => i,1,Voicemail(s0)
```

Any command-line input or output is written as follows:

```
# cp /usr/src/asterisk-addons/configs/cdr_mysql.conf.sample
/etc/asterisk/cdr_mysql.conf
```

New terms and important words are shown in bold. Words that you see on the screen, for example, in menus or dialog boxes, appear in the text like this: "Firebase is a cloud based **backend-as-a-service** (**BaaS**) service provided by Google that provides a structural way to save your data very efficiently and also retrieve it at much faster speeds."

Warnings or important notes appear in a box like this.

Tips and tricks appear like this.

Reader feedback

Feedback from our readers is always welcome. Let us know what you think about this book-what you liked or disliked. Reader feedback is important for us as it helps us develop titles that you will really get the most out of.

To send us general feedback, simply email feedback@packtpub.com, and mention the book's title in the subject of your message.

If there is a topic that you have expertise in and you are interested in either writing or contributing to a book, see our author guide at www.packtpub.com/authors.

Customer support

Now that you are the proud owner of a Packt book, we have a number of things to help you to get the most from your purchase.

Downloading the example code

You can download the example code files for this book from your account at `http://www.packtpub.com`. If you purchased this book elsewhere, you can visit `http://www.packtpub.com/support` and register to have the files emailed directly to you.

You can download the code files by following these steps:

1. Log in or register to our website using your email address and password.
2. Hover the mouse pointer on the **SUPPORT** tab at the top.
3. Click on **Code Downloads & Errata**.
4. Enter the name of the book in the **Search** box.
5. Select the book for which you're looking to download the code files.
6. Choose from the drop-down menu where you purchased this book from.
7. Click on **Code Download**.

Once the file is downloaded, please make sure that you unzip or extract the folder using the latest version of:

- WinRAR / 7-Zip for Windows
- Zipeg / iZip / UnRarX for Mac
- 7-Zip / PeaZip for Linux

The code bundle for the book is also hosted on GitHub at `https://github.com/PacktPublishing/-Expert-Android-Programming`. We also have other code bundles from our rich catalog of books and videos available at `https://github.com/PacktPublishing/`. Check them out!

Downloading the color images of this book

We also provide you with a PDF file that has color images of the screenshots/diagrams used in this book. The color images will help you better understand the changes in the output. You can download this file from `https://www.packtpub.com/sites/default/files/downloads/ExpertAndroidProgramming`.

Errata

Although we have taken every care to ensure the accuracy of our content, mistakes do happen. If you find a mistake in one of our books-maybe a mistake in the text or the code-we would be grateful if you could report this to us. By doing so, you can save other readers from frustration and help us improve subsequent versions of this book. If you find any errata, please report them by visiting `http://www.packtpub.com/submit-errata`, selecting your book, clicking on the **Errata Submission Form** link, and entering the details of your errata. Once your errata are verified, your submission will be accepted and the errata will be uploaded to our website or added to any list of existing errata under the Errata section of that title.

To view the previously submitted errata, go to `https://www.packtpub.com/books/content/support` and enter the name of the book in the search field. The required information will appear under the **Errata** section.

Piracy

Piracy of copyrighted material on the Internet is an ongoing problem across all media. At Packt, we take the protection of our copyright and licenses very seriously. If you come across any illegal copies of our works in any form on the Internet, please provide us with the location address or website name immediately so that we can pursue a remedy.

Please contact us at `copyright@packtpub.com` with a link to the suspected pirated material.

We appreciate your help in protecting our authors and our ability to bring you valuable content.

Questions

If you have a problem with any aspect of this book, you can contact us at `questions@packtpub.com`, and we will do our best to address the problem.

1
Understanding the Gradle System

Google introduced Gradle and Android Studio in order to help make the development process more streamlined. They wanted to ensure that it becomes easier for developers to reuse code and also help them create build variants with ease. Having it closely integrated with an IDE such as Android Studio ensured that Gradle has a good IDE integration without making the build system dependent on the IDE.

In this chapter, we will discuss:

- Setting up Gradle in Android Studio
- Dependent libraries to be used in Android Studio, including Identifiers

If you have been using Eclipse, it's likely that some of you won't know of any alternative to the default APK generation technique within the IDE. But, as such as alternative, you can do this using the command line. The Android build system compiles app resources and source code, and packages them into APKs that you can test, deploy, sign, and distribute.

Stepping into the Gradle world

Gradle is an open source build automation system that is based on the Apache ANT and Maven concept. It introduces a Groovy-based **Domain Specific Language** (**DSL**) instead of the XML which is primarily used by Apache Maven for declaring the project configuration. Gradle was designed keeping in mind the support for multi-project builds which grow to be quite a large size, and it supports incremental builds. Gradle does this by understanding which parts of the build tree are up to date.

This ensures that tasks dependent on those parts will not be re-executed. Gradle determines which tasks need to be run and in which order, using **Directed Acyclic Graph** (**DAG**).

Gradle can automate the building, testing, publishing, deployment, and more of software packages or other types of projects. Using the combination of the power and flexibility of ANT and the dependency management and conventions of Maven, Gradle helps to build in a more effective manner.

First, let's get familiarized with the Gradle environment inside Android Studio. To do that we should first create a new Android Project. I assume you have Android Studio installed by now. Here is the link in case you wish to know more about the install: `https://developer.android.com/studio/install.html`

Now that you have the Android Studio installed, we will first create a new project,

Open Android Studio, create a **New Project**, and give a name to your project as seen in the following figure:

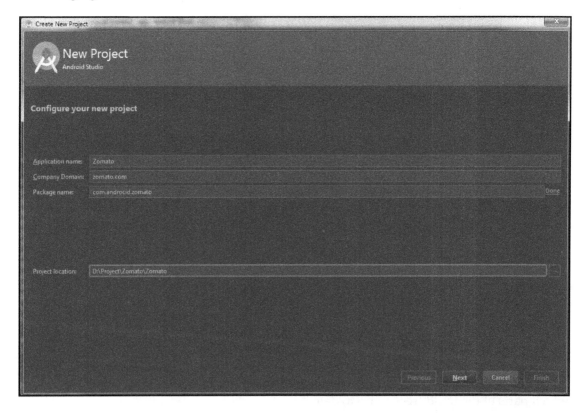

At the **Target Android Devices** screen, without making any changes, just click on **Next:**

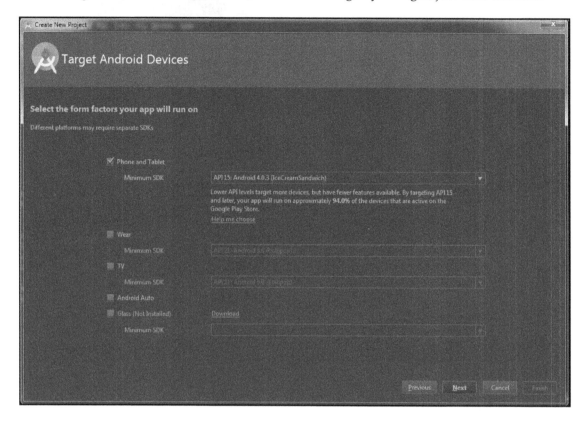

Next, at the **Add an Activity to Mobile** screen, select the Empty Activity option for now:

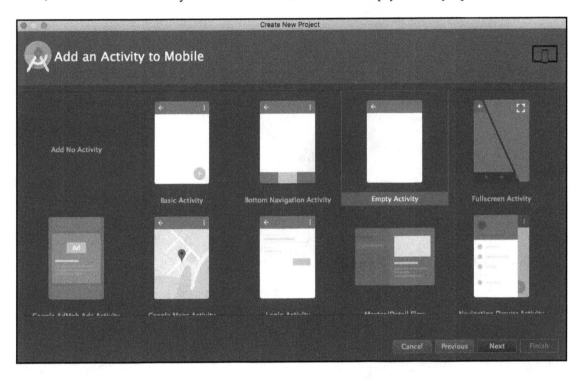

Now, the Activity and an XML file will be generated by default. Just click **Finish** when done:

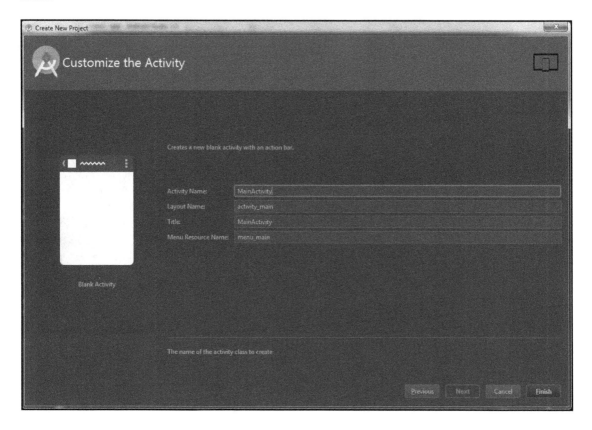

When the project load is complete, just change the view structure to Project. You may leave it at Project Files by default:

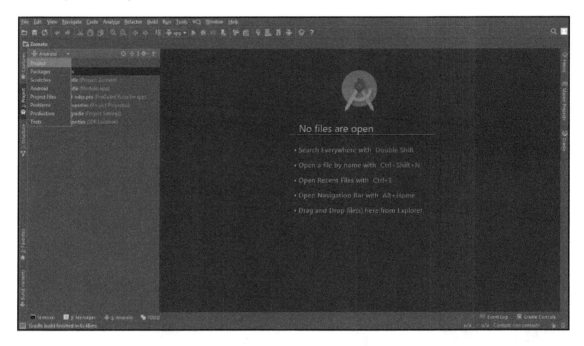

Once this is done open the `build.gradle` file. Here you will see the libraries that are compiled in the project:

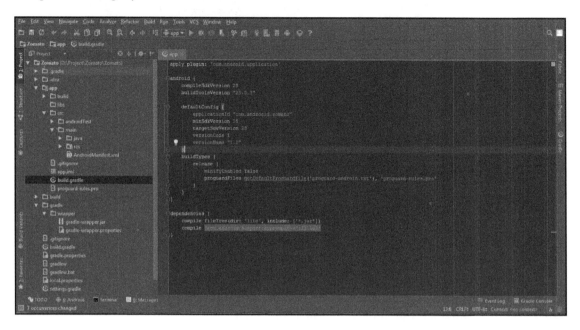

We have completed the launch of a blank project and we now should understand the basic setup of the same. In the next section, we will talk about adding Gradle to this app.

Adding Gradle to your app

You can Gradle build script dependency to your app in the following way:

Open the 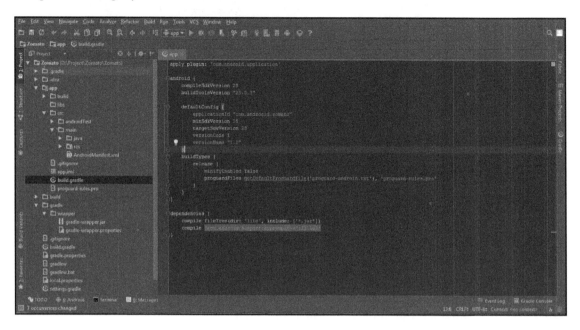 file from your app module.

Here, in the dependencies, add the Gradle identifier for a library that you want to import:

```
dependencies {
    compile fileTree(dir: 'libs', include: ['*.jar'])
    compile 'com.android.support:appcompat-v7:23.1.1'
    compile 'com.android.support:design:23.1.1'
}
```

Let us consider the current Gradle library, for instance:

`com.android.support:appcompat-v7:23.1.1`

The components of this Gradle library could be distributed in sections to ease understanding. Here are a few pointers to make note of:

- `com.android.support` is the package name of the project
- `appcompat-v7` is the project name
- `23.1.1` is the version of the project

We have now completed the setup for Gradle in Android Studio. We will be using several libraries in our App. In the next section, we will see how to add new Gradle Libraries.

Adding a new Gradle library

Making Android Development more awesome, Gradle allows us to incorporate libraries in to Android Studio in different ways. Using these, developers can easily include their libraries using Gradle dependencies. In this section we will discuss the following techniques:

- Adding a Gradle identifier
- Adding as a module

Adding a Gradle identifier

To add a new Gradle library, find the Gradle identifier for the third party library, and add it to the dependencies list.

When you make changes to the build configuration files in your project, Android Studio requires that you sync your project files so that it can import your build configuration changes and run some checks to make sure your configuration won't create build errors.

To sync your project files, click **Sync Now** (as seen in the following figure) in the notification bar (this appears when you make a change), or click **Sync Project** from the menu bar. If Android Studio notices any errors with your configuration--for example, if your code uses API features that are only available in an API level higher than your compileSdkVersion-- the **Messages** window appears to describe the issue:

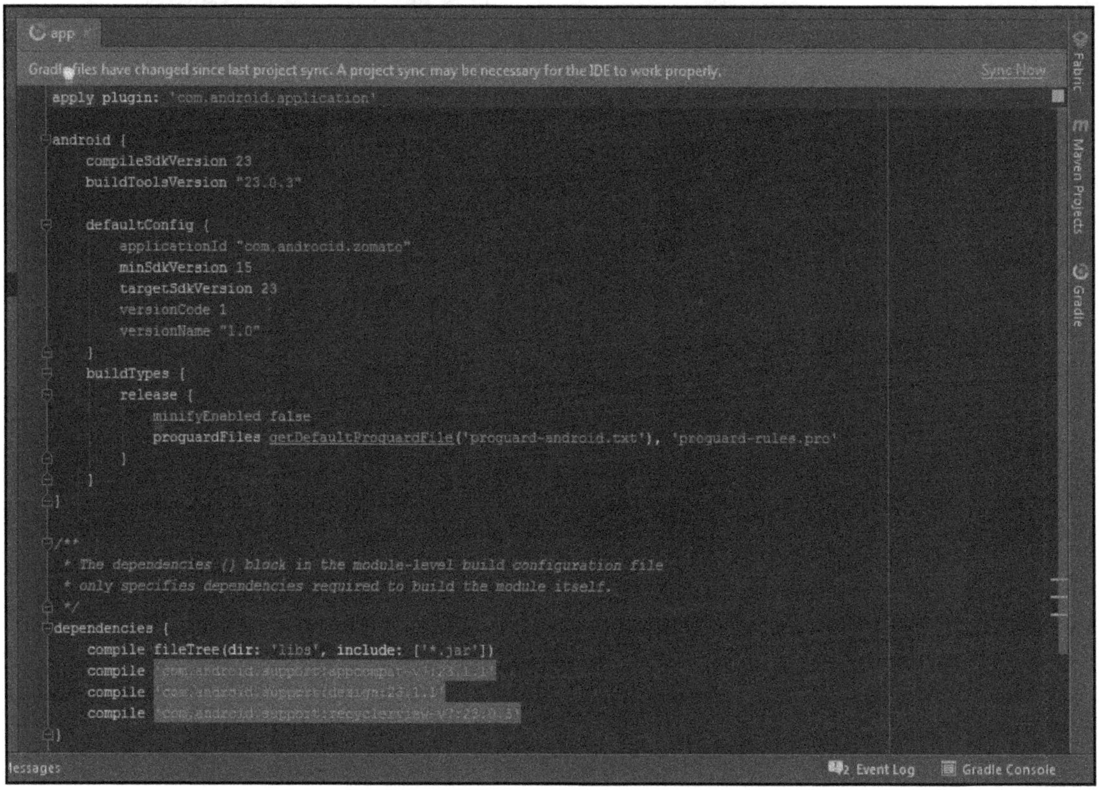

Next, we will discuss how libraries can be added using a module.

Adding as a module

You can also add a library in Android Studio by adding it as a module. To add the module:

1. First, place the library code in any folder of your choice
2. Then, you need to Import the library as a module in your app. The figure below shows the steps to add the library as a Module:

This will open a new window where you need to select the library that you have saved to the directory. When you have selected the directory, click on **Done**. This will import the external library into your project.

As an example, I have added the module crop image to my project, which appears in my project folder.

Next, we need to add the module to the app's dependency list. To do this, right click on the module that has been added and click on the **Open Module Settings** option:

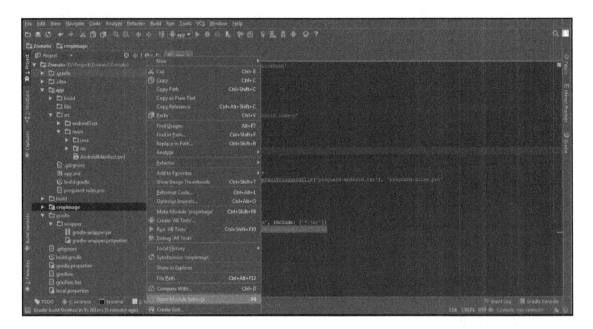

It will open a new window with your app module and library module in the list. Choose you app module, and then select the dependency list.

Next, click on the plus icon which will open another dialog with the module name. Select it and click **OK**:

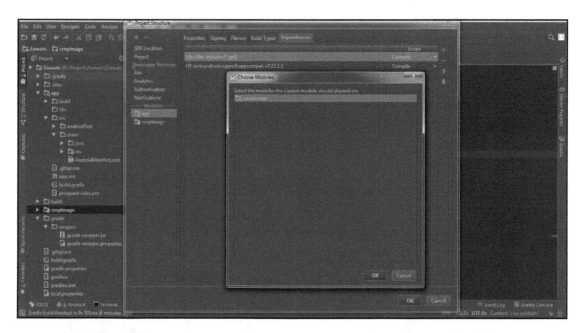

This will build the Gradle and add the module to the `build.gradle`, and it will be seen as a compiled project here:

Note that Core, UI and Util sub projects can also have their own `build.gradle` file, depending on their specific needs. Alternatively, you can also define the dependencies of a project in the root `build.gradle` file, as discussed in the preceding section. In this case, we won't be focusing on these points.

Summary

We started the chapter by looking at what Gradle is and how it is important in project development. We briefly looked at the Android Studio setup and how it can help in building the system along with Gradle. After the introduction, we talked about how developers can set up Gradle in Android Studio. We also created a new project in Android and discussed how Gradle libraries can be added to the project.

In `Chapter 2`, *Exploring Android Studio Developer Tools* we will discuss some of the key developer tools in Android Studio.

2
Exploring Android Studio Developer Tools

According to Statista, one of the leading statistical analysis agencies, designing a smartphone is ultimately a game of trade-offs: screen size vs. portability; battery life vs. data speeds; appearance vs. sturdiness; to name just a few. To make these trade-offs, it's important to know what the consumer wants.

Now that we know how to use Gradle, in this chapter we will discuss some of the tools that provide help in building apps and also help in debugging and performance tooling. We will discuss three important tools:

- APK Analyzer: the tool to analyze the **Android Application Package** (**APK**) file
- Battery Historian: shows the details of how the battery is used in the phone
- Memory Analyzer: understanding memory patterns while using the app

APK Analyzer

An APK is an Android Application package file. Gradle, by default, builds a single APK, no matter what libraries you include. This compiled and packaged file includes all of the application's code (`.dex` files), manifest files, resources, and assets.

The library, within itself, comprises multiple copies of the same native code, optimized for the different architecture. This means that the library is a native binary with multiple architecture such as x86, x86_64, armeabi, and so on, all packed together. A developer can easily run the command unzip <your_APK_name>.APK to understand the content of an APK:

When your app, and the libraries it references, reaches a specific threshold, you encounter build errors that point to the app's limit of the Android App Build Architecture. The most recent Android build system displays an error, trouble writing output:

Too many field references: 152000; max is 65536.

You may try using **--multi-dex** option.

Looking closely at the log, the number **65536** has a significant reason for appearing. This number represents the total number of references that can be invoked by the code within a single **Dalvik Executable** (**dex**) bytecode file.

Both these error conditions display a common number: **65536**. This number is significant in that it represents the total number of references that can be invoked by the code within a single dex bytecode file. If you have built an Android app and received this error, then congratulations, you have a lot of code!

Reducing the APK file size with APK Analyzer

When users download the APK from the Play Store, the package manager is smart enough to install only the code for the architecture it is installed on, but there is no relief for the data consumed if the APK size is large. Memory space on the phone is a competitive area and to make it worse, if users spot the large APK size they may well decide not to bother. Ensure that your app utilizes memory in a way appropriate for making users download and retain the app. The smaller you make your APK, the more likely it is for the user to at least download the app in the first instance.

The APK file is a simple archive file and there's no way of compressing its size further. Hence, the actions that need to be performed should be followed skillfully using some tools like APK Analyser, before the build is shipped.

This tool helps to understand the contents and the sizes of the different components in your APK. With the help of this tool, you can reduce the size of your APK, by identifying the raw file size and estimated download size of each component that combine, to make up your APK.

To use APK Analyser, select **Build>AnalyzeAPK**. Follow this step by selecting the APK you want to take a closer look at. The tool will then output in the main Android Studio window, so that you can explore the various components that make up the APK. Using this information, you can nail down the areas where you think there's a loss of some excess bytes.

You need to understand the contents and sizes of different components in your APK, avoid 64K referenced method limit issues with your dex files, diagnose ProGuard configuration issues, view the merged `AndroidManifest.xml` file, and inspect the compiled resources file. This feature can help you reduce your APK size (you'll see both the raw file size as well as the download size of the various components). You can check out the official reference at `https://developer.android.com/studio/build/shrink-code.html` for more details regarding the preceding topics.

Understanding basic battery drain

Earlier editions of Android OS used to run on Dalvik Runtime, which means apps used to compile at execution time. Post-Lollipop edition, Android has switched to Android runtime (ART), which means the apps are compiled beforehand, ensuring they are launched faster. ART, as the runtime, executes the Dalvik Executable format and dex bytecode specification. Apart from the launch, the entire consumer experience using the app is essential for app retention. One important feature is the battery - a *dear* feature of the phone.

An app which is greedy for power often finds itself in the position of either being uninstalled or lower rated when reviewed on the Google Play Store listing. Take a look at some of the most popular apps on the Store, including Facebook, which has had consistently bad reviews that quote battery drain as one of the top sources of user dissatisfaction. If your app has the reputation of being a battery hog, that might incur a loss of potential users that could otherwise be using the app. Android developers usually neglect the way that their app could impact the battery life of the smartphone. Not that it needs deeper insights in embedded systems, but a few tips can help you to appreciate the impact of an app on battery life.

The battery is part of the user's experience.

If your app is one of the top drainers of the battery in the device, what's the best way to figure it out? The battery setting menu has an information resource to diagnose battery drain issues caused by mobile apps. Simply heading to **Settings** | **Battery** will provide the user with the necessary information in a graphical format, comparing consumption against time. The records are maintained since the last full charge status. There is also an interesting statistical overview of the applications that have contributed to battery drain:

Clicking on the graphs opens an extended section that shows how much time your device has spent in various cellular states. The different color patterns such as green, yellow, and orange indicate the signal strength. It also provides other information like active time using Wi-Fi, Device Awake time, and Screen On time.

A key observation you should make as a developer is of the state when your device is awake but the screen is off. This might be the result of a Wakelock or alarm that uses the device resources when the user might not be actively using the device. If this is frequently seen, it calls for some optimization. We will be talking about the Wakelocks and their impacts during the performance section of this book.

Batterystats and Battery Historian

The Android Settings menu options provide high level measurements of battery drain. However, to gain more insight into battery consuming apps, there are some tools that can be useful. Tools such as Batterystats and Battery Historian come in handy. Batterystats collects battery data from your device, and Battery Historian converts that data into a HTML visualization that helps you understand power consumption graphically.

Batterystats, was introduced in KitKat, but Lollipop brought a large dataset for the users which included data about every Wakelock action on the device.

Please reset the data and enable full Wakelock reporting to receive comprehensive information including how the device utilizes the battery, along with details about all the running processes.

Here are some of the commands you can run after connecting your device:

```
adb shell dumpsys batterystats --reset (Resets all of the data in the
Battery Settings menu before generating the new dataset)
adb shell dumpsys batterystats --enable full-wake-history (Enables full
Wakelock reporting)
adb shell dumpsys batterystats --charged (Enables you to receive the data
since the phone was last fully charged)
```

If you wish to know what a `Batterystats` System Dump looks like, you can run the command using the command line interface in Android Studio. Take a look at the sample as follows:

```
Terminal
  Daily stats:
    Current start time: 2016-09-19-04-20-03
    Next min deadline: 2016-09-20-01-00-00
    Next max deadline: 2016-09-20-03-00-00
    Current daily steps:
      Discharge total time: 11h 29m 52s 400ms  (from 70 steps)
      Discharge screen on time: 3h 15m 57s 300ms  (from 33 steps)
      Charge total time: 1h 28m 17s 100ms  (from 59 steps)
      Charge screen off time: 1h 25m 56s 700ms  (from 56 steps)
    Daily from 2016-09-18-01-36-14 to 2016-09-19-04-20-03:
      Discharge total time: 11h 50m 51s 300ms  (from 143 steps)
      Discharge screen off time: 1d 9h 21m 40s 300ms  (from 1 steps)
      Discharge screen on time: 3h 59m 50s 400ms  (from 65 steps)
      Charge total time: 7h 19m 38s 200ms  (from 133 steps)
      Charge screen off time: 1h 18m 44s 100ms  (from 54 steps)
      Charge screen on time: 12h 12m 24s 300ms  (from 73 steps)
    Daily from 2016-09-17-01-13-09 to 2016-09-18-01-36-14:
      Discharge total time: 14h 23m 39s 0ms  (from 130 steps)
      Discharge screen off time: 1d 15h 41m 13s 600ms  (from 5 steps)
      Discharge screen on time: 3h 25m 26s 600ms  (from 43 steps)
      Charge total time: 12h 5m 41s 400ms  (from 109 steps)
   TODO      Terminal      6: Android Monitor
```

We will be talking more about what each of these components mean during performance in `Chapter 15`, *Understanding App Store Analytics for Optimization* later in the book, where we will cover in detail how each of these elements help users to optimize the Android App for better performance.

Google I/O 2015 saw the launch of an updated tool called Battery Historian 2.0 (Download at: `https://github.com/google/battery-historian`). This was launched with new reports completely rewritten in GO. This tool provides extensive information that helps you drill down into battery data for your specific application.

To run the latest edition of Battery Historian, you will need Android Devices with versions later than Android 5.0 and Golang version 1.8.1. Please follow the installation guide given on the link above to complete the setup.

You can either save the file or check the output right from the terminal window. Exploring each component, the following are the important keywords of the stats:

- **Battery History**: This shows the time series of various power-relevant events, such as the screen being on, radio signals and app launch. You can also get details of each one of these using the Battery Historian graph, which we will discuss in the next section.
- **Per-PID Stats**: Shows how each process ran, including the wake time.

- **Statistics since last charge**: This information provides an overall picture of what's happening with the device, to ensure no external events are affecting your experiments. Some of the statistics include, but are not limited to: phone signal levels, screen brightness, signal scanning time, time on battery, time on battery screen off, Wi-Fi signal levels, Wi-Fi idle time, and Wi-Fi Power drain (in mAh).
- **Estimated power use (mAh) by UID and peripheral**: This is an extremely rough estimate and its use should avoid consideration as an experiment data.
- **Per-app mobile ms per packet**: Shows the Radio-awake-time divided by packets sent - which means, since an efficient app transfers all its traffic in batches, the lower the value, the better it is for the app's performance.
- **All partial wake locks**: All app-held Wakelocks, by aggregate duration and count.

Batterystats collects battery data from your device. It creates a dump of all the battery data of a particular selected device using **Android Debug Bridge** (**ADB**) commands. Using these Batterystats, the battery usage could be discovered using a Battery Historian, which would create a HTML file for viewing the Batterystats results in a browser for user viewing.

A graphical representation from Battery Historian of the live Zomato App is shown in the following screenshot:

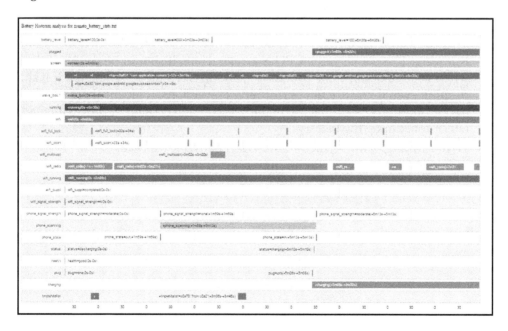

Using the Battery Historian, important statistics can be drawn upon:

- It shows you the processes from the device that consume your battery. Here, you could compare the battery usage for each process.
- It also shows you the tasks from an app that consume more of the battery, so that you can take necessary action on them.

The preceding graph representation shows the readings, based on various categories of the Historian. A few of the major categories to look out for, and to analyze regarding the battery consumption for a device, are listed as follows:

- **Battery level**: This shows the battery level of the device when it was recorded. It is calculated in percent where 099 is 99% battery. It helps you determine how fast the device battery drains out.
- **Screen**: Shows whether the screen was ON.
- **Top**: It shows the application that consumes the most battery usage. Currently the Zomato App is at the top, as the records have been taken, resetting the battery usage and using only the Zomato App.
- **Wake_lock**: This is the most important field to check battery consumption. The usual process of the App is to wake up, do a small amount of work, and then go back to sleep. Waking up the app is very expensive to the battery. So if there are lot of bars showing up, it might be a problem. In this case, the app was continuously awake, hence showing a continuous wake_lock value.
- **Running**: This shows if the CPU is awake. Here, it should be awake at the times when you are doing some processing, and in sleep mode when not. If it shows as running even if you are not performing any actions, it means there are background processes that are making your CPU do a lot of processing, and hence consuming the battery.
- **Wifi_running**: Shows whether the Wi-Fi network was active.
- **Phone_signal_strength**: Shows the signal strength of the mobile device network.

Let us now discuss how we can set up to plot Battery Historian for the App we are going to build:

1. Download the open-source Battery Historion Python script from GitHub (`https://github.com/google/battery-historian`).
2. Unzip the file to extract the Battery Historian folder. Find the `historian.py` file in the folder and move it to the desktop or another writable directory.
3. Connect your mobile device to your computer.
4. On your computer, open a terminal window.
5. Change the directory path to the path where you have saved `historian.py`. For example, if it is on desktop, run:

   ```
   cd ~/Desktop
   ```

6. Shut down your running adb server :

   ```
   adb kill-server
   ```

7. Restart adb and check for connected devices: >adb devices. This will show the list of devices.
8. If you don't see any devices, make sure your phone is connected and USB Debugging is turned on, and then kill and restart adb.
9. Reset battery data gathering by running the command :

   ```
   >adb shell dumpsysbatterystats --reset
   ```

10. Resetting erases old battery collection data; otherwise, the output will be huge.
11. Disconnect your device from your computer so that you are only drawing current from the device's battery.
12. Use the app for a while, until it gathers a sufficient amount of data for your use.
13. Reconnect your phone.
14. Make sure your phone is recognized:

    ```
    >adb devices
    ```

15. Dump all battery data. This can take a while:

    ```
    >adb shell dumpsysbatterystats> batterystats.txt
    ```

16. Create a HTML version of the data dump for Battery Historian:

    ```
    > python historian.py batterystats.txt > batterystats.html
    ```

17. Open the `batterystats.html` file in your browser.
18. The Battery Historian tool makes it simpler to dig into the data for one single process. As a developer, you can easily spot battery drain functions using this tool and work on its resolution. In the next section, we will discuss the memory monitor tools.

Memory Monitor

When you hear the term memory management in an Android app, it is basically the **Random Access Memory (RAM)**. Managing the RAM is the most critical section in the Android app development process, as the physical memory is often constrained. The fundamental principle of memory management is to avoid a memory leak from your app.

In Android Studio there is a tool we can use to check the memory usage in the App. To check this you could follow these steps:

1. Run your app on an Android device connected to an emulator.
2. Open the Android Monitor tab in Android Studio situated at the bottom window.
3. Open the Monitor section within it, and you are there.

Here you'll be able to continuously check the memory usage of the app as and when the app is being used. The following image shows the memory usage for an app:

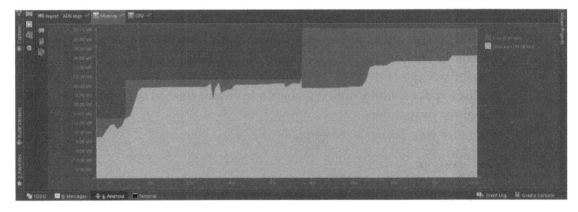

The preceding memory graph shows the memory used by a device against time. This graph shows the memory usage in the app when any process is performed by the app, be it loading data over the network, displaying an image, rendering a view on the screen, or running a background task.

There are two graphs being plotted at the same time here, one with the allocated memory that could be used by the device.

<p>`OutOfMemoryException` error is the most common cause of unconventional crashing of an app due to memory leaks, and the Memory Monitor tool can help you to debug the same.

Wondering what the various causes of memory increase are?

In any app, the memory is bound to increase at various points of time as and when you use it. Do not panic if the memory keeps on increasing when you do some stuff in the app, like loading data over the network, displaying an image, rendering a view on the screen or running a background task. It means that for whatever task you do in the app, for example displaying an image onto the screen, the app needs to allocate some amount of space in the RAM. Now, this allocation is for one particular process. Similar allocations will also happen for other processes. These will increase the memory and, if not handled, may cause a memory leak in your App.

For most of the Apps, Android has a Dalvik garbage collector, which takes care of the memory allocations and releases the memory when done. This will help prevent memory leaks.

By carefully understanding how your Android application handles memory operations, you can ensure that the app is running efficiently on memory contained devices. Eventually, this will also lead to a reduction in out-of-memory crashes.

Logcat

Android Studio has a logcat tab inside Android Monitor that prints system events, such as when a garbage collection occurs, as well as messages your app prints with the Log class, to assist with debugging. Logcat displays messages in real time and also keeps a history so you can view older messages.

Log	Log Level	Description
Log.v(tag, message)	Verbose	Show all log messages (the default).
Log.d(tag, message)	Debug	Show debug log messages that are useful during development only, as well as the message levels lower in this list.
Log.i(tag, message)	Information	Show expected log messages for regular usage, as well as the message levels lower in this list.
Log.w(tag, message)	Warning	Show possible issues that are not yet errors, as well as the message levels lower in this list.
Log.e(tag, message)	Error	Show issues that have caused errors, as well as the message level lower in this list.

Tag and message are the string data-type.

You can search for messages in the logcat by;

- Typing a character sequence in the search field
- Optionally selecting Regex if you want to use a regular expression search pattern

The logcat will reflect the changes accordingly.

Also finer searches can be done by finding the text within the searched text by using the find option, clicking *Ctrl + F* on the keyboard.

Summary

Battery life is an excellent indicator of how your App performs. Apps without optimization can severely impact the battery life of a device. We've walked though in-depth analysis of battery drain in Android Apps. We also looked at Batterystats and the Historian tool to analyse battery usage patterns. Additionally, we explored memory optimization to ensure the app runs smoothly and stays off the memory leaking track.

In the next Chapter 3, Leap into the Android Support Library we will discuss Android Support Libraries.

3
Leap into the Android Support Library

One of the greatest strengths of the Android Platform is its support for a huge variety of devices. These include smartphones, tablets, Smart Wears, smart TV's, and even cars. From just a mobile computing platform, Google has used the powers of Android to a great and deeper extent. Looking at the Android distribution, Android 4.x.x version caters for more than 95% of its share. Comparing smartphone OS global market shares from Q1-09 to Q2-16, Android has grown massively from 1.6% to 86.2%. According to Google, 6M+ users are added every month, and that is a great number. At this pace, we can expect 630M users by 2018.

In this chapter, we will look at the Android Support Library features and how they assist us in the project.

The Android Support Library

Supporting multiple devices can pose issues, particularly when users expect apps to function seamlessly on every device, in the same way. This expectation rises even when users know very well that there is a significant difference in the software and hardware of the phone. While Google releases, latest updates to Android, it is not necessarily true that all OEMs follow up on this update on their smartphone. This leads to the fact that most of the users tend to use releases which are approximately 15 months old or older.

If that is held true, developers would have to compromise a lot in order to support most of their users, running several versions of Android. Fortunately, the Android team is aware of this and endeavors to provide consistent help for the developer in this regard. This is a tricky issue, especially considering the consistency of the app feature that shouldn't affect the architectural structure. Google's Android team has a strategic answer to this: The Android Support Library.

The Android Support Library is a collection of libraries, which are available on several API levels, that help developers to focus on the unique parts of their app, supporting new functionality and compatibility issues that might arise due to different versions running on different devices.

Setting up Android Support Libraries in your development environment depends entirely on what features you want to use and what range of Android platform versions you are targeting with your application. The Android Support Repository package is provided as a supplemental download to the Android SDK, and using the Android SDK manager you can grab the same.

Please follow the steps given as follows to set up the Support Library files:

1. Open the Android SDK Manager option in Android Studio by selecting **Tools** > **Android** > **SDK Manager**.

This will open the window as selected:

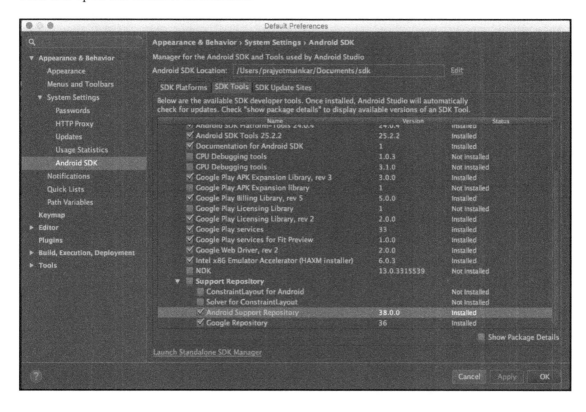

In the **Support Repository** option, select **Android Support Repository**. If you have opened the standalone SDK Manager, this option would be in the `Extras` section, as shown in the following image:

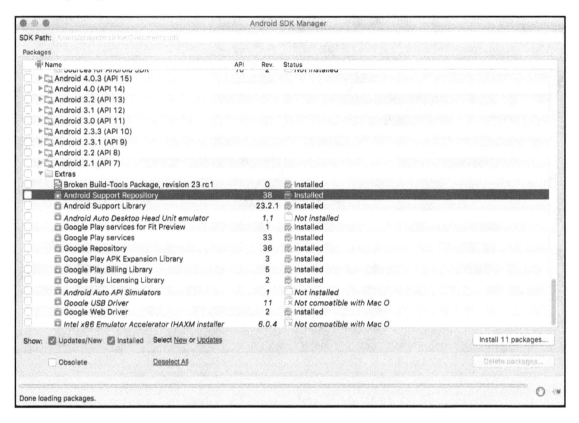

2. Click on the **Install Package** option

After downloading, the tool installs the Support library files to your existing Android SDK directory. To view these library files, you can navigate to the following subdirectory of your SDK:

`<sdk_path_on_your_system>/extras/android/m2repository/com/android/suppo rt/ directory`

Android offers several support library features you can add to your project, specifically:

- v4 Support library
- v7 Support library
- Multidex Support library
- v8 Support library
- v13 Support library
- Annotations Support library
- Design Support library
- Custom Tabs Support library

Let us now take a look at what is offered by these individual support library features:

v4 Support Library

These libraries are designed to be used with Android v2.3 (API Level 9) and above. Here is the list of supported libraries:

Support Library	Description	Gradle Dependency
v4 compat library	Provides compatibility wrappers for a number of framework APIs including `Context.obtainDrawable()` and `View.performAccessibilityAction()`.	com.android.support:support-compat:24.2.1
v4 core-utils library	Provides a number of utility classes, such as `AsyncTaskLoader` and `PermissionChecker`.	com.android.support:support-compat:24.2.1
v4 core-ui library	Supports and implements a variety of UI-related components, such as `ViewPager`, `NestedScrollView`, and `ExploreByTouchHelper`. We will be using these primarily in our app.	com.android.support:support-core-ui:24.2.1
v4 media-compat library	Helps in backporting portions of the media framework such as MediaBrowser and MediaSession.	com.android.support:support-media-compat:24.2.1

v7 Support Library

Like the v4 libraries, these libraries are also designed to be used with Android v2.3 (API Level 9) and above. Here is the list of supported libraries:

Support Library	Description	Gradle Dependency
v7 appcompat library	This will be one library that will play important role in our project. This library supports the Action Bar Design pattern. Moreover, it also includes support for material design user interface implementations. This library depends on the v4 Support Library. Some of the key classes which are part of this library are: `AppCompatActivity`, `ActionBar`, `AppCompatDialog`, and `ShareActionProvider`.	com.android.support:appcompat-v7:24.2.1
v7 cardview library	A very important library that supports card layout as defined in Material Design pattern. This allows us to show up information in the form of cards, which can be supported on any device.	com.android.support:cardview-v7:24.2.1
v7 gridlayout library	Sections in the Zomato App such as Trending this week use grid layout. Using this library adds support for the `GridLayout` class, which allows you to arrange UI elements using a grid styling.	com.android.support:gridlayout-v7:24.2.1

v7 mediarouter library	Though we won't be using this library, it provides `MediaRouter`, `MediaRouteProvider`, and related media classes that support Google cast. In short, it supports streaming and routing of media channels from one device to external devices.	com.android.support:mediarouter-v7:24.2.1
v7 palette library	This library includes support for the Palette class, which extracts prominent colors from an image. This is mainly used in music applications.	com.android.support:palette-v7:24.2.1
v7 recyclerview library	Supports adding of RecyclerView class which will help in efficiently displaying large data sets within the bounds of limited window of data items.	com.android.support:recyclerview-v7:24.2.1
v7 Preference Support Library	This library helps in adding preference objects, such as `CheckBoxPreference` and `ListPreference`, used by the user while modifying the UI settings	com.android.support:preference-v7:24.2.1

Google recommends including the v4 support and v7 appcompat libraries, because they support a wide range of Android versions and provide APIs for recommended design patterns.

Multidex Support library

In Chapter 2, *Exploring Android Studio Developer Tools*, we spoke about Dalvik Executable (dex) files. This library provides support for building apps that support multiple dex files. Apps that have references to more than 65536 methods would be required to use multidex configuration. The gradle dependency identifier for this library is as follows:

```
com.android.support:multidex:1.0.0
```

v8 Support Library

This is compatible with Android 2.3 (API level 9) and higher and can be used independently from other libraries. It has v8 renderscript library - which adds support for the RenderScript computation framework.

For using this, you will need to add the following to your Gradle build script properties:

```
defaultConfig {
renderscriptTargetApi 18
renderscriptSupportModeEnabled true
}
```

v13 Support Library

This library is designed to be used for Android 3.2 (API level 13) and higher, and supports fragment user interface patterns. It supports the FragmentCompat class and additional fragment support classes. The gradle dependency identifier for this library is as follows:

```
com.android.support:support-v13:24.2.1
```

Annotations Support Library

This library provides support to add annotation metadata to your Apps. The gradle dependency identifier for this library is as follows:

```
com.android.support:support-annotations:24.2.1
```

Design Support Library

This is one of the most crucial libraries of the project, which will allow you to add Material Design Components and Patterns to your App, such as navigation drawer, Floating Action Button (FAB), tabs, and snackbars. The gradle dependency identifier for this library is as follows:

```
com.android.support:design:24.2.1
```

Custom Tabs Support Library

This package provides APIs for adding and managing custom tabs in the App. The gradle dependency identifier for this library is as follows:

```
com.android.support:customtabs:24.2.1
```

Summary

In this chapter, we first discussed setting up the Android Support Library in the Android Development Environment. We followed this by discussing several libraries that can help developers to use libraries which can offer backward-compatible versions of new features.

In `Chapter 4`, *Google Play Services*, we will take you through Google Play Services and we will discuss using several Google features in the app such as Maps and Google+ Sign in.

4
Google Play Services

Google Play Services is a boon to app development, especially helping developers with Google-packed features such as Maps, Google+, Drive, Game services and Analytics. With automatic platform updates distributed as an APK on the Google Play Store, developers can easily receive the updates and more easily integrate Google features. In this chapter, we will first see how the Google Play Service architecture works, followed by some of the APIs supported in Google Play Services. This will be followed by learning to incorporate Google Sign-in and Maps API. First, let's see what the architecture of Google Play Services looks like:

The architecture

The Google Play Service Library contains APIs that provide an interface to the individual Google services. This interface also allows you to obtain authorization from users to gain access to these services using the users' credentials. These services include Google Drive, Play Games and more. Since the library derives updates from Google Play, it does contain APIs that help you resolve any issues at runtime. Sometimes you may have come across apps that prompt you to update Google Play Services before proceeding. The Google Play Service APK runs as a background service in the Android OS and you can interact with the background service though the client library. The service performs the desired action on your behalf.

The table below shows the list of services provided by Google Play Services:

Google Play Services API	Description
Google+	com.google.android.gms:play-services-plus:10.0.1
Google Account Login	com.google.android.gms:play-services-auth:10.0.1
Google Actions, Base Client Library	com.google.android.gms:play-services-base:10.0.1
Google Address API	com.google.android.gms:play-services-identity:10.0.1
Google App Indexing	com.google.android.gms:play-services-appindexing:10.0.1
Google App Invites	com.google.android.gms:play-services-appinvite:10.0.1
Google Analytics	com.google.android.gms:play-services-analytics:10.0.1
Google Awareness	com.google.android.gms:play-services-contextmanager:10.0.1
Google Cast	com.google.android.gms:play-services-cast:10.0.1
Google Cloud Messaging	com.google.android.gms:play-services-gcm:10.0.1
Google Drive	com.google.android.gms:play-services-drive:10.0.1
Google Fit	com.google.android.gms:play-services-fitness:10.0.1
Google Location and Activity Recognition	com.google.android.gms:play-services-location:10.0.1
Google Maps	com.google.android.gms:play-services-maps:10.0.1
Google Mobile Ads	com.google.android.gms:play-services-ads:10.0.1

Google Places	`com.google.android.gms:play-services-places:10.0.1`
Mobile Vision	`com.google.android.gms:play-services-vision:10.0.1`
Google Nearby	`com.google.android.gms:play-services-nearby:10.0.1`
Google Panorama Viewer	`com.google.android.gms:play-services-panorama:10.0.1`
Google Play Game services	`com.google.android.gms:play-services-games:10.0.1`
SafetyNet	`com.google.android.gms:play-services-safetynet:10.0.1`
Android Pay	`com.google.android.gms:play-services-wallet:10.0.1`
Android Wear	`com.google.android.gms:play-services-wearable:10.0.1`

In the app we are working on, we would need Google services such as Google+ Login and Google Maps. To begin with, you must first install the Google Play Services library (revision 15 or higher) for your Android SDK. Also, to include a specific dependency for your app, proceed to add specific services in your app's build Gradle.

The various services provided by Google Play Services could be included in an Android app using a Gradle path in the app's `build.gradle`. For example:

```
dependencies {
compile'com.google.android.gms:play-services:10.0.1'
}
```

Make sure these changes are saved and you click **Sync Project** with Gradle Files in the toolbar. Since we are using the Google+ Sign in feature, we are required to provide SHA-1 of your signing certificate to create an OAUTH2 client and API key for your app. To generate your SHA-1, please run the following command using the `KeyTool` utility provided with Java:

```
keytool -exportcert -list -v \ -alias <your-key-name> -keystore<path-to-
production-keystore>
```

Next, proceed to get the debug certificate fingerprint using the following command:

On Linux/Mac:

```
keytool -exportcert -list -v \ -alias androiddebugkey -keystore
~/.android/debug.keystore
```

And on Windows:

```
keytool -exportcert -list -v \
    -alias androiddebugkey -keystore %USERPROFILE%\.android\debug.keystore
```

The key tool utility should now prompt you to enter a password for the keystore. The default password for the debug keystore is android. Post this, you will able to see the fingerprint displayed onto the terminal.

To know more about signing your Android application, please do check this link:

```
https://developer.android.com/studio/publish/app-signing.html
```

Since we are looking to access Google APIs using the users' Google Accounts over HTTP, we have to ensure that the users experience a secure and consistent experience in retrieving an OAuth 2.0 token for your app. To make this possible, you need to register your Android app with the Google Cloud Console by providing your app's package name and the SHA1 fingerprint of the keystore, using which you will sign the release APK.

To register your Android app with Google Cloud Console, follow these simple steps:

1. Login to `Google Cloud Console: https://console.developers.google.com`.
2. Click on **Create project** and enter the project name. In our case, we have named it Zomato Project:

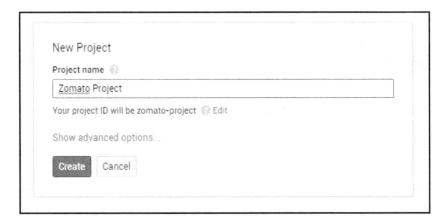

3. Click **Create**. This will create a new project in your Google Developer Console.

Since we have created the project, we will now enable the APIs that are required for the project. To enable the APIs, click on the library tab. Here you will see the list of all APIs that can be added to the app.

Now, let's start by integrating Google+ Login into our app:

1. First go to the library tab in the Google developer console.
2. Select Google+ API under the Social APIs section and click **Enable**. Now, the Google + API is enabled for this project.
3. Next go to the Credentials. Here we will be creating an OAuth credential for the app so that the user can log in from the Android app. Before we create a new credential, we have to fill in OAuth details of the app:

4. After all of these details have been filled, go to the Credentials tab and click on **Create credential**:

5. Then, select the type of application where we are applying the Google+ Login. In our case, it is an Android app, so we would select Android:

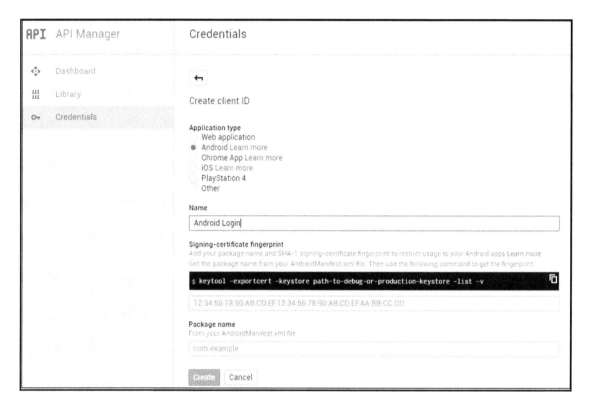

6. Then you will see an option to add the app's package name and signing-certificate fingerprint.

7. Now go to `https://developers.google.com/identity/sign-in/android/start` and click on **GET A CONFIGURATION FILE**:

8. Here you will see an option to select an app and enter the package name. Fill in the details and click on **Choose and configure services**:

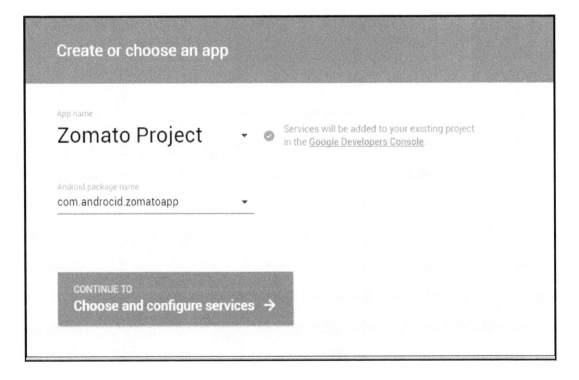

9. At this screen, enable Google Sign In and enter the signing-certificate fingerprint.
10. Then click on Generate configuration file:

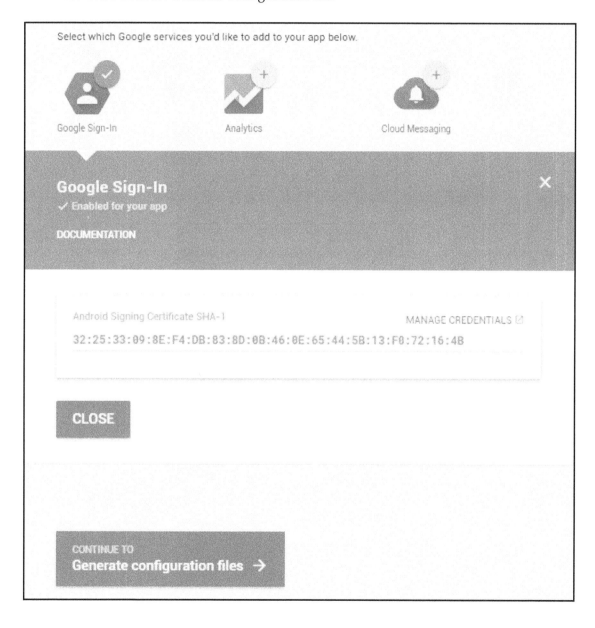

11. You can now download the `google-services.json` file, which we will be using in the app for services like Google+ Sign In and other services enabled from Google the console:

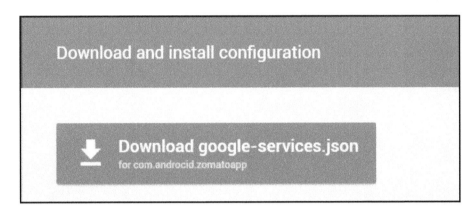

The `google-services.json` file is to be placed in the app directory in your project.

Now, add the dependency to your project-level `build.gradle`: Classpath `com.google.gms:google-services:3.0.0`.

Also, add this plugin in your app-level `build.gradle`: Apply plugin `com.google.gms.google-services`.

Finally, add the dependency into your app-level Gradle: Compile `com.google.android.gms:play-services-auth:9.2.1`.

We have now completed the setup for Google Play Services for this app. In the next section we will discuss the Android Architecture we would follow, along with discussion on the UI patterns for this app.

Google Maps

Google Maps is used in the app for finding the location of a place, or to navigate you to that place. Integrating Google Maps in the app is simple; check out the steps below:

First we need to enable the Google Maps API from the Developer Console link: `https://console.cloud.google.com`. In your project page select Library; then, under Google Maps APIs, select **Google Maps Android API**:

Next, enable the API so that it can be used in our application. After the Google Maps API is enabled, we need to start integrating it into our app:

In Android studio create a new **Google Maps Activity**:

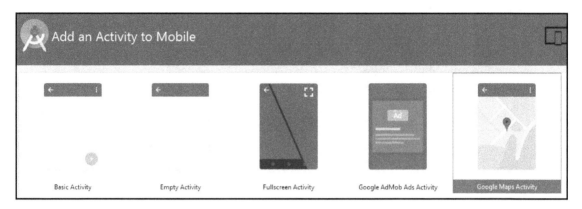

After the activity is created, we need to create an API key from the developer console:

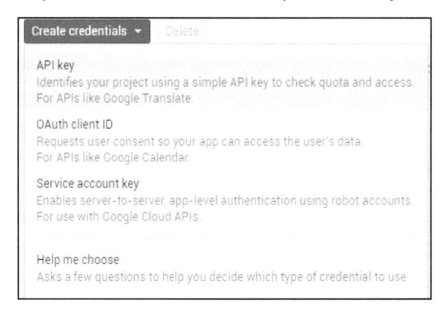

Go to the credentials section in the developer console, and create a new **API key**:

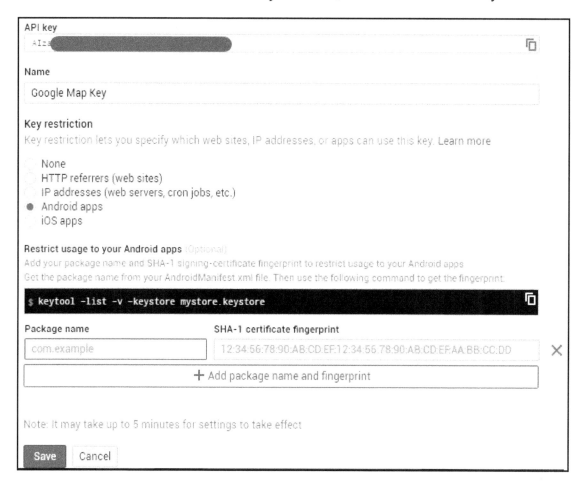

Here, select Android app and enter your app's package name and Sha-1 certificate. After saving the API key, use the key in your app.

Now in your app, add the dependency in your app's `build.gradle` file:

Compile `com.google.android.gms:play-services-maps:10.0.1.`

Create a string resource `google_maps_key strings.xml` with the value of the API key. Save the file.

After adding, save the `AndroidManifest.xml` and re-build your application.

Summary

We started the chapter by discussing what Google Play Services is and which Google Play Services APIs are available. Next, we discussed Google Sign up, followed by Google Maps.

In the `Chapter 5`, *Material Design*, we will talk about Material Designs.

5
Material Design

Material design is a design language developed by Google's Design team to foster uniform design guidelines for App developers. Google has set design principles as guidelines to help developers work with material design for their apps. This principle sets up visual cues, motion, and interaction design across platforms and devices, making it a unified design belief. In this section, we will cover how to incorporate material design into your app.

Wireframing and tools to gather feedback

Wireframing is a technique to plan out the high-level screen hierarchy for your application and display the forms that would be present in your app by providing some mode of navigation, to allow users to effectively traverse your app flow. Some apps have wireframes expressed in a tree structure, a graph, or a flowchart.

The methods of wireframing could vary based on the type and magnitude of the app, but the standard patterns of wireframing remain the same. Also, there are varieties of tools that could be used across different types of apps and different kinds of information that represent the types of things users interact with in your app. Software engineers and data architects often use **entity-relationship diagrams** (**ERDs**) to describe an application's information model. We will understand and learn the various techniques of wireframing in detail in this chapter.

Understanding the wireframing process (tangible and digital)

Before understanding the actual wireframing process, it will be nice to gather some initial information about things that would help draw some effective wireframes. Once you understand what your app will do, the first step is to list the screens present on the app step by step. Doing this will give you a clear idea about the basic outline of the wireframing screens required.

Wireframing is the step in a design process where screens are laid out creatively, by arranging the UI elements to allow users to navigate through your app. These wireframing screens need not be same as the final UI for the app. They could be somewhat rough wireframes, which would give you an idea of what elements would be present on a screen.

The easiest and fastest way to get started is to sketch out your screens by hand using paper and pencils. Once you begin sketching, you may uncover practicality issues in your original screen map or the patterns you use. In some cases, patterns may apply well to a given design problem in theory, but in practice they may break down and cause visual clutter or interactional issues (for example, if there are two rows of tabs on the screen). If that happens, explore other navigational patterns, or variations on chosen patterns, to arrive at a more optimal set of sketches.

After you're satisfied with the initial sketches, it's a good idea to move on to digital wireframing, using software such as Adobe Illustrator, Adobe Fireworks, OmniGraffle, or any other vector illustration tools. When choosing a tool to use, consider the following features:

Material UI for Android developers

Material design for Android includes implementation of visual, motion, and interactive designs for your app on different devices. Android now includes support for material design apps. To use material design in your Android apps, follow the guidelines defined in the material design specification and use the new components and functionality available in Android 5.0 (API level 21) and later versions.

Building meaningful motions

In the following section, we will cover how to provide motions in our app to improve a user's app experience. The Android library provides many components for giving a material experience to the user. We will explain some of the components provided in the Android library in this section.

Floating Action Button (FAB)

Floating Action Buttons are used for a special type of promoted action. They are distinguished by a circled icon floating above the UI and have special motion behaviors related to morphing, launching, and the transferring anchor point.

Floating action buttons come in two sizes: the default and mini. The size can be controlled with the FABSize attribute. As this class descends from ImageView, you can control the icon that is displayed via setImageDrawable(Drawable).

The background color of this view defaults to your theme's colorAccent. If you wish to change this at runtime, you can do so via setBackgroundTintList(ColorStateList).

The FAB could be used to carry out different kinds of transitions on click. The following are a few images that show the different places where the FAB could be used:

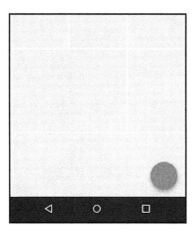

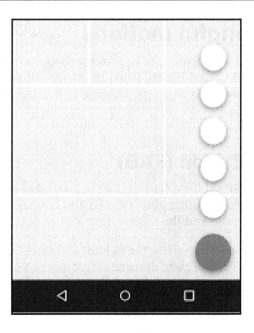

Figure 1.2.1: Fab shows options for animating on top

It could show options in animating on top on click:

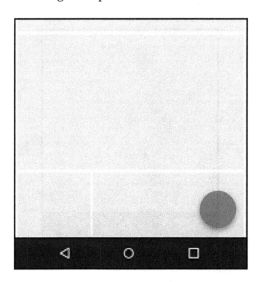

Figure 1.2.2: Fab animates to bottom menu

Let's take a look at how to use the FAB in our Zomato code. Consider the restaurant details screen where we have a FAB button present, as follows; the button can be used at various different places:

Figure 1.2.3. FAB used in the Zomato place detail screen

The FAB animation has a button. Clicking on the button opens up the bottom menu and shows us the various options. Here, the transition from the FAB button to the bottom menu forms the major chunk of its material aspect. The following is the complete transition showing how the FAB gets converted to the bottom menu:

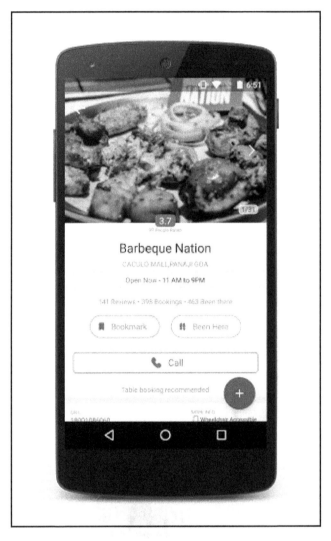

Figure 1.2.4. FAB button initially present on the screen

Figure 1.2.5. Clicking on the FAB button

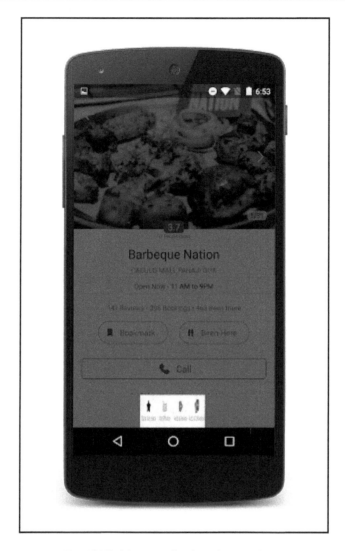

Figure 1.2.6. The in-between transition of the FAB to menu animation

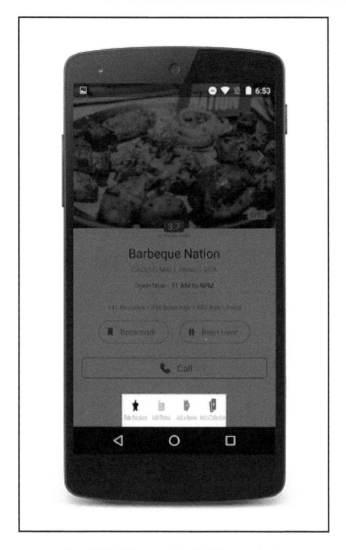

Figure 1.2.7. The in-between transition of the FAB to menu animation

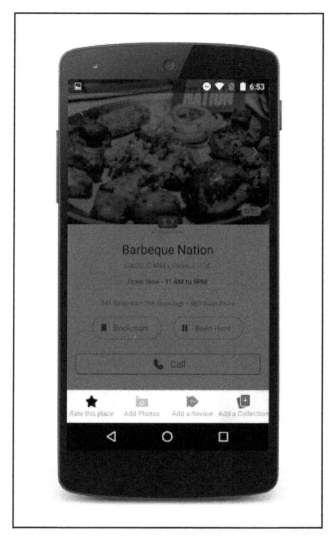

Figure 1.2.8. The formation of the final bottom menu

Let's now look at how to implement FAB in our code. Firstly, make sure that you have added the gradle dependency in your app's `build.gradle` file:

```
compile 'com.android.support:design:25.3.1'
```

Then, in your layout where you need to place the FAB, place the following code:

```
<android.support.design.widget.FloatingActionButton
    android:id="@+id/FAB"
    android:layout_width="wrap_content"
    android:layout_height="wrap_content"
    android:layout_marginBottom="?actionBarSize"
    android:layout_marginRight="20dp"
    android:src="@drawable/ic_add_white_24dp"
    app:backgroundTint="@color/colorPrimary"
    app:layout_anchor="@id/scrollView"
    app:layout_anchorGravity="bottom|end" />
```

Your FAB has been placed in your XML code, and your layout with the FAB is now ready. The next step is to import and initialize it in your Java class:

```
import android.support.design.widget.FloatingActionButton;
```

If you are using Android Studio, the import will be handled automatically, and you don't have to worry about it. Then, initialize the FAB as follows:

```
FloatingActionButton mFab;
mFab = (FloatingActionButton) findViewById(R.id.fab);
```

Once it is initialized, you need to handle what will happen when you click on the FAB button:

```
mFab.setOnClickListener(new View.OnClickListener() {
    @Override
    public void onClick(View v) {
        // Your code
    }
});
```

Now, the menu will appear when you click on the FAB button. The code for the on click of the FAB is mentioned below. Refer to PlaceDetailActivity.java for better understanding of this part of the flow:

```
mFab.setOnClickListener(new View.OnClickListener() {
    @Override
    public void onClick(View v) {
        mFabToolbar.expandFab();

        Animator bottomExpansion =
                ObjectAnimator.ofPropertyValuesHolder(bottomLay,
                        PropertyValuesHolder.ofFloat(View.SCALE_X,
0f, 1f));
        bottomExpansion.setStartDelay(300);
```

```
                bottomExpansion.setDuration(300);

                Animator bottomExpansionFade =
                        ObjectAnimator.ofPropertyValuesHolder(bottomLay,
                                PropertyValuesHolder.ofFloat(View.ALPHA,
        0f, 1f));
                bottomExpansion.setStartDelay(300);
                bottomExpansion.setDuration(300);

                Animator overlayFade =
                        ObjectAnimator.ofPropertyValuesHolder(tra_overlay,
                                PropertyValuesHolder.ofFloat(View.ALPHA,
        0f, 1f));
                overlayFade.setStartDelay(0);
                overlayFade.setDuration(600);

                bottomExpansion.addListener(new Animator.AnimatorListener() {
                    @Override
                    public void onAnimationStart(Animator animation) {
                        bottomLay.setVisibility(View.VISIBLE);
                    }

                    @Override
                    public void onAnimationEnd(Animator animation) {
                    }

                    @Override
                    public void onAnimationCancel(Animator animation) {
                    }

                    @Override
                    public void onAnimationRepeat(Animator animation) {
                    }
                });

                overlayFade.addListener(new Animator.AnimatorListener() {
                    @Override
                    public void onAnimationStart(Animator animation) {
                        tra_overlay.setVisibility(View.VISIBLE);
                    }

                    @Override
                    public void onAnimationEnd(Animator animation) {

                    }

                    @Override
                    public void onAnimationCancel(Animator animation) {
```

```
                }

                @Override
                public void onAnimationRepeat(Animator animation) {

                }
        });


        AnimatorSet animSet = new AnimatorSet();
        animSet.playTogether(bottomExpansion, bottomExpansionFade,
overlayFade);
        animSet.start();


    }
});
```

Before the preceding activity, you need to initialize the FAB toolbar menu and set the FAB to the toolbar, as follows:

```
mFabToolbar = (FooterLayout) findViewById(R.id.fabtoolbar);
mFabToolbar.setFab(mFab);
```

Once this is done, the animation of opening the menu will be executed smoothly. Also, we need to close the bottom menu when clicking anywhere outside. For that, we need to define an overlay layout, which when clicked on will contract the bottom menu to the FAB:

```
tra_overlay.setOnClickListener(new View.OnClickListener() {
    @Override
    public void onClick(View v) {
            tra_overlay.setVisibility(View.INVISIBLE);
            bottomLay.setVisibility(View.INVISIBLE);

            mFabToolbar.contractFab();
    }
});
```

Implementing Search in Zomato

The search screen in Zomato opens up when you click on the search icon on the Toolbar on the home page. Clicking on the search icon will produce a ripple effect, which helps a user to get a better experience:

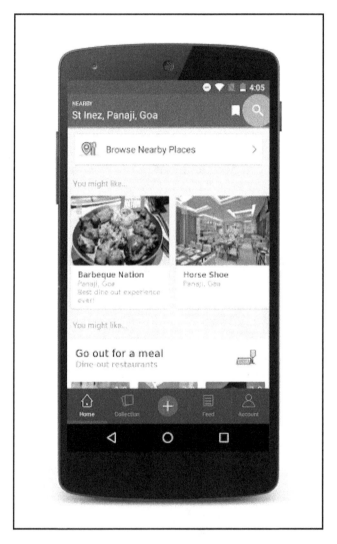

Figure 1.2.9. The search icon on the home screen with the ripple effect

When you click on the search icon, it opens up a new screen of search. When this screen opens up, there is a smooth transition that takes place as each of the components appears on the screen. The search icon first opens up smoothly to form the toolbar:

Figure 1.2.10. The in-between transition when the search icon opens up smoothly

The search icon's in-between transition shows that the ripple wave grows gradually until it completely covers the toolbar:

Figure 1.2.11. The search icon completely opens up to form the toolbar

Once the search icon translates to form the toolbar, the `EditText` translates down from the top to the bottom and the quick search options simultaneously translate up, creating a smooth transition effect:

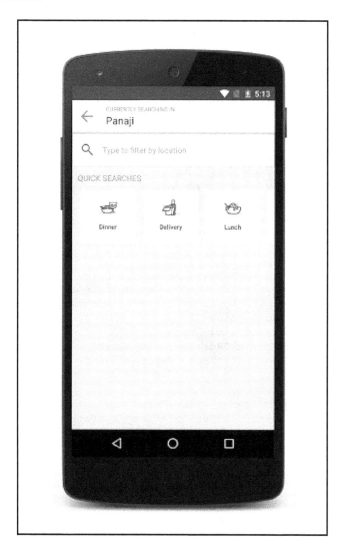

Figure 1.2.12. The Search icon completely opens up to form the toolbar

The XML layout of the search view is shown in the following code:

```xml
<RelativeLayout xmlns:android="http://schemas.android.com/apk/res/android"
    android:layout_width="match_parent"
    android:layout_height="match_parent"
    android:background="@color/app_bg_color">

    <LinearLayout
        android:layout_width="match_parent"
        android:layout_height="match_parent"
        android:orientation="vertical">

        <LinearLayout
xmlns:android="http://schemas.android.com/apk/res/android"
            android:layout_width="match_parent"
            android:layout_height="wrap_content"
            android:background="@color/colorPrimary"
            android:gravity="center_vertical"
            android:minHeight="?attr/actionBarSize"
            android:orientation="horizontal">

            <ImageButton
                android:layout_width="wrap_content"
                android:layout_height="wrap_content"
                android:background="?attr/selectableItemBackground"
                android:padding="10dp"
                android:onClick="closeClick"
                android:src="@drawable/im_close"
                android:tint="@color/white" />

            <LinearLayout
                android:layout_width="0dp"
                android:layout_height="wrap_content"
                android:layout_weight="1"
                android:orientation="vertical"
                android:paddingLeft="8dp"
                android:paddingRight="8dp">

                <TextView
                    android:id="@+id/title"
                    android:layout_width="wrap_content"
                    android:layout_height="wrap_content"
                    android:text="Panaji"
                    android:textColor="@color/white"
                    android:textSize="18sp"
                    android:textStyle="normal" />

            </LinearLayout>
```

```
    </LinearLayout>

    <LinearLayout
        android:id="@+id/searchViewLay"
        android:layout_width="match_parent"
        android:layout_height="wrap_content"
        android:background="@drawable/ripple_white_button"
        android:gravity="center"
        android:padding="10dp">

        <ImageView
            android:layout_width="wrap_content"
            android:layout_height="wrap_content"
            android:padding="5dp"
            android:src="@drawable/im_search_72" />

        <EditText
            android:id="@+id/searchText"
            android:layout_width="match_parent"
            android:layout_height="wrap_content"
            android:background="@color/transparent"
            android:hint="Type to filter by location"
            android:padding="10dp"
            android:textSize="14dp" />

    </LinearLayout>

    <RelativeLayout
        android:layout_width="match_parent"
        android:layout_height="match_parent">

        <android.support.v7.widget.RecyclerView
            android:id="@+id/searchList"
            android:layout_width="match_parent"
            android:layout_height="match_parent" />

    </RelativeLayout>

    </LinearLayout>

</RelativeLayout>
```

The major components on this screen are the `EditText`, for typing the text for searching. Another important component is the `RecyclerView`, which displays the list of all the details. Here, we are concerned more about the way the UX for the search gives a smooth experience to a user. For this, various animations are used:

```
//ANIMATIONS
private void enterViews() {
    showTop(searchViewLay);
    showBottom(mightLike, new AnimatorListenerAdapter() {
        @Override
        public void onAnimationStart(Animator animation) {
            super.onAnimationStart(animation);
        }
    });
}
```

The `enterViews` method animates the are being used f

The `showTop` method inside the `enterViews` method is described as follows:

```
private void showTop(View view) {
    view.setVisibility(View.VISIBLE);
    Animator iconAnim = ObjectAnimator.ofPropertyValuesHolder(view,
                PropertyValuesHolder.ofFloat(View.TRANSLATION_Y, -
view.getHeight(), 0f));
    iconAnim.setDuration(VIEW_ANIMATION);
    iconAnim.start();
}
```

The `showTop` method makes the view visible. The view being passed to the method as a parameter is the `searchViewLayout`, which means that it makes the search view visible. Then it adds the animation to that particular search view layout. The animation is set to make a translate animation, which means that the search view layout will be translated along the Y axis for a distance of the `searchViewLayout`'s height, for the duration of `VIEW_ANIMATION`'s time. Then, the animation is started using the `start()` method. The following is the explanation of the `showBottom` method inside the `enterViews` method:

```
private void showBottom(View view, Animator.AnimatorListener listener) {
view.setVisibility(View.VISIBLE);
Animator iconAnim = ObjectAnimator.ofPropertyValuesHolder(view,
PropertyValuesHolder.ofFloat(View.TRANSLATION_Y, view.getHeight(), 0f));
iconAnim.setDuration(VIEW_ANIMATION);
iconAnim.addListener(listener);
iconAnim.start();
}
```

The `showBottom()` method, similar to the `showTop()` method, will do the same translation animation for the `mightLike` layout. This animation will have a listener, which will let you know when the animation starts and when it ends. The `exitViews()` method will be called when the search view has to be closed. These animations will show up just before the search view closes:

```
//EXIT
private void exitViews() {
    hideTop(searchViewLay);
    hideBottom(mightLike, new AnimatorListenerAdapter() {
            @Override
            public void onAnimationStart(Animator animation) {
                    super.onAnimationStart(animation);
            }

            @Override
            public void onAnimationEnd(Animator animation) {
                    super.onAnimationEnd(animation);
            }
    });
    new Handler().postDelayed(new Runnable() {
            @Override
            public void run() {
                    finish();
                    overridePendingTransition(0, 0);
            }
    }, 50);

}
```

Here, both the `searchViewLay` and the `mightLike` layouts should be hidden, showing the closing animations:

```
private void hideTop(final View view) {
    view.setVisibility(View.VISIBLE);
    Animator iconAnim = ObjectAnimator.ofPropertyValuesHolder(view,
                PropertyValuesHolder.ofFloat(View.TRANSLATION_Y, 0f, -
view.getHeight()),
                PropertyValuesHolder.ofFloat(View.ALPHA, 1f, 0f));
    iconAnim.setDuration(VIEW_ANIMATION);
    iconAnim.start();
}
```

In the `hideTop()` method, the `searchViewLay` will be made to animate along the Y-axis in the opposite direction with respect to the preceding translation:

```
private void hideBottom(final View view, Animator.AnimatorListener
listener) {
    view.setVisibility(View.VISIBLE);
    Animator iconAnim = ObjectAnimator.ofPropertyValuesHolder(view,
                PropertyValuesHolder.ofFloat(View.TRANSLATION_Y, 0f,
view.getHeight()),
                PropertyValuesHolder.ofFloat(View.ALPHA, 1f, 0f));
    iconAnim.setDuration(VIEW_ANIMATION);
    iconAnim.addListener(listener);
    iconAnim.start();
}
```

Building the UX Design

With the increased expectation of users who are becoming more accustomed to high quality apps, and as UX plays a very important part in making a user's app experience better, it is necessary to build a proper UX pattern. Android library provides many ways and built-in libraries for building a good UX. Besides these, you need to build your own UX patterns depending on the flow of your app. To build a good UX, you need to use animations in the right places.

Understanding UX principles and how it's different from UI

The user experience is very important for keeping a user engaged with the app by making them understand what is happening on the screen. Here is another simple material aspect of UX, where a user gets a very good experience when they click on **view** on the screen; the UX shows a ripple effect when the user clicks on the view:

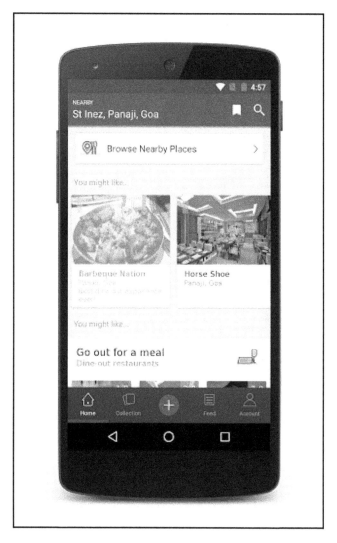

Figure 3.1.2. The Ripple effect

The ripple effect starts from the point of contact with the screen. The ripple is high at the point of contact and gradually decreases its force. Firstly, a user should know when they click on a button and should not have a doubt whether they have clicked or not. Having this effect gives a user a very good experience when they click on a button.

Let's see how to integrate the ripple effect on the button click of any views. We will use the `CardView` as the outermost clickable view. The following is the code to do that:

```
<android.support.v7.widget.CardView
    android:layout_width="0dp"
    android:layout_height="wrap_content"
    android:layout_margin="3dp"
    android:layout_weight="1"
    android:clickable="true"
    android:foreground="@drawable/place_foreground"
    android:padding="0dp"
    app:cardBackgroundColor="@color/white"
    app:cardCornerRadius="0dp"
    app:cardElevation="0dp"
    app:cardPreventCornerOverlap="false"
    app:cardUseCompatPadding="true"
    app:contentPadding="0dp">
```

We will use the foreground attribute of the `CardView` to make the ripple effect when the user clicks on the `CardView`:

```
android:foreground="@drawable/place_foreground"
```

We will check the drawable file `@drawable/place_foreground`, placed in the `drawable` folder:

```
<inset xmlns:android="http://schemas.android.com/apk/res/android"
    android:drawable="@drawable/place_foreground_selector"
    android:insetBottom="4dp"
    android:insetLeft="2dp"
    android:insetRight="2dp"
    android:insetTop="4dp" />
```

An inset is used when you need a background that is of smaller bounds than the actual view's bounds. We need to set a `drawable` for the inset. The `place_foreground_selector drawable` is used to do that:

```
<?xml version="1.0" encoding="utf-8"?>
<selector xmlns:android="http://schemas.android.com/apk/res/android">
    <item android:state_pressed="true">
        <shape android:shape="rectangle">
            <solid android:color="@color/place_item_ripple_color" />
            <corners android:radius="@dimen/card_corner_radius" />
        </shape>
    </item>
    <item android:state_enabled="true" android:state_focused="true">
        <shape android:shape="rectangle">
```

```
        <solid android:color="@color/place_item_ripple_color" />
        <corners android:radius="@dimen/card_corner_radius" />
      </shape>
    </item>
</selector>
```

This `drawable` is a selector, which checks three states. `state_pressed="true"` is
executed when the view is clicked. At this point, the following shape is seen in the view:

```
<shape android:shape="rectangle">
    <solid android:color="@color/place_item_ripple_color" />
    <corners android:radius="@dimen/card_corner_radius" />
</shape>
```

It gives a color to the view, which is set is the `colors.xml` and has a corner radius, which is
set from the `dimens.xml` file present in the values folder. The color defined is the hex code
of the color that needs to be displayed when the view is pressed:

```
<color name="place_item_ripple_color">@color/white_ripple</color>
<color name="white_ripple">#96ffffff</color>
```

The `ffffff` color set is a white color, and 96 is the alpha value set to give transparency to
the white color. `state_enabled="true"` and `state_focused="true"` are states to check
when the view is enabled and focused. Only when these two conditions are satisfied, is the
shape drawn:

```
<shape android:shape="rectangle">
    <solid android:color="@color/place_item_ripple_color" />
    <corners android:radius="@dimen/card_corner_radius" />
</shape>
```

`shape` as defined here is a rectangle, as the `CardView` is a rectangle with rounded corners.
The drawable `file-@drawable/place_foreground-is` also placed in the `drawable-`
`v21` folder. The `@drawable/place_foreground` file placed in the `drawable` folder is used
to generate the ripple effect in devices prior to Android version 21, as the ripple effect is not
supported on older versions of Android. For Android versions later than v21, the ripple
effect is built-in:

```
<ripple xmlns:android="http://schemas.android.com/apk/res/android"
    android:color="@color/place_item_ripple_color"
    android:drawable="@drawable/place_foreground_selector" />
```

Here, the ripple is a built-in class, which defines the ripple effect. It needs to set a drawable and a color. The ripple color is the same one defined earlier. Also, the `@drawable/place_foreground_selector` drawable needs to be placed in the `drawable-v21` folder:

```xml
<?xml version="1.0" encoding="utf-8"?>
<selector xmlns:android="http://schemas.android.com/apk/res/android">
    <item android:state_pressed="true">
        <shape android:shape="rectangle">
            <solid android:color="@color/place_item_ripple_color" />
        </shape>
    </item>
    <item android:state_enabled="true" android:state_focused="true">
        <shape android:shape="rectangle">
            <solid android:color="@color/place_item_ripple_color" />
        </shape>
    </item>
</selector>
```

Both the `@drawable/place_foreground_selector` folders are similar, except that the corners do not have to be specified.

Summary

Material design plays an important part in how a user is able to use an app easily, and hence it makes sure that they use the app more often. In this chapter, we covered material design and followed with the material design animation. We then processed this animation to build animation in the app. In the next section, we will cover building the core features of the foodspotting app.

6

SOLID Android Development and Its Design Principles

SOLID is a mnemonic acronym that helps define the five basic object-oriented design principles:

- Single Responsibility Principle
- Open-Closed Principle
- Liskov Substitution Principle
- Interface Segregation Principle
- Dependency Inversion Principle

Single Responsibility Principle

The Single Responsibility Principle states that:

A class should have one, and only one, reason to change.

The idea behind this principle is to design a class that has one responsibility or various methods with unique functionality. According to this principle, a method should not do more than one task at a time. Each function must be designated a unique task.

Let's take, for example, the adapter of a `recyclerView`:

```
@Override
public void onBindViewHolder(final ViewHolder holder, final int position) {
    PlaceItem item = list.get(position);

    String name = item.getName() != null ? item.getName() : "";
```

```
      String description = item.getDescription() != null ?
  item.getDescription() : "";
      String location = item.getAddress() != null ? item.getAddress() : "";
      String rating = String.format("%.02f", item.getRating());
      String distance = item.getDistance()+"km";
      holder.name.setText(name);
      holder.location.setText(location);
      holder.description.setText(description);
      holder.rating.setText(rating);
      holder.distance.setText(item.getDistance());
      Picasso.with(context)
            .load(R.drawable.im_backdrop)
            .placeholder(R.drawable.placeholder_200)
            .error(R.drawable.placeholder_200)
            .into(holder.image);
  }
```

The preceding code is the `onBindViewHolder` of the adapter of a `recyclerView`. It does not satisfy the single responsibility principle, as we are formatting the values as we are setting the text to the views. The `onBindViewHolder` of the `recyclerView` adapter is mainly responsible for binding the view with the values of its object class.

In the preceding code, the `onBindViewHolder` is doing more tasks than it should. If we have kept the same format in more than one place and there comes a need to make changes to the format, then we will have to make the changes everywhere and this may result in software logic duplication issues. If we don't update the code in some places, it may cause an error. If the code was a logical change that had been replicated, the entire flow of the app would change. To prevent this, we have to write the code in a way that we don't have to make many changes if the features are changed.

As in the case of the preceding example, we can refactor it by the following:

```
  @Override
  public void onBindViewHolder(final ViewHolder holder, final int position) {
      PlaceItem item = list.get(position);

      holder.name.setText(CommonFunctions.checkNull(item.getName()));
  holder.description.setText(CommonFunctions.checkNull(item.getDescription())
  );
      holder.location.setText(CommonFunctions.checkNull(item.getAddress()));
      holder.rating.setText(CommonFunctions.formatRating(item.getRating()));
      holder.distance.setText(
  CommonFunctions.formatDistance(item.getDistance()));

      Picasso.with(context)
            .load(R.drawable.im_backdrop)
            .placeholder(R.drawable.placeholder_200)
```

```
            .error(R.drawable.placeholder_200)
            .into(holder.image);
    }
```

Now, as can be seen, the code checking and formatting are not done in the `onBindViewHolder` function but they are being done elsewhere. Due to this, the change of the functionality or format can be done in the common function instead of each instance of the code.

Open-Closed Principle

The Open-Closed Principle states that:

Software entities (classes, modules, functions, etc) should be open for extension, but closed for modification.

This principle basically states that we have to design our modules, classes, and functions in a way that when a new functionality is needed, we should not modify our existing code but rather write new code that will be used by existing code

Now let us discuss the Open-Closed Principle in the following example.

Let us assume we are trying to calculate the area of some shapes. So let's take the example of a rectangle and a circle. The classes for these have been formed in the following code:

```
public class Rectangle {
    private double length;
    private double height;
    // getters/setters ...
}

public class Circle {
    private double radius;
    // getters/setters ...
}
```

So a common function used to calculate the area of both the rectangle and the circle would look something like this:

```
public class AreaManager {
    public double calculateArea(ArrayList<Object>... shapes) {
        double area = 0;
        for (Object shape : shapes) {
            if (shape instanceof Rectangle) {
                Rectangle rect = (Rectangle)shape;
```

```
            area += (rect.getLength() * rect.getHeight());
        } else if (shape instanceof Circle) {
            Circle circle = (Circle)shape;
            area += (circle.getRadius() * cirlce.getRadius() * Math.PI;
        } else {
            throw new RuntimeException("Shape not supported");
        }
    }
    return area;
    }
}
```

As can be seen from the preceding function, as new shapes are introduced, the calculateArea function will grow bigger and lots of handling and changes will be required. This violates the Open/Closed Principle

A way to resolve this is by using a common interface:

```
public interface Shape {
    double getArea();
}
```

Both the rectangle and circle can implement this interface by which the method to calculate the area will remain inside the object class instead of the AreaManager.

So now the rectangle and circle classes will look something like this:

```
public class Rectangle implements Shape {
    private double length;
    private double height;
    // getters/setters ...

    @Override
    public double getArea() {
        return (length * height);
    }
}

public class Circle implements Shape {
    private double radius;
    // getters/setters ...

    @Override
    public double getArea() {
        return (radius * radius * Math.PI);
    }
}
```

Now, as the methods for calculating the areas are present inside the objects, the `AreaManager` will look something like this:

```
public class AreaManager {
    public double calculateArea(ArrayList<Shape> shapes) {
        double area = 0;
        for (Shape shape : shapes) {
            area += shape.getArea();
        }
        return area;
    }
}
```

Now we can calculate the total area without ever needing to change the `calculateArea` method. The same shape interface can be now used in new classes to calculate the area without changing the `AreaManager`.

Liskov Substitution Principle

The Liskov Substitution Principle states that:

Child classes should never break the parent class' type definitions.

According to this principle, a subclass should override the parent class's methods in a way that does not break functionality from a client's point of view.

According to this principle, if a class is extending another class, the functionality of the child class should not conflict with that of its parent.

We can demonstrate this with the following example:

```
public class Rectangle {
    private double length;
    private double height;

    public void setLength(double length) {
        this.length = length;
    }

    public void setHeight(double height) {
        this.height = height;
    }

    public double getLength() {
```

```
        return length;
    }

    @Override
    public double getHeight() {
        return height;
    }

    public double getArea() {
        return (length * height);
    }
}
```

Here we have a rectangle. As we know, a square is also a type of rectangle, so it can extend the `Rectangle` class. Also we know that the height and the width of the square have to be the same so the getter can be written like this:

```
public class Square extends Rectangle {

    @Override
    public void setHeight(double height) {
        this.length = height;
        this.height = height;
    }

    @Override
    public void setLength(double length) {
        this.length = length;
        this.height = length;
    }
}
```

As can be seen from the preceding definition, we can get a rectangle also from the square implementation.

So now let's get an instance of Rectangle from the `Square` class:

```
Rectangle r = new Square();
r.setHeight(5);
r.setLength(10);
```

Now if we try to get the area, we will get 100 instead of 50, as a square has both the same length and height, which is not the case with a rectangle, and this violates the Liskov Substitution Principle.

A simple example of the Liskov Substitution Principle would be a List and ArrayList. An ArrayList implements a List but it does not change the basic functionality of the List.

Interface Segregation Principle

The Interface Segregation Principle states that:

No client should be forced to depend on methods it does not use.

According to this principle, if an interface has too many methods, then we need to divide the interface into smaller interfaces with fewer methods. A simple example of this principle is shown next.

Let us assume we are using a custom interface to detect various states of a view:

```
public interface ClickListener {
    public void onItemClickListener(View v, int pos);
    public void onItemLongClickListener(View v, int pos);
    public void onItemPressListener(View v, int pos);
    public void onSelectedListener(View v, int pos);
}
```

Now, while implementing this listener, we only want the `onItemClickListener` or the `onItemLongClickListener;` the others are not required but we still have to use them in the code. This violates the Interface Segregation Principle.

Now we can easily resolve this by splitting the interface into smaller interfaces, like this:

```
public interface ClickListener {
    public void onItemClickListener(View v, int pos);
    public void onItemLongClickListener(View v, int pos);
}
public interface HoldListener {
    public void onItemPressListener(View v, int pos);
    public void onSelectedListener(View v, int pos);
}
```

Now we will only initialize the `ClickListener` and use its methods instead of the old interface where we had to utilize four methods. Here we have segregated them into two different interfaces.

Dependency Inversion Principle

The Dependency Inversion Principle states that:

1. *High-level modules should not depend on low-level modules. Both should depend on abstractions.*

2. *Abstractions should not depend upon details. Details should depend upon abstractions.*

The best way to explain this principle is by giving an example. Let's assume we have a `Worker` class that is a low level class and a `Manager` class that is a high level class. The `Manager` class contains many complex functionalities which it implements along with the `Worker` class, so the classes will look something like this:

```
class Worker {

    public void work() {
        // ....working
    }
}

class Manager {
    //--Other Functionality
    Worker worker;

    public void setWorker(Worker w) {
        worker = w;
    }

    public void manage() {
        worker.work();
    }
}
```

Here the `Manager` class has been implemented and is directly associated with the `Worker` class due to which changes in the `Worker` class directly affect the `Manager` class.

If we have to add another class which would be a parent of the `Worker` class, and the `Worker` class does similar work to that of the `Manager` class, it will require lots of changes.

To make it easier to add the `Manager` class, we will use interfaces:

```
interface IWorker {
    public void work();
}

class Worker implements IWorker{
```

```
    public void work() {
        // ....working
    }
}

class SuperWorker  implements IWorker{
    public void work() {
        //.... working much more
    }
}

class Manager {
    IWorker worker;

    public void setWorker(IWorker w) {
        worker = w;
    }

    public void manage() {
        worker.work();
    }
}
```

Now the both the worker and SuperWorker class implement the `IWorker`, while the `Manager` class directly uses the `IWorker` to complete its functionality by which changes to the `Worker` and `SuperWorker` do not affect the `Manager` class.

Summary

The SOLID principles are five principles that one should follow while coding. They are at times tough to put into practice when it comes to the usage of each individual principle, but making a habit of following these principles will keep your code readable, reusable, and easy to maintain.

7
Understanding MVC, MVP, MVVM and Clean Arch Patterns

A design pattern is a reusable form of a solution to a design problem. It is a style of coding by which we can manage various components of the system we are making. Here we will discuss four of those design patterns: MVC, MVP, MVVM, and Clean Arch.

MVC (Model View Controller)

This is one of the most widely used approaches in software development. The MVC consists of three main components:

- **Model**: The model represents the object in the application. This has the logic of where the data is to be fetched from. This can also have the logic by which the controller can update the view. In Android, the model is mostly represented by object classes.
- **View**: The view consists of the components that can interact with the user and is responsible for how the model is displayed in the application. In Android, the view is mostly represented by the XML where the layouts can be designed.
- **Controller**: The controller acts as a mediator between the model and the view. It controls the data flow into the model object and updates the view whenever data changes. In Android, the controller is mostly represented by the activities and fragments.

All of these components interact with each other and perform specific tasks, as shown in the following figure:

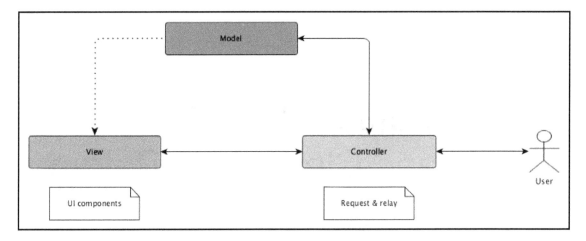

Figure 2.2.1

It has been noticed that Android is not able to follow the MVC architecture completely, as activity/fragment can act as both the controller and the view, which makes all the code cluttered in one place. Activity/fragment can be used to draw multiple views for a single screen in an app, thus all different data calls and views are populated in the same place. Therefore, to solve this problem, we can use different design patterns or can implement MVC carefully by taking care of conventions and following proper programming guidelines.

The following shows a basic example of how MVC is used in Android :

Model:

```
public class LocationItem {
String name;
String address;
public LocationItem(String name, String address) {
this.name = name;
this.address = address;
}
public String getName() {
return name;
}
public String getAddress() {
return address;
}
}
```

View:

```
<TextView
android:id="@+id/name"
style="@style/HorizontalPlaceTitleTxtStyle"
android:layout_width="wrap_content"
android:layout_height="wrap_content" />
```

Controller:

```
TextView name = (TextView)findViewById(R.id.name);
name.setText(LocationUtil.getLocationName(list.get(position)));
//Function In LocationUtil(Controller Class)
public class LocationUtil {
public static String getLocationName(LocationItem item) {
return item.getName();
}
}
```

To explain the MVC pattern components shown in the preceding code; the model here is `LocationItem`, which holds the name and address of the location. The view is an XML file, which contains a `TextView`, through which the name of the location can be displayed. The activity, which is the controller, contains a `LocationItem`. It gets the name of the `LocationItem` at a specific position in the list and sets it up in the view, which displays it.

MVP (Model View Presenter)

Model View Presenter (**MVP**) is derived from the MVC pattern. MVP is used to minimize the high dependency on the view, which is the case in the MVC. It separates the view and model by using the presenter. The presenter decides what should be displayed on the view.

- **Model**: The model represents the objects in the application. This has the logic of where the data is to be fetched from.
- **View**: The view renders information to users and contains a UI Component .xml file, activity, fragments, and dialog under the View Layer. It does not have any other logic implemented.
- **Presenter**: The presenter layer performs the task of the controller and acts as the mediator between the view and model. But unlike the controller, it is not dependent on the view. The view interacts with the presenter for the data to be displayed, and the presenter then takes the data from the model and returns it to the view in a presentable format. The presenter does not contain any UI components; it just manipulates data from the model and displays it on the view.

The interaction between the various components of the MVP are shown in the following figure:

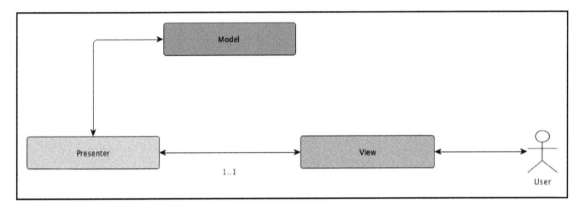

Figure 2.2.2

In the MVP design, the presenter communicates with the view through interfaces. The interfaces are defined in the presenter class, to which it passes the required data. The activity/fragment or any other view component implements the interfaces and renders the data in a way they want. The connection between the presenter and the view is one to one.

The following provides an example to enable a better understanding of the MVP design:

In this example, we will show how the MVP design can be used to display a list into a `recyclerview`:

```
public interface LocationInteractor {

    interface OnLoadFinishedListener {
        void onSuccess(List<LocationItem> items);
        void onFailed();
    }
    void loadLocations(OnLoadFinishedListener listener);

}
```

Here we have a `LocationInteractor` class that is used by the presenter to communicate with the model:

```
public class LocationInteractorImpl implements LocationInteractor {

    @Override
    public void loadLocations(final OnLoadFinishedListener listener) {
```

```
        RetroInterface.getRssFeedApi().getFeed("", new
Callback<LocationResponse>() {
            @Override
            public void success(LocationResponse locationResponse, Response
response) {
                if (listener != null) {
                    if (locationResponse != null) {
                        listener.onSuccess(locationResponse.getDetails());
                    } else {
                        listener.onFailed();
                    }
                }
            }

            @Override
            public void failure(RetrofitError error) {
                if (listener != null) {
                    listener.onFailed();
                }
            }
        });
    }
}
```

This is the `LocationInteractorImpl` class which is the model. This class interacts with the presenter to provide the list of locations.

The `loadLocations` function is used by the presenter to interact with the model and fetch the list of locations.

The model (`LocationInteractorImpl`) then uses the `listener.onSuccess` and `listener.onFailed` methods to send results back to the presenter:

```
public interface LocationInterface {

    void showProgress();
    void hideProgress();
    void locationLoaded(List<LocationItem> items);
}
```

The `LocationInterface` class is used by the presenter to communicate with the view:

```
public interface LocationPresenter {
    void loadLocations();
    void onDestroy();
}
```

The `LocationPresenter` class is used by the view to communicate with the presenter. Depending on the functions called by the view, the presenter will communicate with the model and get the responses:

```
public class LocationPresenterImpl implements LocationPresenter,
LocationInteractor.OnLoadFinishedListener {

    private LocationInterface locationInterface;
    private LocationInteractor locationInteractor;

    public LocationPresenterImpl(LocationInterface locationInterface) {
        this.locationInterface = locationInterface;
        this.locationInteractor = new LocationInteractorImpl();
    }

    @Override public void loadLocations() {
        if (locationInterface != null) {
            locationInterface.showProgress();
        }
        locationInteractor.loadLocations(this);
    }
    @Override public void onDestroy() {
        locationInterface = null;
    }

    @Override
    public void onSuccess(List<LocationItem> items) {
        if (locationInterface != null) {
            locationInterface.locationLoaded(items);
            locationInterface.hideProgress();
        }
    }

    @Override public void onFailed() {
        if (locationInterface != null) {
            locationInterface.locationLoaded(null);
            locationInterface.hideProgress();
        }
    }
}
```

The `LocationPresenterImpl` class is the presenter class which communicates between the view and the model. This class implements `LocationPresenter` with which the view communicates with the presenter and the `LocationInteractor.OnLoadFinishedListener` from which the model communicates with the presenter.

When the view calls the `loadLocations` function of the presenter, the presenter interacts with the model and calls the `loadLocations` method of the model, indicating that the model is to return the list of locations to be displayed.

The `onSuccess` and `onFailed` functions are then called by the model after the list has been fetched successfully or has failed. Then the presenter communicates with the view through the `locationLoaded` function. Here, it passes the list that has been fetched by the model:

```
public class LocationListActivity extends Activity implements
LocationInterface{
    private ProgressBar progressBar;
    RecyclerView recyclerView;
    List<LocationItem> items;
    AddPlacesAdapter adapter;
    private LocationPresenter presenter;
    @Override
    protected void onCreate(Bundle savedInstanceState) {
        super.onCreate(savedInstanceState);
        setContentView(R.layout.activity_login);

        progressBar = (ProgressBar) findViewById(R.id.progress);
        recyclerView = (RecyclerView) findViewById(R.id.recyclerView);
        items = new ArrayList<>();
        adapter = new AddPlacesAdapter(this, items);
        adapter.setClickListener(new AddPlacesAdapter.ClickListener() {
            @Override
            public void onItemClickListener(View v, int pos) {
                //Handle Click events
            }
        });
        recyclerView.setLayoutManager(new LinearLayoutManager(this));
        recyclerView.setAdapter(adapter);
        presenter = new LocationPresenterImpl(this);
        presenter.loadLocations();
    }

    @Override
    protected void onDestroy() {
        presenter.onDestroy();
        super.onDestroy();
```

```
    }

    @Override
    public void showProgress() {
        progressBar.setVisibility(View.VISIBLE);
    }
    @Override
    public void hideProgress() {
        progressBar.setVisibility(View.GONE);
    }

    @Override
    public void locationLoaded(List<LocationItem> items){
        if(items!=null) {
            this.items = items;
            adapter.refresh(items);
        }
    }
}
```

The `LocationListActivity` is the view where all the interaction with the user will happen. The view implements the `LocationInterface`, by which it gets the responses from the presenter. The view uses an instance of the presenter:

```
presenter = new LocationPresenterImpl(this);
```

It then calls the `presenter.loadLocations();` to tell the presenter that it wants the list of locations to be displayed.

MVVM

MVVM stands for **Model-View-View-Model**. It is similar to the MVC model, the only difference being it has two-way data binding with the view and view-model. The changes in the view are being propagated via the view-model, which uses an observer pattern to communicate between the view-model and the model. The view in this case is completely isolated from the model.

The major advantage of using MVVM is it enables automatic changes in the view via the view-model:

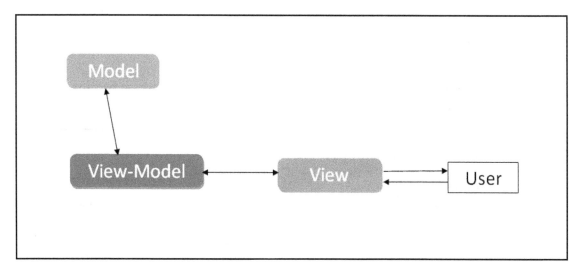

Figure 2.2.3

MVVM has the following components:

- **Model**: The model represents the objects in the application. This has the logic of where the data is to be fetched from.
- **View**: The view is similar to the MVC pattern view, which renders information to users and contains a UI Component .xml file, activity, fragments, and dialog under the View Layer. It does not have any other logic implemented.
- **View-model**: The view-model helps in maintaining the state of the view and does changes to the model based on the inputs gained from the view.

Many views can be linked to one view-model, which creates a many-to-one relation between the view and a view-model. Also, a view has information about the view-model but the view-model does not have any information about the view. The view is not responsible for the state of information; rather, that is being managed by the view-model and the view and the model are only reflected via the changes made to the view-model.

In developer's terminology, one can say that the view-model is the interface between a designer and a coder.

Clean Architecture Pattern

The Clean Architecture Pattern, in its simplest terms, means to write a clean code, by separating it into layers, with the outer layer being your implementations and the inner layer being the business logic. An interface connects these two layers, controlling how the outer layers use the inner layers.

This kind of code architecture pattern is also known as Onion Architecture because of its different layers, as seen in the following figure:

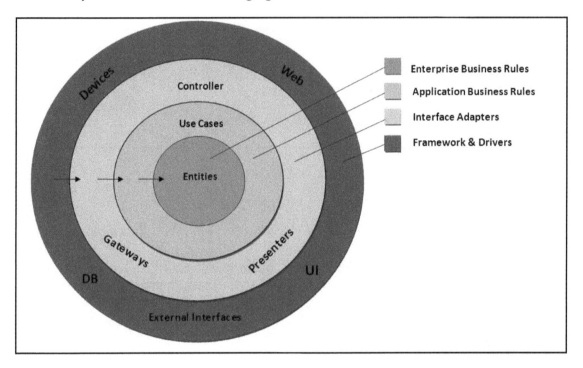

Figure 2.2.4

The inner layers have no idea about the outer layers. The outer layer uses the components from the inner layers based upon its needs, meaning the outer layers are dependent on the business logic implementations of the inner layers. Hence, the dependency points inwards.

Understanding the layers of Clean Architecture

Understanding the various layers present in this architecture helps to achieve a code implementation that is clean and independent. I will outline the layers in the figure, but focus more on the Clean Architecture core conceptual rules: The Dependency Rule, Abstraction Principle, and communication between the layers:

- **Entities**:
  Entities form the core of your app, which means they define what exactly your app is doing. Entities are basically objects created to make a data model to hold the business logic and the functionality that would be carried out on it. Some of the entities for an app could be a user entity, a restaurant entity, a place entity, and so on.

- **Use cases**:
  Use cases are in the layer that forms objects using the core entities. The use cases may contain one or more entities based upon their use. The use cases are a direct object used for forming a business logic. A simple use case could be order, which books a restaurant for a user. Hence, this use case may contain entities such as user and restaurant.

- **Presenter**:
  This layer is the one that presents a use case for its use. This means that it may have a business logic which would be using the entities to give an output data to the UI for rendering.

- **UI**:
  This is basically the output that you see and is formed by the components such as activities, fragments, views, adapters, and so on.

All of these components form the core of the architecture. This could be forming the way the structure should look like when things are being coded. But a Clean Architecture Pattern is formed only when some major principles are put to best use.

The crux of the Clean Architecture is formed by the following principles:

- **Dependency Rule**:
  The Dependency Rule makes up a major chunk of the Clean Architecture pattern. What it says is that the outer layers should depend on the inner layers.
  The inner layers should have no idea about the outer layers. But the outer layers can use, or can see, or know about the components of the inner layers, and, based upon their needs, could make use of them. It also means that the outer layers are dependent on the business logic implementations of the inner layers. Hence, the dependency points inwards, as shown in figure 2.2.4.

- **Abstraction Principle**:
  The Abstraction Principle says that as you are moving towards the center, the code becomes more abstract as the inner circle contains business logic and the outer circle contains implementation details. The inner layers are abstract because the outer layer does not know anything about the business logic used by the inner layers. It only knows the key features of what it does.
  Let us have a simple example to understand this layer. Let us consider the case where a user can increase or decrease the brightness of the device. The brightness could be changed using a code that has already been written with some business logic that is completely abstract. But the feature that we know is that changing the slider values will increase or decrease the brightness of the device.

- **Communication between the layers**:
  The two layers need some kind of interface between them in order to enable communication between the inner layers and the outer layers.
  From the Dependency Principle, we know that the outer layers should communicate with the inner layers, and to communicate with the inner layer, the outer layer needs an interface. This interface acts as a communication mode between the outer layers with the inner layers.
  As mentioned by the dependency rule, the dependency points inwards; that is, the outer layers communicate with the inner layers, but there is a small twist here. The inner layers pass back the result to the outer layer after applying the business logic; that is, the inner layers have an output port. The inner layer will return a use case to the outer layer. The use case to be returned at the output port could be decided by the inner layer. The inner layer would still not know, what the outer layer will do with it.

To better understand the aforementioned principles, check out this code reference as an example to show the Abstraction Principle. Consider the following line of code:

```
ratingTextView.setText(CommonFunction.formatRating(restaurant.getRating()))
;
```

This is a statement in Android code that displays the rating for a restaurant in a `TextView` in an Android app. It seems to be a complex one when you just look at it but would be really simple when split up in to sections.

`ratingTextView` is the `TextView` and `.setText` sets the text for this `ratingTextView`.

The rating value to be set needs to be provided to this `ratingTextView` and is decided by `restaurant.getRating()`. Here `restaurant` is an object of the entity Restaurant and `.getRating()` gives the rating value for that restaurant. `CommonFunction.formatRating` formats the rating to a specific rounded value that should be displayed in `ratingTextView`.

Once you have roughly understood this line of code, let me now explain to you how and where the principles are being applied in this case. The `formatRating` is a function name that does the work of taking the rating value as input, applying some business logic to it, and giving back a result in the form of a specific rounded value. Now this business logic is abstract to the outer layer. Hence, the Principle of Abstraction is applied.

The inner layer is a `formatRating` function that would take input as the rating value and give output as a rounded value of the rating. The outer layer is just making a call to that function to get a rounded value and then display it. The dependency is from the outer layer to the inner layer, and the inner layer does not know what the outer layer is going to do with the rounded value. Hence, the Dependency Rule is applied.

The outer layer has to call the inner layer function that is written in the `CommonFunction` class. The `CommonFunction` class calls the `formatRating` function, which makes the communication between the outer layer and the inner layer

The preceding example is applied at a code level with one statement. The same could be applied at different levels where the outer layer and inner layers would be different.

Summary

What you can learn from the architectural patterns described in this chapter, is that you keep the code segregated to avoid dependencies. What is asked from a user, what it does internally, and what is presented back to the user are all independent pieces of code that are linked to one another by a thin crust. All these patterns have some features in common.

8
Decision Making

Have you asked yourself some of the following questions anytime in your coding career?

Why do I code the way I code? Am I coding the correct way? If I am not coding the right way, what is the right way to code? If you have ever asked yourself such questions, then that is the best thing you might have ever done.

Decision making is a very important part of your coding career: deciding how to code and what the best practices are, why to code following some standard patterns, and why not to code in a certain way. I will help you classify the various patterns here.

How to begin

It is important to follow a proper code pattern to make your code structured, more efficient, non-redundant, reusable, and less time-consuming when maintaining it. It is obvious that you may revisit a code after a long time, for one reason or another.

In such a case, you should be happy that the code you have written is structured and easily reusable for yourself. You should not have to spend time finding out all the dependencies of the code that you are looking at.

To follow a proper structure and pattern, these are the strategies that you may need to use while building your app structure:

- Creational patterns
- Builder
- Dependency injection
- Singleton

Structural patterns:

- Adapter
- Facade

Behavioral patterns:

- Command
- Observer
- Model View Controller
- Model View View-Model

Creational patterns

The creational pattern is the pattern to be followed for the creation of code.

It pertains to how you create an object, by making use of the existing code and by creating an instance of the existing code. It's basically reusing code by creating objects instead of repeating code.

Using a creational pattern, objects may be created making use of the existing code by following some standard patterns.

Builder

The builder pattern separates the construction of a complex object from its representation.

This means that creating a construction makes use of a builder to build the structure. This builder could be customized to create different representations of the same construction.

Consider the following piece of code to show an alert dialog in Android:

```
AlertDialog.Builder builder = new AlertDialog.Builder(this)
        .setTitle("Dialog Title")
        .setMessage("Description for the dialog.")
        .setNegativeButton("Cancel", new DialogInterface.OnClickListener() {
            @Override public void onClick(DialogInterface dialogInterface,
    int i) {
                // Call back when "Cancel" button is clicked
            }
        })
        .setPositiveButton("OK", new DialogInterface.OnClickListener() {
```

```
            @Override public void onClick(DialogInterface dialogInterface,
    int i) {
                // Call back when "OK" button is clicked
            }
        });
    builder.show();
```

This `AlertDialog.Builder` helps you specify parts of your `AlertDialog` that matter to you. For instance, you may input your own title and description that need to be created for the dialog. Also, you can customize buttons such as `OK` and `Cancel`, and you can also customize it to not show the `Cancel` button. With these customizations, the builder is created. Once the builder is created, it is used to create the main construction; that is, the `AlertDialog`.

The preceding code block produces the following alert:

Providing different inputs to the builder would give you different outputs.

Dependency injection

Dependency injection gives you the objects required by instantiating a new object. Here, the new object created does not need customizations to be made use of. It can be directly made use of in your code wherever you need it.

Android SDK provides you with many standard classes that may be made use of by creating its objects. For example, a network class provided by Android, `ConnectivityManager`, provides you with predefined functions to give you all the network related data. You just need to create an object of that class and make use of the functions provided by it to get the network data:

```
boolean haveConnectedWifi = false;
boolean haveConnectedMobile = false;
```

```
ConnectivityManager cm = (ConnectivityManager)
getSystemService(CONNECTIVITY_SERVICE);

NetworkInfo[] netInfo = cm.getAllNetworkInfo();
for (NetworkInfo ni : netInfo) {
      if (ni.getTypeName().equalsIgnoreCase("WIFI"))
         if (ni.isConnected())
            haveConnectedWifi = true;
      if (ni.getTypeName().equalsIgnoreCase("MOBILE"))
         if (ni.isConnected())
            haveConnectedMobile = true;
}
boolean isNetworkAvailable = haveConnectedWifi || haveConnectedMobile;
```

The preceding piece of code creates an object of the `ConnectivityManager` that is `cm` class, and using this object, it gets the network info of the mobile device. It checks if the device has mobile data available and also checks if it has Wi-Fi data available. Then, if it has at least one network available, it saves it as a Boolean value in `isNetworkAvailable`, which could be used in your code to check if the network is available.

Many other dependency injection codes are provided by the Android SDK, which provides the network info, app info, stored data in `SharedPreferences`, load image, and so on. These can be used anywhere in your code as per your requirements.

Singleton

The singleton pattern says that a class should have only a single instance that is globally accessible.

A creation of an object of a class is useful when you require only one instance of the class. An example of a class to create a singleton instance is shown here:

```
public class SingletonClass {
   private static SingletonClass instance = null;
   private SingletonClass() {
      // add your initialization data over here
   }
   public static SingletonClass getInstance() {
      if (instance == null) {
         instance = new SingletonClass();
      }
      return instance;
   }
}
```

The preceding class uses a static way of accessing the class, which will create only one instance of the class, as its constructor method is not public. This prevents the creation of multiple instances by making a check of the instance if it is null. In your code, you could then access the singleton instance in the following manner:

```
SingletonClass.getInstance();
```

This will create the instance of the class only once, and you may use that instance anywhere in your app.

You may also have functions in the `SingletonClass` making use of the singleton instance, which will call it only once. In the following code, the same class is extended with a function that you may write to add the functionality to be made use of only once:

```
public class SingletonClass {
    private static SingletonClass instance = null;
    private SingletonClass() {
        // add your initialization data over here
    }
    public static SingletonClass getInstance() {
        if (instance == null) {
            instance = new SingletonClass();
        }
        return instance;
    }

    private boolean isDebug = false;
    public void isDebugMode(boolean isDebugEnabled) {
        this.isDebug = isDebugEnabled;
    }
}
```

The additional code here is the `isDebugMode` function that accepts a Boolean and stores it in a global variable, `isDebug`, of the class. This could be made use of later in the class. This value could be set using the same instance in the following manner:

```
SingletonClass.getInstance().isDebugMode(true);
```

For the same instance, it sets the debug mode to true. This class could be extended accordingly to handle many such singleton instances.

Structural patterns

These patterns are structured to understand exactly what they are doing, and can be made use of in multiple places because of their organized patterns. They create objects in a familiar arrangement that perform typical tasks. In Android, the structural patterns are Adapter and Facade.

Adapter

The word adapter says it all: it adapts itself to be a bridge between the data source and the type of view this data has to be displayed in; basically, the adapter view.

The data here might be of any kind, but it needs to be displayed in the same view, for which an adapter plays an important role.

The following figure identifies how the adapter binds the data with the view:

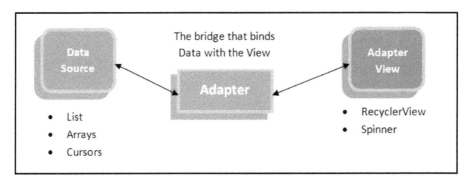

The data could be in any form, such as List, ArrayList, Array, Cursor, and so on. This kind of data needs to be displayed in the RecyclerView, Spinner, and so on, to display the data in a list.

The adapter does not know what kind of data it is going to handle. It will handle and display the type of data it is asked to display. For instance, if a user's list needs to be displayed, then it will require the list of all the users whose lists need to be displayed.

The `RecyclerView` has its own adapter which can be used to display the data in the `RecyclerView`. The following is the code of an adapter class, which explains how to display a user's list using a `RecyclerViewAdapter` into a `RecyclerView`:

```java
public class UserListAdapter extends
RecyclerView.Adapter<UserListAdapter.ViewHolder> {

    private Context context;
    private List<User> userList;

    public UserListAdapter(Context context, List<User> userList) {
        this.context = context;
        this.userList = userList;
    }

    @Override
    public ViewHolder onCreateViewHolder(ViewGroup parent, int viewType) {
        LayoutInflater inflater = LayoutInflater.from(parent.getContext());
        View view = inflater.inflate(R.layout.item_user, parent, false);
        return new ViewHolder(view);
    }

    @Override
    public void onBindViewHolder(final ViewHolder holder, final int
position) {
        final User user = userList.get(position);
        holder.nameTextView.setText(user.getName());
    }

    @Override
    public int getItemCount() {
        return userList.size();
    }

    class ViewHolder extends RecyclerView.ViewHolder {
        protected TextView nameTextView;
        public ViewHolder(View itemView) {
            super(itemView);
            nameTextView = (TextView)
itemView.findViewById(R.id.nameTextView);
        }
    }
}
```

In the code, there is a constructor that takes the `userList` as input:

```
public UserListAdapter(Context context, List<User> userList) {
        this.context = context;
        this.userList = userList;
    }
```

Then the `item_user` layout displays the list in a specified way:

```
View view = inflater.inflate(R.layout.item_user, parent, false);
```

It displays the name of the user in the list using:

```
holder.nameTextView.setText(user.getName());
```

Facade

A facade basically provides an interface so that all the other interfaces can be made use of within it. It is a top layer interface that can be made use of in order to prevent a functionality change affecting any view.

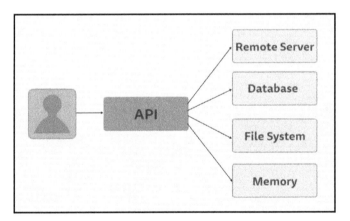

Fig something.something

The preceding figure shows the API interface that becomes a higher-level interface to all the other interfaces, such as databases, servers, or file systems.

For an example of a facade, we will consider a `Retrofit` class that converts your HTTP API into a Java interface:

```
public interface YourAppApi {
    @FormUrlEncoded
    @POST("/login")
    void login(
            @Field("email") String email,
            @Field("password") String password,
            Callback<RetroLogin> cb
    );
}
```

The `YourAppApi` is the higher-level interface within which all the other interfaces will be comprised. Here, an instance of the login API that takes the params as `email` and `password` gives the response in the `RetroLogin` class is given:

```
RestAdapter restAdapter = new RestAdapter.Builder()
        .setLogLevel(RestAdapter.LogLevel.FULL)
        .setEndpoint("http://www.your_website_name.com/")
        .setClient(new OkClient(new OkHttpClient()))
        .build();
```

A `RestAdapter` is created to make the call to the API hosted on a server, which would be the endpoint of your website. It would create an object of the `RestAdapter` class, which you would be using to create the instance of the `YourAppApi` interface:

```
RestClient.YourAppApi appApiInstance =
restAdapter.create(RestClient.YourAppApi.class);
```

Using this `appApiInstance`, the login interface would be called using the following code:

```
appApiInstance.login(email, password,
        new Callback<RetroLogin>() {
            @Override
            public void success(RetroLogin retroLogin, Response response) {
                // Your code on successfully getting the response
            }

            @Override
            public void failure(RetrofitError error) {
                // Your code if any errors occur while getting the response
            }
        });
```

It would take the user's email and password and give out a response in JSON format that is parsed into a model class provided by you. In our case, `RetroLogin` is the model class that would be getting the response.

Behavioral pattern

This pattern helps you to define the behavior of your code, or why a particular code is written in the way is has been written.

Command

When you write code, it should be commanding other code to give some expected result based on the inputs that are provided. This type of pattern coding has some inputs called parameters. They are being sent to some functionality to process the result and give it back to us.

A simple example is the process of making toast. You provide the toaster with the bread. The toaster does its work of heating the bread and gives out the result as toast.

Observer

The observer pattern is a pattern where multiple objects subscribed to one observer change based on changes made on that observer.

It basically works like a one-to-many pattern, where changes made to the observer lead to the necessary changes on all the subscribed objects.

The two major components here are the Observable and the Subscribers.

The Observable is a piece of code that contains a major chunk of functionality to perform a task. Those who want to make use of this Observable need to subscribe to it. Those who subscribe are called the Subscribers.

Subscribers listen to the Observable for the changes, and whenever changes happen to the Observable, the Subscribers are notified.

Model View Controller

The **Model View Controller** (**MVC**) pattern is a pattern that divides the code into its three components, we will briefly go through it here:

- **Model**: The model represents the object in the application. This has the logic of where the data is to be fetched from. This can also have the logic by which the controller can update the view. In Android, the model is mostly represented by object classes.

- **View**: The view consists of the components that can interact with the user, and it is responsible for how the model is displayed in the application. In Android, the view is mostly represented by the XML where the layouts could be designed.

- **Controller**: The controller acts as a mediator between the model and the view. It controls the data flow into the model object and updates the view whenever data changes. In Android, the controller is mostly represented by the activities and fragments.

Model View Presenter

Model View Presenter (**MVP**) is derived from the MVC pattern. MVP is used to minimize the high dependency on the view that is the case in the MVC. It separates the view and model by using the presenter. The presenter decides what will be displayed on the view. The MVP model is discussed as follows:

- **Model**: The model represents the objects in the application. This has the logic of where the data is to be fetched from.
- **View**: The view renders information to users and contains the UI Component .xml file, activity, fragments, and dialog come under the view layer. It does not have any other logic implemented.
- **Presenter**: This layer performs the task of the controller and acts as the mediator between the view and the model. Unlike the controller, it is not dependent on the view. The view interacts with the presenter for the data to be displayed, and the presenter then takes the data from the model and returns it to the view in a presentable format. The presenter does not contain any UI components; it just manipulates the data from the model and displays it on the view.

Model View View-Model

The **Model View View-Model** (**MVVM**) is an improvement over the MVC model, as discussed here.

The MVVM has the following components:

- **Model**: The model represents the objects in the application. It has the logic of where the data is to be fetched from.

- **View**: The view is similar to the MVC pattern view, which renders information to users and contains the UI Component .xml file, activity, fragments, and dialog come under the view layer. It does not have any other logic implemented.

- **View-Model**: This helps in maintaining the state of the view and does changes to the model based on the inputs gained from the view.

Many views can be linked to one view-model, which creates a many-to-one relationship between the view and the view-model. Also, a view has information about the view-model, but the view-model does not have any information about the view.

Summing up MVP and MVC

Looking at the various patterns to code, you need to find the best practice to be used depending on the use cases. Some of the coding patterns are formed based on the architectural patterns followed by the inherited classes. In those cases, you are restricted to follow one pattern, but there might be instances where you need to make use of certain patterns based on the applicability.

The Model View Presenter pattern is based on the Model View Controller pattern. Since they share several concepts, it can be hard to differentiate between them. The presenter and the controller have a similar role. They are responsible for the communication between the model and the view. That being said, the controller doesn't manage the model and the view as strictly as the presenter does. Separating interfaces from logic in Android is not easy, but the Model-View-Presenter pattern makes it a little easier to prevent our activities from degrading into very coupled classes consisting of hundreds, or even thousands, of lines. In large applications, it is essential to organize our code well. If not, it becomes impossible to maintain and extend.

Refactoring your app

When you hear the term refactoring your app, you may get confused with what exactly is going to get refactored in Android. It all compiles to code refactoring. To define it, refactoring is the process of restructuring the code without changing the behavior of the existing code. Refactoring improves the readability of the code. Also, it makes complex code simple. What it also does is it reduces code duplication; it makes use of the same code at two or more different places instead of writing the same code at those places.

What are the advantages of refactoring?

Refactoring is a process of improving your code without writing new functionality.

Refactoring helps to clean your code and use a simple code design for you app. Making code simple makes it more readable and understandable. Hence, it also helps a third person to quickly understand it.

A refactored code will follow the **DRY** principle; that is, Do not Repeat Yourself. Hence, it will not have duplicated code. As there is no, or minimal, duplication in refactored code, such code is very easy to maintain.

Also, you save a lot of time in the future if you have your code refactored, as you may reuse the code written in multiple places without having to test it again for its functionality. Also, it saves time when maintaining such code.

Another advantage of refactoring is it reduces the size of the classes, and this reduces the size of your whole application.

How is refactoring done?

Refactoring can be done in various ways by doing a series of minor changes. With each of these minor changes, the functionality is not affected, but the existing code is improved bit by bit. And when these small bits are combined, it is refactored code.

Refactoring should abide by the following three key components. If the three components are met, then you have correctly refactored your code:

- New functionality should not be created during refactoring
- After refactoring, all the existing test cases should be successfully executed
- The code must be simple to read, understand, and use

When should you refactor?

- **Rule of Three**:
  This states that you must refactor your code if you write the same code, or duplicate your code, for the third time.
  For the first time, you write code to get done. The second time, when you write a similar code, you know that it would be duplicate code, but you still write it again. But if you are repeating the same code for a third time, you should be refactoring that code.

- **When adding a feature**:
  You must refactor your code before adding a new feature to existing code that is not refactored.
  Refactoring helps in order to easily read and understand a piece of code. When a piece of code is unclear, it takes a lot of effort to understand it and is time-consuming. So the best time to refactor code that is not refactored is when adding a new feature within that piece of code. This will help make things obvious for you and easy to understand for those coming after you.
  Refactoring also makes it a lot easier and smoother to add new features by putting in minimal effort and therefore saving a lot of time.

- **When fixing a bug**:
  Again, you must refactor code when you are fixing a bug in the code that has not been previously refactored.
  A bug might be hidden in the deepest and innermost places of your code. And having to find that bug in the code that is not refactored would be the deadliest nightmare you would ever have. So the best thing to do when you need to find a bug is to first check if the code is refactored, and if it is not, then do a code refactor first and then try finding the bug. It will help save a lot of time and the bug might find itself.

- **During code review**:
  Code review is a very important step for refactoring and is probably the last chance to refactor your code before it's shared.
  It's your responsibility to do a code review from your end before it is done by the reviewer, and you should refactor as much as possible. The reviewer will then review along with the author of the code and propose changes and decide, together with the author, how difficult it will be to implement various refactoring techniques.

What code needs to be refactored?

When code is not refactored, that code smells. There are different ways to identify the smell of your code. What I mean is your unrefactored code can be classified into categories which may then help you to identify how to refactor that code. We will go through these categories one by one.

Bloaters

Bloaters are codes, methods, and classes that have increased largely in size and have become hard to work with. They accumulate over time as the functionality increases and nobody tries to resolve it:

- **Long method**:
  A long method is a method that contains too many lines of code. Generally, any method longer than 10 lines is long.

- **Large class**:
  A class that contains many lines of code formed by many fields and methods.

- **Primitive obsession**:
  Primitive obsession occurs if primitives (for example, string and int) are used instead of small objects for simple tasks (such as user first names, user last names, user emails, user phone numbers, and so on). They could be clubbed in separate objects, such as users use of string constants as field names for use in data arrays.

- **Long parameter list**:
  More than three or four parameters for a method is too many.

- **Data clumps**:
  Different parts of the code with identical groups of variables with similar causes. These clumps should be turned into their own classes.

Object-orientation abusers

These pieces of code smell because the application of object-oriented programming principles is not being applied on the code correctly:

- **Switch statements**:
  Your switch statement has been made complex, or the operator used is complex. It could also occur if a sequence of if statements is used instead of a switch.

- **Temporary fields**:
  Temporary fields are being used in the code which are not used at all times, but they get their values only under certain circumstances. If these circumstances do not occur, then these objects or fields lead to code smell.
- **Refused bequest**:
  A subclass may have access to multiple methods from its parent class. But what if it is actually using only a few of the methods from it, and the others are just present because they are given to the subclass. If a subclass uses only some of the methods and properties inherited from its parents, the unneeded methods may simply go unused.
- **Alternative classes with different interfaces**:
  The code smells if two or more classes have the same functionality, but what differs is only either the name of the class or the functions.

Change preventers

If you change the code in one place, then you will need to change it in the other places where the code is dependent. This affects the development process because it requires unnecessary additional handling, which is time consuming:

- **Divergent change**:
  If you have to make many unrelated methods while making a change in one class then the change is divergent. For example, when adding a new restaurant type, you have to change the methods for finding, and displaying, restaurants.
- **Shotgun surgery**:
  If you need to do a small modification at one place, then it requires that you make many small changes to many different classes.
- **Parallel inheritance hierarchies**:
  When creating a subclass for a class, if it requires creating a subclass for another class related to it, then it is parallel inheritance.

Dispensables

Dispensables are codes that are unnecessary or useless and can be directly removed to make the code more understandable and efficient:

- **Comments**:
  Comments that are too large and unnecessary at multiple places in a method or a class.
- **Duplicate code**:
  More than one codes that are almost identical used in different places.
- **Lazy class**:
  If a class is not performing any major functionality and the functionality written seems to be unnecessary, then such a class should be deleted.

Data class

A data class refers to a class that contains only fields and crude methods for accessing them (getters and setters). These are simply containers for data used by other classes. These classes do not contain any additional functionality and cannot operate independently on the data that they own:

- **Dead code**:
  If a variable, field, method, or class is not made use of anywhere in your code, or if there is an old code that is no longer used, then that code is dead and should be deleted using a good IDE.
- **Speculative generality**:
  A class, method, field, or parameter which was speculated to be made use of in the future but was never made use of. Such unused code is categorized as speculative generality.

Couplers

Excessive coupling between classes and methods leads to code smell that is categorized into coupling smells:

- **Feature envy**:
  Data of another object is made use of by a method, more than its own data. Such code smells after fields are moved to a data class.

- **Inappropriate intimacy**:
  One class uses the internal fields and methods of another class.

- **Message chains**:
  A code makes a series of calls, like one method calling another, and that method in turn calling another method: `method1()` || `method2()` || `method3()`.

- **Middle man**:
  If a class calls another class, and performs only the one function of calling the other class, then the middle class smells.

How do I refactor my code?

Once you identify the category your smelling code falls into, it's time for you to refactor it and remove all code smells. Here we will find how to do some minor tweaks in our code, and they will solve a lot of your problems.

Refactoring of methods

One of the causes of code smells is the way in which methods are written: how the code has been written in these methods, whether the methods have been written correctly, whether some necessary methods have been written where they should be written, whether too many unnecessary methods have been written, how complex a method has been made, (making difficult to understand), or how long and extensive a method is made by adding long code. Thus, the refactoring in these would comprise of solving the issues in these methods. Some of these techniques are described next.

Extract method

- What is the issue?
  You have a long piece of continuous code that becomes too lengthy to be used as a single piece of code. This long code does one kind of work but it is in between or along with the other code that performs another functionality.

- How do you solve it?
  Create a new method and write the code in this new, separate method, which will not affect the current functionality. This method can be called from the place where you were actually writing the lengthy code. This will make the code get clubbed into a method, and make it more readable.

Consider the following code, which hides the user views:

```
// Get the list of user images and store in list
List<Image> userImages = user.getImages();
// Hide my user details
firstNameTextView.setVisibility(View.GONE);
lastNameTextView.setVisibility(View.GONE);
emailTextView.setVisibility(View.GONE);
```

Here, hiding the user views could be clubbed into one method:

```
// Get the user details
List<Image> userImages = user.getImages();
hideUserViews();


private void hideUserViews() {
firstNameTextView.setVisibility(View.GONE);
lastNameTextView.setVisibility(View.GONE);
emailTextView.setVisibility(View.GONE);
}
```

Inline method

- What is the issue?
  When the content of a method is very small or it doesn't serve a purpose, keeping it in that method and clubbing it along with some other piece of code.
- How do you solve it?
  Here, the method could be completely removed and the content from the method could be directly replaced in the code where the method was called.

The `inline` method could be explained using the following code. We have a method to check if the stock is limited. The stock is limited if the stock count is less than 10:

```
private boolean isLimitedStock(int count) {
if(isLessThanTen(count)) {
return true;
}
return false;
}

private boolean isLessThanTen(int count) {
return count<10;
}
```

Here, the `isLessThanTen` function is not serving much purpose, and the same conditional check could be performed inside the `isLimitedStock` function itself in the following manner:

```
private boolean isLimitedStock(int count) {
if(count<10) {
return true;
}
return false;
}
```

Extract variable

- What is the issue?
  An expression is too complicated to understand.
- How do you solve it?
  Divide the expression into separate parts and each part will have its result stored. Later, you could combine these parts to get the final result. This will make the expression easier to understand.

The following is an example of a complex validation step at the time of user registration. It checks for multiple conditions to validate user data:

```
if (!firstname.isEmpty() && firstname.length() > 1 && !lastname.isEmpty()
&& lastname.length() > 1 && !email.isEmpty() && email.isValidFormat() &&
!password.isEmpty() && password.length()>6) {
return true;
}
```

Looking at it, it looks very complex. But if we segregate it into sections, then it becomes simple to understand:

```
boolean isValidFirstName = !firstname.isEmpty() && firstname.length() > 1;
boolean isValidLastName = !lastname.isEmpty() && lastname.length() > 1;
boolean isValidEmail = !email.isEmpty() && lastname.isValidFormat();
boolean isValidPassword = !password.isEmpty() && password.length() > 6;

if (isValidFirstName && isValidLastName && isValidEmail && isValidPassword)
{
return true;
}
```

Inline temp

- What is the issue?
  The result of an expression, which is simple and direct to understand, is stored in a temporary variable, and that variable is made use of only once.
- How do you solve it?
  Delete the temporary variable by making use of the expression itself, instead of the variable.

Consider the example of an `inline` method `here`, `where`, and `once again`, whose functions are finding if the stock is limited. The following code has been changed slightly to explain the case of the inline temp:

```
private boolean isLimitedStock(int count) {
boolean isCountLessThan10 = count<10;
if(isCountLessThan10) {
return true;
}
return false;
}
```

Here, the variable `isCountLessThan10` becomes a temporary variable that stores a Boolean if that number is less than 10, and then directly uses it in the following condition to check. It should be used with the expression directly, as seen previously:

```
private boolean isLimitedStock(int count) {
if(count<10) {
return true;
}
return false;
}
```

Replace temp with query

- What is the issue?
  A code or expression that gives a result has been stored in a temporary variable, but that temporary variable has been made use of in multiple places in your code.
- How do you solve it?
  Since you are making use of the result from the expression or code, you should create a new method that does the work of the expression, and this method has to be called wherever required. Such a method may also be used in some other part of the code at a later stage.

Consider the code that finds you the area of a rectangle. You know that the area of the rectangle is the length multiplied by the breadth:

```
float areaOfRectangle = length * breadth;
if(areaOfRectangle>100) {
float amount = areaOfRectangle * 700;
}
else {
float amount = areaOfRectangle * 800;
}
```

Here, the area of the rectangle is used to find the amount. This should be replaced by a method:

```
private float areaOfRectangle() {
return length * breadth;
}
```

Then this method should be made use of instead of the temporary variable:

```
if(areaOfRectangle()>100) {
float amount = areaOfRectangle() * 700;
}
else {
float amount = areaOfRectangle() * 800;
}
```

Split temporary variable

- What is the issue?
  One local variable inside a method saves values of different expressions for the statements at various places.
- How do you solve it?
  Different variables need to be created for each of the statements inside the method. The same variable should not be reused.

The following code makes use of the same local variable in a function:

```
private float getValue(int number) {
int tempValue = number*10;
if(tempValue>1000) {
// do something
}
tempValue = number / 5;
if(tempValue<20) {
```

```
// Do something
}
return tempValue;
}
```

The `tempValue` variable is first storing one value and then again, at a later point, storing another value. Instead, a separate variable should be used to store the second value. This helps at a later point when you revisit the code for rechecking, or have to do some changes using this variable, as it would waive off the need for checking if the correct values are stored in the variable at the point where the change or check needs to be performed:

```
private float getValue(int number) {
int tempValue = number*10;
if(tempValue>1000) {
// do something
}
int tempValueNew = number / 5;
if(tempValueNew<20) {
// Do something
}
return tempValueNew;
}
```

Remove assignments to parameters

- What is the issue?
  A new value is added to a parameter of a method.
- How do you solve it?
  A parameter value should not be replaced with any other value inside a method. Instead, a new variable should be created that holds the same value as the parameter value, if required.

The following code assigns a newly calculated value to the parameter:

```
private float getValue(int number) {
if(number>1000) {
number = number * 10;
}
return number;
}
```

Instead, a variable has to be used which would first hold the parameter's value:

```
private float getValue(int number) {
int numberTemp = number;
if(number>1000) {
numberTemp = number * 10;
}
return numberTemp;
}
```

This is important because in the near future, if you have to make changes to this method and do some calculations using the parameter, you won't be able to make them, as you will have lost the value of the original parameter after the reassignment.

Replace method with method object

- What is the issue?
  Here, the problem is similar to the problem you had for the extract method: the code in a method has become too long, but in this case you cannot club the code into a method, as the local variables are dependent on each other at multiple places.
- How do you solve it?
  The whole code in the method can be compiled into a separate class, as a dependent local variable could be made use of inside that class as per your needs. So this is an extraction of the code into a class instead of a method.

The following code has some local variables that are interdependent of each other:

```
private void computeScale() {
int width = 10;
int height = 20;
int ratio = height/width;
if(width>height) {
ratio = width/height;
}
// Then using this 3 variables a complex computation is carried out
}
```

This could be solved by creating a separate class:

```
class Image {
int width;
int height;
int ratio;
```

```
public Image(int width, int height) {
this.width = width;
this.height = height;
calculateRatio();
}

private void calculateRatio() {
ratio = height/width;
if(width>height) {
ratio = width/height;
}
}

public int computeScale() {
// Return some value after calculation using the fields of this class
}
}
```

And then in the method, just call it to compute the value:

```
private void computeScale() {
int width = 10;
int height = 20;

int scale = new Image(width, height).computeScale();
}
```

Substitute algorithm

- What is the issue?
  The problem here is that the current algorithm written in your method is not the best way to write it. You might have a better way to write the same algorithm.
- How do you solve it?
  Change the existing code in the method with a new code, without changing the output of the method, but by changing the algorithm.

If we want to find the remainder of a division operation, the following code could be used:

```
private int getRemainder(int dividend, int divisor) {
int integerResult = dividend/divisor;
int remainder = dividend - integerResult * divisor;
return remainder;
}
```

It would give you the correct remainder value after the division. But is the algorithm used here the best one to get the remainder? It is not, because the remainder could be found using the mod operator directly. Therefore, change the algorithm written with this new one:

```
private int getRemainder(int dividend, int divisor) {
int remainder = dividend % divisor;
return remainder;
}
```

I know that the preceding code violates the inline temp technique, but I have kept it that way so that you can understand it properly. The code could be written better in the following way:

```
private int getRemainder(int dividend, int divisor) {
return dividend % divisor;
}
```

Summary

Refactoring becomes a very important part of your coding life cycle, as it is the one responsible for keeping your code clean. Keeping your code clean is very important, as it improves the readability of the code. It also has other advantages in that it makes your code simple and reduces code duplication. It could reduce the number of lines in the code, thus reducing the size of your whole final product. First, you need to understand and learn where your code smells and what smell your code has. Then, apply the right refactoring technique to remove the code smell. Thus, understanding the refactoring methods turns out to be crucial.

9
Performance Matters

An app is dear to an end user, especially when it performs better than its expectations. A lot of apps today are resource eaters. Even though they might be the best at the user interface and experience, if they end up eating too many of resources of the phone, the app might just face an uninstalled state within no time. The battery is one such dear factor to the user and still remains a point of consideration while choosing a smartphone.

In this section, we will discuss several performance avenues in an app that we must cater to to ensure that we are building a performance-centric app which is resource friendly. We will list some of the tools we can use to improve the app performance too.

Improving display performances

After the UIs are designed, the most common issues developers face is the performance of UIs on devices. This chapter will help to identify problems in an app's layout performance and improve the UI responsiveness.

Optimizing layouts

Optimizing layouts becomes the most important part, as far as user experience is concerned, because the layout is the aspect of the app which is finally seen by the user. They are the interface between the user and the app. How the app looks and how it plays with the user's experience is all decided by the layout. So, making the layout user friendly and optimized is important.

Optimizing layout hierarchies

Android has many standard layouts that can be used to design the layout. Using these layouts means that each layout has to be added to your application. The app is also required to initialize it, and the layout later requires to be drawn.

Layout hierarchy is making use a layout within another parent layout. For example, using `nested` instances of `RelativeLayout` or `LinearLayout`. Using such nested layouts is a very costly way of doing layout drawing work, because it requires a lot of processing to be done. Furthermore, if `LinearLayout` uses the `layout_weight` parameter, then it is more expensive, as each child needs to be measured twice. The `android:layout_weight` attribute assigns a value to a view in terms of how much space it can occupy on the screen and carries a default value of zero. A larger weight value means that it allows the layout to be expanded to fill any remaining space in the parent view. It is more important to optimize the layout when it is used in a list or a grid as, otherwise, it can lead to lagging of the view.

Optimization of such layouts requires us to perform stepwise checking of the layout and improve it by changing the layout code wherever possible. Android Studio provides you with tools to check for hierarchies in your layout, analyze them, and fix them based on the analysis. Two of `sthe` tools provided are mentioned and explained below:

- Hierarchy Viewer: Hierarchy Viewer is a tool that Android Studio provides to analyze the layouts in Android. Once your layouts are ready, you need to inspect those layouts in Hierarchy Viewer. Hierarchy Viewer allows you to analyze your layout while your application is running. This tool finds out the cost for drawing each of the layouts and analyzes the performance of each of the elements in the layout.
  The Hierarchy Viewer tool is present in Android Device Monitor. It asks user to select running processes on a connected device or emulator. It then displays the layouts from all these processes, in a layout tree. Once the hierarchy viewer draws the layouts, it analyzes it and shows the performance of each layout using traffic lights. The traffic lights on each block indicate its Measure, Layout, and Draw performance. This can be understood by considering the example of an item in `RecyclerView`:

Figure 5.1.1. Layout item of a RecyclerView.

- Consider Figure 5.1.1, which shows a layout used as an item in a `RecyclerView`. The layout shows a bitmap image on the left and two `TextViews` to display text on the right. As in a `RecyclerView`, the same layout has to be inflated multiple times. Such a layout need to be optimized as it would otherwise increase the performance.

  Once you open Hierarchy Viewer, it will show a list of available devices and their running components. Choose your component and click Hierarchy View to view the layout hierarchy of the selected component. Figure 5.1.2 shows the Hierarchy View of the above `RecyclerView` item:

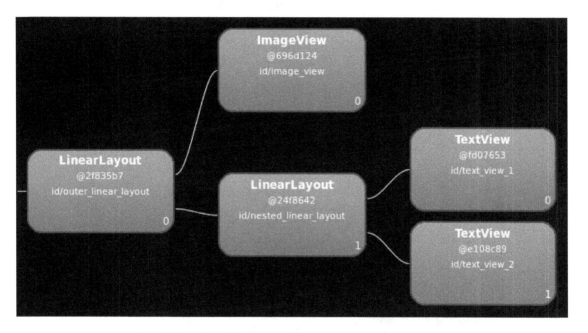

Figure 5.1.2. Layout hierarchy for the layout in Figure 5.1.1 using nested instances of LinearLayout.

- The layout performance of the above view is slow, because of nested LinearLayouts. The above layout has to be improved on performance by changing the layout code and removing the nested layout in the code. This can be done using a **RelativeLayout** instead of a LinearLayout, keeping the layout design intact. When this design is converted to use **RelativeLayout**, the layout becomes a two-level hierarchy. After changing the code and running the Hierarchy Viewer the view is as shown in Figure 5.1.3:

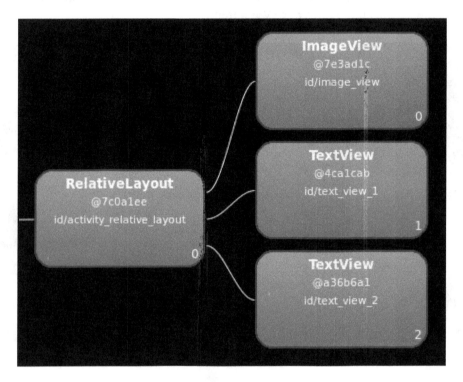

Figure 5.1.3. Layout hierarchy for the layout in Figure 5.1.1, using RelativeLayout.

- The nested view of the layout is removed in this case, and the performance of the layout is improved. But this performance improvement is a small one, considering this single layout. However, its value increases as it is used in a `RecyclerView`, and this layout would be inflated multiple times. The `LinearLayout` becomes inefficient because of its use of `layout_weight`, which can slow down the speed of measurement. Hence, one should mostly avoid the use of `layout_weight` wherever possible and use it only if it is of utmost use.

- Lint:

  Lint is another tool provided by Android to search for possible view hierarchy optimizations. Lint is a tool that it is integrated into Android Studio and you need to write rules which run automatically whenever you compile your program. With Android Studio, lint can perform inspections for a specific build variant or for all build variants. Some examples of lint rules are:

  - Use compound drawables: A `LinearLayout` which contains an `ImageView` and a `TextView` can be more efficiently handled as a compound drawable.
  - Merge root frame: If a `FrameLayout` is the root of a layout and does not provide background or padding, it can be replaced with a merge tag which is slightly more efficient.
  - Useless leaf: A layout that has no children or no background can often be removed (since it is invisible) for a flatter and more efficient layout hierarchy.
  - Useless parent: A layout with children that has no siblings, is not a `ScrollView` or a root layout, and does not have a background, can be removed and have its children moved directly into the parent for a flatter and more efficient layout hierarchy.
  - Deep layouts: Layouts with too much nesting are bad for performance. Consider using flatter layouts such as `RelativeLayout` or `GridLayout` to improve performance. The default maximum depth is 10.

Lint has inspection profiles that can be configured within Android Studio by navigating to the **File** | **Settings** | **Project** Settings option. The Inspection Configuration page appears with the supported inspections:

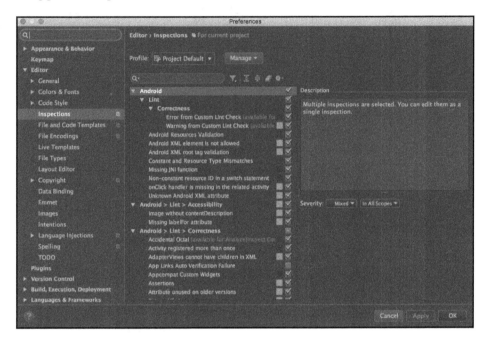

Lint has the ability to automatically fix some issues, provide suggestions for others, and jump directly to the offending code for review.

The layout optimization could also occur by reusing some layouts that are already present, as that makes the layout more efficient. Reusing layouts allows you to create reusable complex layouts, such as an action bar panel or a custom progress bar with a description. Here, the elements of your application that are common across multiple layouts can be extracted and managed separately and later be included in each layout. So, while you can create individual UI components by writing a custom view, you can do it even more easily by re-using a layout file. The methods to make a reusable layout are mentioned below.

- Re-using layouts with `<include/>`:
  This method of re-using of a layout can be done using an `<include/>` statement in your XML code and including the already existing layout file into the current layout.

In order to create a reusable layout using `<include/>`, there are two methods. One is by creating a new layout, which you know you will be reusing, from scratch, and the second is to make a piece of existing code into a separate layout file and later use it at another place.

If you know that you are making a reusable layout, then create a new XML file and name the layout file `my_reusable_layout.xml`:

```
<FrameLayout xmlns:android="http://schemas.android.com/apk/res/android"
    xmlns:tools="http://schemas.android.com/tools"
    android:layout_width="match_parent"
    android:layout_height="wrap_content"
    android:background="@color/black"
    tools:showIn="@layout/activity_main" >

    <ImageView android:layout_width="wrap_content"
        android:layout_height="wrap_content"
        android:src="@drawable/mylogo" />
</FrameLayout>
```

- The is exactly what the layout should look like, and that needs to be directly included in the other layout file where it needs to be reused. That could be done by using the `<include>` tag in the code where the layout has be included. Reusing layout is a powerful feature that allows developers to create reusable complex layouts. For example, if you are building a survey app which has a layout which accepts Yes/No questions, or a custom progress bar with description text, you can reuse the layout. A point to be noted is that any elements of your app that are common across multiple layers can be extracted and managed separately. Afterwards, they can be included in each layout.

The above layout is included in another layout, as shown in the code below:

```
<LinearLayout xmlns:android="http://schemas.android.com/apk/res/android"
    android:orientation="vertical"
    android:layout_width="match_parent"
    android:layout_height="match_parent"
    android:gravity="center_horizontal">

    <include layout="@layout/my_reusable_layout"/>

    <TextView android:layout_width="match_parent"
        android:layout_height="wrap_content"
        android:text="@string/settings" />

    ...

</LinearLayout>
```

You can also override all the layout parameters of the included layout's root view by specifying them in the `<include/>` tag. For example:

```
<include android:id="@+id/my_reusable_id"
    android:layout_width="match_parent"
    android:layout_height="match_parent"
    layout="@layout/my_reusable_layout"/>
```

However, if you want to override layout attributes using the <include> tag, you must override both `android:layout_height` and `android:layout_width` in order for other layout attributes to take effect.

- Use the `<merge>` Tag:

  The layout can be also reused using the `<merge/>` tag; this helps to eliminate redundant view groups in your view hierarchy. The merge is useful mostly when your main layout is a vertical `LinearLayout` in which two consecutive views can be reused in multiple layouts. In this case, the reusable layout in which you place the two views requires its own root view. However, using another `LinearLayout` as the root for the re-usable layout would result in a vertical `LinearLayout` inside a vertical `LinearLayout`. This can slow performance. Instead, a `<merge>` tag could be used to avoid this redundancy. A code example of a merge has been show in the following code example below:

```
<merge xmlns:android="http://schemas.android.com/apk/res/android">
    <Button
        android:layout_width="match_parent"
        android:layout_height="wrap_content"
        android:text="@string/ok"/>

    <Button
        android:layout_width="match_parent"
        android:layout_height="wrap_content"
        android:text="@string/cancel"/>
</merge>
```

- The `<merge>` tag is used to mitigate the number of the levels and to increase the performance of rendering layout. The merge layout should also be included in the layout using the `<include>` tag. When you include this layout in another layout, the system ignores the `<merge>` element and places the two buttons directly in the layout, in place of the `<include/>` tag. Note that `<merge/>` can only be used as the root tag of an XML layout.

Views on demand

Some of the layouts need to be loaded in another layout only when required. Such layouts are the ones which are loaded in the layout on demand. Loading views on demand increases the performance of the layout, as the views are not present in the layout beforehand. Hence, there is no processing of those layouts involved.

The performance of a layout is increased a lot more if the view that is included on demand is a complex view. Also, the view might not be required until a certain condition is met and it would be no use to include that view in the layout and hamper the performance. A few examples of such views are item details, progress bars, and display messages.

This technique of loading views on demand can be implemented by defining a `ViewStub` for complex and rarely used views.

Define a ViewStub

`ViewStub` is a lightweight view. It has no dimensions and, hence, doesn't draw anything on the layout. This view is very cheap to inflate and include in a view hierarchy. Each `ViewStub` needs to include the `android:layout` attribute to be included in the layout to inflate. Instead of choosing to inflate views manually and add them to your view hierarchy at runtime, use `ViewStub`. Its ease of use comes in very handy while developing. One point to be noted here is that it does not support the `<merge/>` tag.

The following `ViewStub` is for a translucent progress bar overlay. It should be visible only when the server call is to be made to fetch data:

```
<ViewStub
    android:id="@+id/stub_id"
    android:inflatedId="@+id/stub_import_id"
    android:layout="@layout/progress_layout"
    android:layout_width="match_parent"
    android:layout_height="wrap_content"
    android:layout_gravity="center" />
```

The layout specified by the `ViewStub` can be called, either by making it visible by calling `setVisibility(View.VISIBLE)` or by calling `inflate()`:

```
findViewById(R.id.stub_id)).setVisibility(View.VISIBLE);
```

or

```
View myStubProgress = ((ViewStub) findViewById(R.id.stub_id)).inflate();
```

Once visible/inflated, the `ViewStub` element is no longer part of the view hierarchy. It is replaced by the inflated layout and the ID for the root view of that layout is the one specified by the `android:inflatedId` attribute of the `ViewStub`. The ID `android:id` specified for the `ViewStub` is valid only until the `ViewStub` layout is visible/inflated.

Improving scrolls and other elements in the app

As seen earlier, an item of a list plays a very important part in the performance of a `RecyclerView`. If the item view is made as efficient as possible, then the list will scroll very smoothly; otherwise, there will always be a lag while scrolling the list. The list scroll will be hampered more if the item view is very complex. Here, in the following section, we will concentrate on improving this smoothness of scrolls in the app by focusing on some other important aspects besides that.

The key to smooth scrolling is to keep the application's main thread free from heavy processing. Any kind of network calls, disk access, and database access must not be performed on the main thread.

Using a background thread

The tasks performed on the Android device in the foreground are all called the tasks on the main thread. These include loading tasks and any kind of user action. If a heavy processing task is performed on the main thread, then there will definitely be lag on the device. All such tasks have to be performed in a background thread which does not affect the main thread but still performs the task in the background. Once the background thread's task is completed, it informs the main thread to perform an appropriate action with the result. Using a background thread allows the main thread to focus on drawing the UI. Android has a built-in class for performing tasks on the background thread. It is called `AsyncTask` and provides a simple way to perform your work outside the main thread. `AsyncTask` automatically queues up all the `execute()` requests and performs them serially.

An example of a class using `AsyncTask` is shown in the code below. The code below makes a call to the Local database and fetches the profile information of a random profile:

```
// Using an AsyncTask to load the slow images in a background thread
new AsyncTask<ViewHolder, Void, Profile >() {
    private ViewHolder viewHolder;

    @Override
    protected Profile doInBackground(ViewHolder... params) {
        viewHolder = params[0];
        return MyLocalDb.getProfileData();
    }

    @Override
    protected void onPostExecute(Profile profile) {
        super.onPostExecute(result);
        if (profile!=null) {
            // If profile data has been correctly fetched then display the
name
            viewHolder.nameTextView.setText(profile.getName());
        }
    }
}.execute(holder);
```

The above code shows that the database access is done via the `doInBackground` method and, once the data is fetched, then the `onPostExecute` method is called which is used to display the details.

Holding view objects in a ViewHolder

Calling the `findViewById()` method frequently during the scrolling of `RecyclerView`, can slow down performance and scrolling. This method looks up the elements after they are inflated and then updates them. This could be avoided by not repeatedly calling the method `findViewById()` but, instead, using a `ViewHolder`.

A `ViewHolder` object stores each of the component views inside the tag field of the Layout, so you can immediately access them without the need to look them up repeatedly. First, you need to create a class to hold all sets of views. For example:

```
static class ViewHolder {
  TextView name;
  TextView aboutMe;
  ImageView image;
  ProgressBar progress;
  int position;
}
```

Then, populate the `ViewHolder` and store it inside the layout:

```
ViewHolder holder = new ViewHolder();
holder.name = (TextView) convertView.findViewById(R.id.name);
holder.aboutMe = (TextView) convertView.findViewById(R.id.aboutMe);
holder.image = (ImageView) convertView.findViewById(R.id.image);
holder.progress = (ProgressBar) convertView.findViewById(R.id.progress);
convertView.setTag(holder);
```

Once the `ViewHolder` saves these views, they can be reused in the code as and when required.

Understanding network requests, computation and memory

This chapter will highlight key areas of app performance, such as network requests, computational algorithms, and memory leak issues. These components play an important role in the performance of the app and can considerably reduce the speed of an app, if end-to-end cases are not handled well. We will go through each of the topics one by one in order to use the best practices to improve the performance of the app.

Collecting, analyzing and optimizing the network and network traffic

To collect, analyze and optimize the network, we would first look at how the network traffic affects the app's performance. Every app will have a network call at some place in their app. A network call is a delayed process, which means that it involves the time between when the network call is made and when the response comes back to the user. This in-between delay could vary depending on the speed of the network. Hence, properly handling all these end-to-end cases is required for a better app performance.

Collection network traffic information

Collecting the network traffic flow data in an app is very important for optimizing the network traffic on a device and the app, as it impacts battery life. In order to optimize that traffic, you need to both measure it and identify its source. In order to communicate on a network, it should make a request. This request could be from your app or from a user on doing some action and triggering a request with the server. In order to monitor this traffic, Android Studio has a network traffic tool known as DDMS.

Taging network requests

Optimization of network resource utilization has to be tracked and handled properly in an app. Therefore, it is required that you check where your app is using the network, how your app is making use of the network, and the frequency of its usage.
For performance analysis, network hardware should be divided into these categories:

- User-initiated network requests: A network request that is initiated by the user performing an action. For example, clicking on a button to fetch user profile details.
- App-initiated network requests: A network request that is initiated within your app code without direct interaction by the user. For example, a call made by the app to send the device details on to the server.
- Server-initiated network requests: A network request that is initiated by a server to your app without any interaction by the user. For example, a notification coming up about a good restaurant near you.

Categorizing these network initiators is important when trying to understand the source of network use. Hence, these categories need tags to differentiate them. Based on the tags for each of these three types of network traffic, a specified color is devised to each of them. Later, in any graphical representation of network usage, these help to distinguish between the types of network traffic initiator.

The three constants for the three types of categories could be mentioned in your app's android code in the following manner:

```
public static final int USER_INITIATED_REQUEST      = 0x1000;
public static final int APP_INITIATED_REQUEST       = 0x2000;
public static final int SERVER_INITIATED_REQUEST    = 0x3000;
```

Then, in all parts of your code, search and identify the three types of network categories. You could use regular expression to find the network codes in your app. Android Studio provides you with a way to find that:

1. Go to **Edit** | **Find** | **Find in Path**.
2. Paste the regular expression string given below in the input box in the dialog that appears:
   ```
   extends GcmTaskService|extends
   JobService|extendsAbstractThreadedSyncAdapter|HttpUrlConnection
   |Volley|Glide|HttpClient
   ```
3. Check the checkbox for **Regular expression**.
4. Check the checkbox for **File mask(s)** and type *.java.
5. Then click on the **Find** button.

Then, based on your findings, tag each of your apps, use of network traffic, the constants that are defined using the method:

```
setThreadStatsTag(int)
```

The use case of tagging has been shown in the example below:

```
if (BuildConfig.NETWORK_TEST && Build.VERSION.SDK_INT >= 14) {
    try {
        TrafficStats.setThreadStatsTag(APP_INITIATED_REQUEST);
        // Once tag has been applied, network request has to be made
request
    } finally {
        TrafficStats.clearThreadStatsTag();
    }
}
```

This method is supported from API level 14 and above, hence the check has to be made for the same in the code.

The `BuildConfig.NETWORK_TEST` is a boolean value defined in your app's gradle dependencies, as shown in the code below:

```
defaultConfig {
    ...
    buildConfigField('Boolean', 'NETWORK_TEST', 'True')
}
```

Configuring a network test build type

You need to create an Android build to test your network performance. This build should be as close as possible to the final production build. Now, create a test build for network testing by creating a `network_test` build type, rather than using debug build type. To do that, open your app's `gradle` file and in the `buildTypes` add the code shown below:

```
android {
    ...
    buildTypes {
        network_test {
            debuggable true
        }
        debug {
            //  For debug buildType, debuggable is true by default
        }
    }
    ...
}
```

Deploying the network test APK

This step involves the deployment of the `network_test` build type APK generated, onto the device. In order to do that, follow the steps below:

1. Connect your device to the system running Android Studio. Make sure that the device comes up in the connected devices list in the Android Monitor section. If it doesn't, then make sure you have enabled USB Debugging mode in the Developer Options in the settings of your mobile device.

2. Once the device is connected, select **Build Variants** on the left edge of the window, in Android Studio. You will see a list of modules along with the build variants:

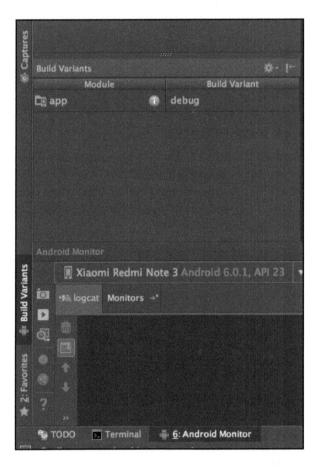

3. Your configured `buildType network_test` will be visible in the list of build variants. Choose that option. If it is not visible, then make sure you have synced the project after writing the code in the build gradle file.

4. Deploy the debuggable version of your app to your device by choosing **Run** | **Debug**.

5. Run the network traffic tool (this will be mentioned in the next section).

6. The network traffic tool in Android Studio will show how the network resources are used by your app in real time, while it is running.

Runing the network traffic tool

The network traffic tool will give you all the network traffic info of all the apps running on a device. In order for the tool to give a reading of your app from the beginning, so that it knows the start of the initial state for your app, you can clear the app data. After doing this, all of your app's cached data will be cleared up, and it will need to perform any initial network requests all over again. This will give you the complete network reading correctly.

Perform the steps below to run the network traffic tool and visualize the network requests:

1. Open the network traffic tool in Android Studio by navigating to **Tools** |**Android** | **Android Device Monitor**. When asked, allow incoming network connections.

2. In the Android Device Monitor window, click the **DDMS** button at the top. Then, select the **Network Statistics** tab. If you don't see this tab, widen the window and then try **Window** | **Reset Perspective**.

3. Select your app to debug from the list of debuggable apps on your device in the Devices tab, then click the Start button in the **Network Statistics** tab.

4. Clear your app's data using the adb command: `adb shell pm clear com.zomato.app`.
   Use your package name instead of `com.zomato.app`.

5. The final step is to start your network debug app and open the app to run the test cases of network traffic flow. Your plan should also allow for app idle time, where the user is not interacting with the app, to allow app-initiated and server-initiated network access to occur.

Repeat the test by clearing the app data and running your test plan again. Tagging helps you to identify the type of request that is using a lot of network traffic, as it is distinguished by colors. You can then, based on these findings, analyze the network usage in your app and improve upon it.

The Network Traffic for the Zomato app for the three types of network traffic is as shown in Figure 5.2.1:

Figure 5.2.1

Analyzing Network Traffic Data

Some apps make network requests even when they are in an idle state, or after a certain interval of time. It is important to analyze these types of network calls, as they affect the performance of the app and the device. A lot of battery is consumed in starting up or waking up the device and making a network call. If kept up for long periods, sending or receiving data will cost a lot of battery. If the app is not accessing the network efficiently, you should make sure that the network calls are grouped together with minimal calls and have the maximum interval time between calls.

The network traffic tool, as seen in the previous section, gives the network traffic based on various network types. Using this graphical tool, you can analyze a lot of network traffic flow. For demonstration purposes, we have increased some server calls that make the app make a lot of inefficient server calls more frequently.

This network traffic flow is continuous and hence does not allow the device to switch to a standby, low-power mode. Such network access behavior is likely to keep the device on for extended periods of time, which is battery-inefficient.

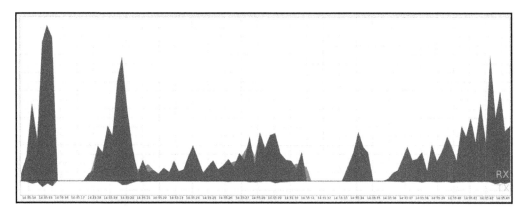

Figure 5.2.2

Figure 5.2.2 shows an optimal network traffic pattern. Here, the network requests are sent in bursts, separated by long periods of no traffic where the device can switch to standby. The graphical representation in Figure 5.2.1 shows that with the same amount of work, it can be made more efficient by clubbing the requests together and allowed the device to be in standby most of the time.

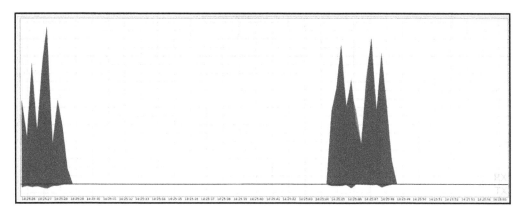

Figure 5.2.3

The best case would be to have the network calls after long periods, if possible, as seen in Figure 5.2.3. It makes a network call after long periods of times as required. The app calls with high network traffic data as shown in Figure 5.2.1 is very inefficient and should be avoided; you need to optimize your network calls in your code.

Analyzing network traffic types

In order to analyze the different network traffic types, you need to understand the different use cases of using the network traffic. For instance, making network calls for any user actions like clicking a button is correct, as the app is in the foreground and the user knows that the app is making use of the network. However, if your app is making network calls when it is not in foreground, then there is network traffic flowing without the user's consent; if used excessively, it could also affect the performance. In order to understand the use case, the analysis of network traffic for different types becomes of the utmost importance. We will understand the network types and analyze them:

- **User-initiated network traffic**:
  When a user interacts with an app, he expects the app to be working smoothly and as fast as possible. There is a normal tendency of a user that, when an app makes a network request as a result of some user action and there is no response within 2 to 4 seconds, then the user will stop using the app. Hence, it is important to analyze what network calls are being made upon any user action, how frequently they are being made, and the amount of data that flows for the network call.
  As the number of requests made is not fixed and the period of making network requests is not definite, it is very difficult to analyze this kind of network traffic flow. However, it is important, because the user expects the app to be fast. Some of the techniques that could be used in this case to optimize use of the network are as follows:
    - Pre-fetch network data - In this technique of optimization, the data is pre-fetched in the app on a user's action and used for the next user action.
    - Check for connectivity - Check if your device has network connectivity before making a network call.
    - Reduce the number of connections - Have a minimal number of network calls.

The details of the above optimization points will be discussed in a later section.

- **App-initiated network traffic**:
  Most network calls take place using this type of network traffic type, as it makes up the major data that is displayed on any app from the server. Hence, it is necessary to have optimal network usage. As with user initiated network traffic, the amount of data sent over the network makes a lot of difference to performance and user experience. As mentioned earlier, as a user expects quick response for a better experience, the network call should have minimal requirements for transferred data. The app also needs to make network calls based on the period of inactivity. If the app is inactive, and there are calls being made, then performance could be affected.. Some ways to optimize app-initiated network traffic include:
    - Batch and schedule network Requests - the network requests have to be made periodically with longer intervals to prevent excessive battery usage.
    - Allow the system to check for connectivity - check for network connectivity before making a network call to avoid a blank network call that simply consumes battery.

The details of the above optimization points will be discussed in a later section.

- **Analyzing server-initiated network traffic**:
  Some network calls are initiated from the server to communicate with the app. These have to be tackled in the server code effectively to avoid excessive battery usage. Notifications from servers are the server-initiated network traffic type. If there is consistent network activity from servers then, to allow the device to switch into low power mode, the network calls must be spaced out.

Optimizing network use

We have seen the different types of network traffic flow and how it could affect the performance of the app and device if not handled correctly. We have also briefly looked at points to optimize the network traffic in the app. Now, we will have a detailed understanding of the optimization methods for different types of network traffic data.

- **Optimizing user-initiated network use**:
  A good experience to a user is when any app works as fast as possible. In the user-initiated network, the request is made when the user does some kind of action within the app. Here, we will see the methods that best improve the user experience by optimally executing network calls when the user performs any action.

  - Pre-fetch network data:
    One method by which a user could get a quick response is by pre-fetching the data required by a user to perform the next set of user actions. This is done for logically anticipating all of the data required by the app if the user does a particular action.
    This method of fetching data is very effective and contributes to a better performance of an app, as it reduces the battery power consumption in the following ways:
    - It helps to reduce the number of independent data transfers performed by the app.
    - The app performs pre-fetching of data only when the device is awake by the user's action. This prevents the overhead of waking up the device, as waking up a device consumes a lot of battery.
    - As the data is pre-fetched, it reduces the number of separate requests for data that would be otherwise required, and which would wake up the device for each call.

- Check for connectivity or listen for changes:
  The second method of optimizing is avoiding making a very costly, battery-draining call searching for a mobile signal. This can be done by making a check to see if the device has a signal or connectivity. This should be done only for a network call on a user action. If a scheduler is used, then it performs that check automatically.

Android has a connectivity manager to check if any network connection is present on a device. Using this, you could create your own function to check if a device has any kind of network. If there is no network connection, then it could directly inform the user about the lack of connectivity on the device and save the battery by avoiding the network call. The following is a code base where, using the connectivity manager, the function checks if the device has internet connectivity:

```
public static boolean isNetworkAvailable(Context context)
   {
   boolean haveConnectedWifi = false;
   boolean haveConnectedMobile = false;

   ConnectivityManager cm = (ConnectivityManager)
   context.getSystemService(context.CONNECTIVITY_SERVICE);
   NetworkInfo[] netInfo = cm.getAllNetworkInfo();
   for (NetworkInfo ni : netInfo) {
      if (ni.getTypeName().equalsIgnoreCase("WIFI"))
      if (ni.isConnected())
         haveConnectedWifi = true;
      if (ni.getTypeName().equalsIgnoreCase("MOBILE"))
      if (ni.isConnected())
         haveConnectedMobile = true;
    }
    return haveConnectedWifi || haveConnectedMobile;
   }
```

- A better approach to performing a user initiated request is to use a scheduler. A scheduler performs a network request only if connected to a network. If there is no connectivity, then they use a technique called exponential back off to save battery. Here, each time a connection attempt fails, the scheduler doubles the delay before the next retry.

  Another method for checking network connectivity is to use Broadcast Receivers on Demand. In this technique, the device listens for connectivity changes when the current activity is in the foreground. If the app finds that network connectivity has been lost, then it disables all of its receivers, except for the connectivity-change receiver. The other receivers are only enabled when connectivity is back.

- Reduce the number of connections:
  An obvious last method to avoid a battery drain and enhance the user experience is by reducing the number of network calls. There might be a case wherein two separate calls give separate data. These could be clubbed into one single call, avoiding the additional call. Reusing connections also makes the network react more intelligently to congestion and network data issues.

- **Optimizing app-unitiated network use**:
  App-initiated network traffic is a type of network traffic that can be optimized a lot, as it is controlled completely by your app. Here, you know how much and what network resources are required and so can set a schedule for them with significant periods of rest for the device, thus saving power:

  - Batch and schedule network requests:
    On a mobile device, there are some heavy, battery-draining tasks, like the process of making a network request, keeping the device awake, waking up the device, and so on. The processing of these tasks may use up a lot of battery. Hence, these tasks have to be performed in batches by queuing them individually.

    For making scheduled network requests, a network access scheduler API could be used. The scheduler would queue and process your app data requests to increase the efficiency of your app. Schedulers group several requests together for the system to process and thus save battery. They further improve efficiency by delaying some requests until other requests wake up the device, or waiting until the device is charging.

- Choose a batch-and-scheduling API:
  There are several different APIs that are provided by Android to perform the scheduling task. Android provides three different APIs for your app to batch and schedule network requests, which are listed in the following table with the most highly recommended first:

Scheduler	Requirements	Implementation Ease
GCM Network Manager	GCM Network Manager requires that your app use the Google Play services client library, version 6.1.11 or higher - use the latest available version.	Straightforward
Job Scheduler	Job Scheduler does not require Google Play services, but is available only when targeting Android 5.0 (API level 21) or higher.	Straightforward
Sync Adapter for scheduled syncs	Sync Adapter does not require the Google Play services client library and has been available since Android 2.0 (API level 5).	Complex

- Allow the system to check for connectivity:
  This is one of the most dangerous battery drainers, as it performs very heavy tasks and wakes up the device frequently. Here, the device searches for the nearest network tower for connectivity. This usually occurs while travelling from one network tower to another. Searching for a cell signal is one of the most power-draining operations there is.
  Prevent this by using a scheduler, which automatically uses a connectivity manager to check for connectivity before calling into your app. As a result, if there's no network, the connectivity manager conserves battery because it performs the connectivity check itself, without loading the app to run the check. The battery is also saved as a scheduler uses an exponential back off technique which has already been mentioned previously.

- **Optimizing server-initiated network use**:
  Server initiated network requests are tough to resolve from Android code. They need to mostly be resolved from the server end, but whatever can be done from the Android end has to be executed. A solution to this problem is for your app to periodically poll the server to check for updates. An efficient approach would be to notify your app when it has new data. This was never an easy job before the introduction of the **Google Cloud Messaging** (**GCM**) service, which solves this communication problem by allowing your servers to send notifications to instances of your app wherever they are installed, enabling greater network efficiency and lowering power usage.
  - Send server updates with GCM:
    Google Cloud Messaging (GCM) is a mechanism used to transmit brief messages from an app server to your app. GCM could be used by your apps wherein the server sends a message to notify your app that there is new data available. This approach eliminates network traffic that your app would perform, by not contacting a backend server for new data when no data is available.
    GCM is more efficient because it prevents the polling method and polling the server would involve a lot of network requests and thus a lot of performance that would drain the battery. The GCM service eliminates unnecessary connections where polling would return no updates and it avoids running periodic network requests.
    Also, GCM is a widely-used technology and is supported by many apps. However, the newer version of sending the messages is using **Firebase Cloud Messaging** (**FCM**), which has already been covered in the previous section.

Batching and Job Schedulers

In this section, we will discuss scheduling jobs which are not required to be completed immediately, but can be done later when more resources are available.

Currently, Android has two APIs with which we can schedule jobs:

- `AlarmManager` API
- `JobScheduler` API

In `AlarmManager` API, we can schedule a task to be done by the system at a given time in the future.

The `AlarmManager` requires a broadcast receiver to capture the task and perform the required action. We can also schedule repetitive jobs which are to be performed at certain intervals.

While we are scheduling an alarm, we must pass the type, the time when the alarm is scheduled, and a `PendingIntent`.

The `AlarmManager` has two types of alarms:

- `RTC`: In this type, the alarm is set as per the system times but will not be called if the device is asleep.
- `RTC_WAKEUP`: In this type, the alarm is set on the system time and it will wake the device up when the alarm is scheduled.

The `AlarmManager` uses a `PendingIntent` to call a specific intent; the intent must pass a call to a receiver class.

The various methods available with the `AlarmManager` are as follows:

Method	Description
cancel(`PendingIntent` operation)	This method removes any alarms with a matching intent.
cancel(`AlarmManager.OnAlarmListener` listener)	This method removes any alarm scheduled to be delivered to the given `AlarmManager.OnAlarmListener`.

set(int type, long `triggerAtMillis`, `PendingIntent` operation)	This method schedules an alarm with the given parameters Int type : Type of alarm Long `triggerAtMillis` : When the alarm will trigger `PendingIntent` operation : Intent passed to be called on alarm
set(int type, long `triggerAtMillis`, `String` tag, `AlarmManager.OnAlarmListener` listener, Handler `targetHandler`)	This is a direct callback version of set (int, long, `PendingIntent`).
`setAlarmClock`(`AlarmManager.AlarmClockInfo` info, `PendingIntent` operation)	This method schedules an alarm that represents an alarm clock.
`setAndAllowWhileIdle`(int type, long `triggerAtMillis`, `PendingIntent` operation)	This methods is like set (`int`, `long`, `PendingIntent`), but will be allowed to execute even when the system is in low-power idle modes.
`setExact`(int type, long `triggerAtMillis`, `PendingIntent` operation)	This methods chedules an alarm to be delivered precisely at the stated time.
`setExact`(int type, long `triggerAtMillis`, `String` tag, `AlarmManager.OnAlarmListener` listener, Handler `targetHandler`)	This is a direct callback version of `setExact`(int, long, `PendingIntent`).
`setExactAndAllowWhileIdle`(int type, long `triggerAtMillis`, `PendingIntent` operation)	This method is like `setExact`(int, long, `PendingIntent`), but will be allowed to execute even when the system is in low-power idle modes.
`setInexactRepeating`(int type, long `triggerAtMillis`, long `intervalMillis`, `PendingIntent` operation)	This method chedules a repeating alarm that has inexact trigger time requirements; for example, an alarm that repeats every hour, but not necessarily at the top of every hour.
`setRepeating`(int type, long `triggerAtMillis`, long `intervalMillis`, `PendingIntent` operation)	This method schedules a repeating alarm.
`setTime`(long millis)	This method sets the system wall clock time.

setTimeZone(**String** timeZone)	This method sets the system's persistent default time zone.
setWindow(**int** type, **long** windowStartMillis, **long** windowLengthMillis, PendingIntent operation)	This method schedules an alarm to be delivered within a given window of time.
setWindow(**int** type, **long** windowStartMillis, **long** windowLengthMillis, String **tag**, AlarmManager.OnAlarmListener **listener**, **Handler** targetHandler)	This is a direct callback version of setWindow(int, long, PendingIntent).

As can be seen in the form above, the AlarmManager can be set with respect to time only and no other conditions are being checked before it is first triggered.

Here is sample of how AlarmManager is initialized and used:

1. Initialize an alarm with a pending intent and set action so as to call the proper receiver using the setAction method of intent:

```
private void createAlarm(Context context) {
Intent intent = new Intent(context, MyBroadcastReceiver.class);
intent.setAction("my.content.update.action");
PendingIntent pendingIntent = PendingIntent.getBroadcast(context,
100, intent, PendingIntent.FLAG_UPDATE_CURRENT);
Calendar calendar = Calendar.getInstance();
calendar.setTimeInMillis(System.currentTimeMillis());
calendar.add(Calendar.MINUTE,1); //To start first alarm after 1 minute
AlarmManager alarmMgr =
(AlarmManager)context.getSystemService(Context.ALARM_SERVICE);
alarmMgr.cancel(pendingIntent); // Cancel any pending alarms if required
int currentapiVersion = android.os.Build.VERSION.SDK_INT;
if (currentapiVersion >= Build.VERSION_CODES.KITKAT){
alarmMgr.setInexactRepeating(AlarmManager.RTC_WAKEUP,
calendar.getTimeInMillis(),
Constant.INTERVAL_ONE_MINUTES,
pendingIntent);
} else{
alarmMgr.setRepeating(AlarmManager.RTC_WAKEUP,
calendar.getTimeInMillis(),
Constant.INTERVAL_ONE_MINUTES,
pendingIntent);
}
}
```

2. Next, we have to add the receiver to be called in the manifest:

```
<receiver android:name=".receiver.MyBroadcastReceiver">
<intent-filter>
<action android:name="my.content.update.action" />
</intent-filter>
</receiver>
```

3. We also add the receiver class to receive the intent:

```
public class MyBroadcastReceiver extends BroadcastReceiver {
private static final String TAG =
MyBroadcastReceiver.class.getSimpleName();
@Override
public void onReceive(Context context, Intent intent) {//Perform Action
}
}
```

Next, we will see how to use the `JobScheduler`.

The `JobScheduler` API was introduced in Android 5.0 Lollipop (API 21). The `JobScheduler` operates at the system level, so it has many features by which it can intelligently schedule and trigger the jobs that have been assigned.

The `JobScheduler` API does not work solely on time scheduled tasks, but checks whether the correct conditions are met before triggering a task. The `JobScheduler` API runs on the main thread of the application, so it can interact with the app more easily and reduce the chances of being stopped by the system to free memory.

The `JobScheduler` consists of three main sections:

- `JobInfo`
- `JobService`
- `JobScheduler`

Let us look into each one of them in detail.

JobInfo

All the parameters that are to be used while scheduling the Job by the scheduler are defined in the `JobInfo` class. We can use `JobInfo.Builder` to create an instance of `JobInfo`. This builder requires the `jobId` and the service component as its parameters. `JobId` can be used to uniquely identify jobs that are scheduled to perform a task. They can be also used to monitor whether the job has been successfully called or not by the app when the conditions are met.

The following are the parameters that can be set using the JobInfo class:

- `setBackoffCriteria` (long `initialBackoffMillis`, int `backoffPolicy`):
  Back-off Criteria is the policy that checks when a job is finished or a retry is requested. You can set the initial back off time and whether it is linear or exponential.
  The default is 30 sec and exponential.
  The max back-off capacity is five hrs.
  Also, setting this method for a job along with `setRequiresDeviceIdle(boolean)` will throw an exception when you call `build()`, as back off typically does not make sense for these types of jobs.
  The back off policy can be set one of the two values:
    - `JobInfo.BACKOFF_POLICY_LINEAR` will use the same back off time for the next retry attempt.
    - `JobInfo.BACKOFF_POLICY_EXPONENTIAL` will retry after exponentially increasing the back off time.
- `setExtras(PersistableBundle extras)`:
  A Bundle of extras. This lets you send specific data to your job. As this is persisted, only primitive types are allowed.
    - Here is a code example of how a `JobInfo` object can be initialized in the code:

- `setMinimumLatency(long minLatencyMillis)`:
  A minimum amount of time your job should be delayed. Calling this method for a periodic job will throw an exception when you call `build()`.

- `setOverrideDeadline(long maxExecutionDelayMillis):`
A maximum amount of time to wait to execute your job. If you hit this time, your job will be executed immediately regardless of your other parameters. Calling this method for a periodic job will throw an exception when you call `build()`.

- `setPeriodic(long intervalMillis):`
If you want the job to be repeated, you can specify the interval between repeats. You are guaranteed to be executed within an interval but cannot guarantee at what point during that interval this willl occur. This can sometimes lead to jobs being run closely together. Setting this function on the builder with `setMinimumLatency(long)` or `setOverrideDeadline(long)` will result in an error.

- `setPersisted(boolean isPersisted):`
You can persist the job across boot. This requires the `RECEIVE_BOOT_COMPLETED` permission to be added to your manifest.

- `setRequiredNetworkType(int networkType):`
The network type you want the device to have when your job is executed. You can choose between:

  - `NETWORK_TYPE_NONE:` No network connection is required for the job. This is the default value set for the job.
  - `NETWORK_TYPE_ANY:` This specifies that the Job requires an internet connection, but it can be of any type, such as Wi-Fi, mobile network, or any other type of connection.
  - `NETWORK_TYPE_UNMETERED:` This is specified when a job has to be triggered when the network type is unmetered, for example, Wi-Fi.
  - `NETWORK_TYPE_NOT_ROAMING:` This is added in API 24. It is specified when network should not be roaming to trigger the Job.

- `setRequiresCharging(boolean requiresCharging):`
Whether or not the device should be charging.

- setRequiresDeviceIdle(boolean requiresDeviceIdle):
  If the device should be idle when running the job. This is a great time to do resource heavy jobs.

```
ComponentName serviceComponent = new ComponentName(context,
MyJobService.class);
JobInfo jobInfo = new JobInfo.Builder(0, serviceComponent)
.setBackoffCriteria(30*1000,JobInfo.BACKOFF_POLICY_EXPONENTIAL)
.setMinimumLatency(5 * 1000) // wait at least
.setOverrideDeadline(10 * 1000) // maximum delay
.setRequiredNetworkType(JobInfo.NETWORK_TYPE_UNMETERED) // require
unmetered network
.setRequiresDeviceIdle(true) // device should be idle
.setRequiresCharging(false) // we don't care if the device is charging or
not
.build();
```

Next, we will see about the `JobService`.

JobService

The `JobService` is the actual service that is going to run our Job. The new `JobService` must be registered in the `AndroidManifest` with the `BIND_JOB_SERVICE` permission. This service has different methods to implement than a normal service:

- onStartJob(JobParameters params):
  This method is what gets called when the `JobScheduler` decides to run your job based on its parameters. You can get the `jobId` from the `JobParameters` and you will have to hold on to these parameters to finish the job later.
  The `jobId` can be used to identify each job.

- onStopJob (JobParameters params):
  This will get called when your parameters are no longer being met. In our previous example. this would happen when the user switches off of Wi-Fi, unplugs, or turns the screen off on their device.

Here are some important things to know when using a JobService:

- The JobService runs on the main thread:
  It is your responsibility to move your work off-thread. If the user tries to open your app while a job is running on the main thread. they might get an **Android Not Responding** (**ANR**) error . This can be done by performing the tasks to be done in the service in a background thread within the service itself, using a Handler or an AsyncTask.
- You must finish your job when it is complete:
  The JobScheduler keeps a wake lock for your job. If you don't call jobFinished (JobParameters params, boolean needsReschedule) with the JobParameters from onStartJob (JobParameters params) the JobScheduler will keep a wake lock for your app and burn the device's battery. Even worse, the battery history will blame your app. So, remember to call jobFinished when the job has completed its work.
- You have to register your job service in the AndroidManifest:
  If you do not, the system will not be able to find your service as a component and it will not start your jobs. You'll never even know as this does not produce an error.

Here is a code example to show how the JobService class looks:

Firstly, we add the service in the AndroidManifest:

```
<service
android:name=".service.MyJobService"
]android:permission="android.permission.BIND_JOB_SERVICE" />
Next, we create the service:
public class MyJobService extends JobService {
private static final String TAG = MyJobService.class.getSimpleName();
JobParameters params;
@Override
public boolean onStartJob(JobParameters params) {
MyLg.e(TAG, "Job Started");
this.params = params;
updateComplete();
return true;//Return
true if using background thread else return false
```

```
}
@Override
public boolean onStopJob(JobParameters params) {
MyLg.e(TAG, "Job Force Stopped");return true;// Reschedule job return true
else return false
}
private void updateComplete() {
List<PhotoItem> allList =
DaoController.getPhotoItems(getApplicationContext());
if (allList.size() != 0) {
PhotoItem item = allList.get(0);
String finalName = "Photo" + new Date().getTime() + "U" +
SessionPreference.getUserId(getApplicationContext()) + ".jpg";
String path = item.getPath();
String tag = item.getTag();
item.setName(finalName);
item.setStatus(true);
uploadPhoto(item);
}else{
jobFinished(params, false);
}
}
private void uploadPhoto(final PhotoItem photo) {
String name = photo.getName();
String content = getImageFromPath(photo.getPath());
if(content!=null) {
RetroInterface.getImageApi().uploadImage(
""+content,
"" + name,
new Callback<NormalResponse>() {
@Override
public void success(NormalResponse menuDetailResponse, Response response) {
photo.setStatus(1);
DaoController.updatePhotoItems(getApplicationContext(), photo);
updateComplete();
}
@Override
public void failure(RetrofitError error) {
photo.setStatus(2);
DaoController.updatePhotoItems(getApplicationContext(), photo);
updateComplete();
}
});
}
else {
MyLg.e(TAG, "Could not decode image..");
photo.setStatus(1); //Skip Image
DaoController.updatePhotoItems(getApplicationContext(), photo);
```

```
updateComplete();
    }
  }
}
```

From the above service, we upload a list of images sequentially.

Next, we will see how to schedule the Job using the `JobScheduler` class.

JobScheduler

We now have our `JobInfo` and our `JobService`, so it is time to schedule our job. All we have to do is get the `JobService` the same way you would get any system service and hand it our `JobInfo` with the schedule (`JobInfo` job) method.
After we have got the instance of the `JobScheduler` class, we have to call the schedule method to schedule the job.

Here is a code example showing how the job has to be scheduled:

```
JobScheduler jobScheduler =
(JobScheduler)getSystemService(Context.JOB_SCHEDULER_SERVICE);
jobScheduler.schedule(jobInfo);
```

Effective use of Extended Doze and Standby

So far, you might have understood that improving the performance of an app is as simple as saving as much of a device's battery as possible by using effective coding techniques. Hence, in the latest versions of Android, starting from Android 6.0 (API level 23) there are two power-saving features included which could extend battery life for users, by managing how apps behave when a device is not connected to a power source:

- Doze: Doze reduces battery consumption when the device is not being used for a long time, by temporarily suspending the background tasks performed by CPU and network calls for apps.
- App Standby Standby temporarily suspends the background network calls for apps that are not used or interacted with recently.

To make sure that the latest versions of Android can make use of both these features effectively, there need to changes made to your code if there is any performance deficit that occurs due to improper code that violates use for these key features.

Understanding Doze

Doze mode in an Android device is a state which is satisfied if these three conditions are met:

- If the device screen is off.
- If the user is not using the device for a period of time.
- If the device is in a non-charging state.

In Doze mode, the device reduces the use of battery by restricting the apps from accessing the network and prevents the apps from doing tasks that use the CPU of the device. It also suspends all the apps jobs, syncs, and alarms. But doze mode gives a breather space to the apps periodically. It exits the doze mode for a short period of time and allows the apps complete their suspended tasks like syncs, jobs, and alarms, and lets apps access the network.

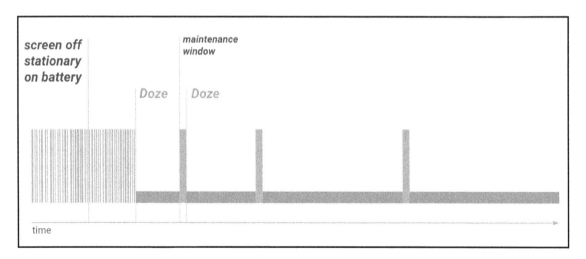

Figure 5.2.4: Doze Mode

Figure 5.2.4 above shows the doze mode for a device. We know that the doze mode exits periodically; this is called the maintenance window. At the end of the maintenance window, the device again moves in doze mode. If the device is not used for a very long time, the maintenance window keeps on decreasing as the time progresses and thus reduces the use of battery when the device is not connected to a charger. Doze mode is exited, as soon as the user wakes up the device or if the device is connected to a charger; at this point all the suspended tasks resume.

Doze restrictions

There are several restrictions applied to your app by the device when the device is in doze mode. The restrictions are as follows:

- Network access is suspended
- The device ignores wake locks
- Standard `AlarmManager` alarms are temporarily suspended to the next maintenance window
  The alarms could be overridden in doze mode by writing this statement in the code: `setAndAllowWhileIdle()` or `setExactAndAllowWhileIdle()`
- Wi-Fi scans are not performed
- Sync adapters are not allowed to run
- The system does not allow `JobScheduler` to run

Adapting your app to Doze

Doze mode may affect an app that uses some services that are controlled by Doze mode. In such cases, there is a need to modify your code in such a way that your app works correctly in Doze mode or after exiting doze mode. However, in a normal case Doze mode does not differently affect app functionality. Mostly, the apps that make use of network, alarms, jobs, and syncs are the apps that need to be well-tested for Doze mode. In those cases, the apps should be able to efficiently manage activities during each maintenance window.

Doze mode is likely to affect activities that make use of `AlarmManager` and timers, because alarms in Android 5.1 or lower do not fire when the system is in Doze. To schedule alarms from Android 6.0 onwards, Android introduces two new `AlarmManager` methods: `setAndAllowWhileIdle()` and `setExactAndAllowWhileIdle()`. With these methods, you can set alarms that will fire even if the device is in doze.

Doze mode also restricts the use of network access and hence may affect services like showing notifications in an app. The solution for this is to make use of `Firebase Cloud Messaging` (FCM) to get notifications from server if possible.

Understanding App Standby

The App Standby feature allows a device to determine if an app is idle. It checks if the user is actively using the app or not by determining if the user touches the app for a certain period of time and none of the following conditions applies:

- The user explicitly launches the app.
- The app has a process currently in the foreground (either as an activity or foreground service, or in use by another activity or foreground service).

A foreground service for a task should be implemented only when a task executes immediately or without interruption. For example, uploading a photo or playing music even while the music-player app is not in the foreground. Foreground service should not be used to determine whether your app is idle.

The Standby mode is exited when the user plugs the device for charging, allowing them to freely access the network and to execute any pending jobs and syncs. If the device is idle for long periods of time, the system allows idle apps network access around once a day. In a Standby state, the app generates a notification that users see on the lock screen or in the notification tray. All the other apps move into standby, but the device admin app never enters App Standby, because it must remain available to receive data from a server at any time.

Testing with Doze and App Standby

Your app may get affected by Doze mode and App Standby if you use some services. So, your app needs to handle these cases to ensure that the app functions smoothly in these conditions. Hence, it is required to test your app in these conditions. An app moves into doze mode, or App Standby, after some time, but a developer cannot wait every time for these conditions to occur. Therefore, it is required to simulate these conditions to test your app fully in Doze and App Standby to ensure a great experience for users.

You can test Doze mode by following these steps:

1. Make sure you have a hardware device or virtual device with an Android 6.0 or higher system image.
2. Connect the device to your development machine and install your app.
3. Run your app and leave it active.
4. Now the device should be forced into idle mode. This can be done by running the following command:

```
$ adb shell dumpsys deviceidle force-idle
```

5. Observe the behavior of your app after you reactivate the device.
6. Verify that your app opens up smoothly and as expected without any issues when it exits Doze mode.

To test App Standby mode with your app:

1. Make sure you have a hardware device or virtual device with an Android 6.0 or higher system image.
2. Connect the device to your development machine and install your app.
3. Run your app and leave it active.
4. Now the app should be forced into App Standby mode. This can be done by running the following commands:

```
$ adb shell dumpsys battery unplug
$ adb shell am set-inactive com.zomato.app true
```

Use your package name instead of com.zomato.app.

5. Now the app should be simulated to wake up using the following commands:

```
$ adb shell am set-inactive com.zomato.app false
$ adb shell am get-inactive com.zomato.app
```

Use your package name instead of com.zomato.app.

6. Observe the behavior of your app after waking it.
7. Verify if your app opens up smoothly and as expected without any issues when it exits the standby mode. In particular, you should check if your app's notifications and background jobs continue to function as expected.

Threads and Pools

A thread is a path followed to execute any task in Android. The Android device functions on a thread. Everything that you see on an Android device works on a thread called the Main thread or a UI thread. If the UI thread performs the task of displaying the UI, then any app functions smoothly. However, if you ask the UI thread to perform other long-running, extensive data operations, then it will affect the performance of the app. The speed and efficiency could be thus improved by splitting these into smaller operations and then running each one of them on multiple threads. On a device that has a CPU with multiple processors, it can run the threads in parallel, instead of making each sub-operation wait for a chance to run its task.

Specifying the Code to Run on a Thread

A separate thread could be written to execute some operation using the functions from a `Runnable` class. The `Runnable` class has a `function, run()`, in which you could write the code that needs to be executed on a separate thread. Similarly, multiple runnable objects could be created and could be run independently to perform their specified operation. The runnable could also be passed to another object that can then attach it to a thread and run it. One or more runnable objects that perform a particular operation are sometimes called a task.

Threads and `Runnable` are encapsulated classes which form the base for creation of some important classes that help to execute a task in a separate thread. A few examples of such classes are `AsyncTask`, `HandlerThread`, `IntentService`, `ThreadPoolExecutor`, and so on. These classes automatically manage threads and task queues and can even run multiple threads in parallel.

In order to create a class on a separate thread using `Runnable`, create a new class that implements `Runnable` as shown in the following code:

```
public class MyRunnable implements Runnable {
    ...
    @Override
    public void run() {
        /*
         * Write your code that needs to run on separate thread
         */
        ...
    }
    ...
}
```

Then, override the `run()` method of this class and write your code that needs to be executed on the separate thread. The `Runnable` won't be running on the UI thread, so it cannot directly modify UI objects such as view objects.

In order to reduce the resource competition between the `Runnable` object's thread and the UI thread.

Set the thread to use background priority by calling `Process.setThreadPriority()` with `THREAD_PRIORITY_BACKGROUND`, at the beginning of the `run()` method.

Also, a reference to the `Runnable` object's Thread should be stored in the `Runnable`, by calling `Thread.currentThread()`.

The following snippet shows how to set up the `run()` method:

```
class MyRunnable implements Runnable {
...
    @Override
    public void run() {
        // Write this line to move the current Thread into the background
android.os.Process.setThreadPriority(android.os.Process.THREAD_PRIORITY_BAC
KGROUND);
        ...
        /*
         * Save the current Thread in the Task instance.
         */
        mTask.setMyThread(Thread.currentThread());
        ...
    }
...
}
```

Creating a Thread Pool

Multiple threads have to be created when you need to run multiple tasks simultaneously. Android has built different classes for multi-threading. To run a task on different data, but with only one execution running at a time, an `IntentService` has to be used.

`ThreadPoolExecutor` could be used to automatically run tasks when the resources become available, or to allow multiple tasks to run at the same time. This class runs a task by adding it to the queue, when a thread in its pool becomes free. A thread pool can run multiple parallel instances of a task, so you should ensure that your code is thread-safe. Enclose variables that can be accessed by more than one thread in a synchronized block. This approach will prevent one thread from reading the variable while another is writing to it. Typically, this situation arises with static variables, but it also occurs in any object that is only instantiated once.

A `ThreadPoolExecutor` could be started by creating an instantiation of `ThreadPoolExecutor` in its own class. In this class, do the following:

- Use static variables for thread pools: In your app, make use of a single instance of your thread pool to control the whole class and its methods. Using the same instance, execute different methods of the class. If you have different Runnable types, you would have a thread pool for each one but each of these can be a single instance. For example, create a global field declaration of the instance:

```
public class MyManager {
    ...
    static  {
    ...
        // Create a single static instance of MyManager class
        mInstance = new MyManager();
    }
```

- Use a private constructor: You need to create a single instance of the constructor, that is, to create a Singleton constructor. So, to satisfy this condition, make the constructor private, which means that you don't have to enclose accesses to the class in a synchronized block:

```
public class MyManager {
    ...
    /**
     * The constructor is made private, so it is unavailable
     * to other classes, even in the same package.
     */
    private MyManager() {
    ...
}
```

- Add tasks that have to be performed in the `Runnable` thread. These tasks must be initiated by calling the methods in the thread pool class. Add a method in the `ThreadPool` class that adds a task to a thread pool's queue as shown in the code below:

```
public class MyManager {
    ...
    // Used to fetch data from local database
    static public MyTask fetchData(LocalDb localDb) {
        ...
    // Adds a task to the thread pool for execution
      mInstance.
            mThreadPool.
            execute(mTask.getMyTaskRunnable());
    ...
    }
```

- Then, create a Handler by instantiating it in the constructor. Attach the handler to the app's UI thread as it safely calls the methods of UI objects:

```
private MyManager() {
    ...
        // A new Handler object is created and
        // it is attached to the UI thread.
        mHandler = new Handler(Looper.getMainLooper()) {
         /*
          * handleMessage() method handles the operations
          * to be performed when it receives a new Message
          * to process.
          */
            @Override
             public void handleMessage(Message message) {
                ...
            }
        ...
        }
}
```

- The next step is to create a thread pool. You could do that by instantiating the `ThreadPoolExecutor` class and defining an object of the class. The following parameters are required to instantiate that class:

- Initial pool size and maximum pool size:
  In order to define a pool, a definite pool size must be initially known. The maximum pool size must also be known. If these are known. then only the pool can be allocated with threads. The maximum number of threads that a thread pool can have depends on the number of cores available for your device. This number is available from the system environment at runtime, as shown:

```
public class MyManager {
 ... /*
 * Gets the number of available cores
 */
 private static int NUMBER_OF_AVAILABLE_CORES =
 Runtime.getRuntime().availableProcessors();
}
```

- Keep alive time and time unit:
  A thread should remain alive for a certain period of time, after which it shuts down. This duration for which a thread will remain idle before it shuts down needs to be mentioned using the time unit value.

- A queue of tasks:
  The third parameter is a queue of tasks that ThreadPoolExecutor takes. These should be a queue of Runnable objects. A thread pool manager takes a Runnable object from a first-in, first-out queue and attaches it to the thread. You provide this queue object when you create the thread pool, using any queue class that implements the BlockingQueue interface. To match the requirements of your app, you can choose from the available queue implementations; to learn more about them, see the class overview for ThreadPoolExecutor. This example uses the LinkedBlockingQueue class:

```
public class MyManager {
 ...
private MyManager() {
 ...
 // Declare a queue of Runnables
 private final BlockingQueue<Runnable> mDecodeWorkQueue;
 ...
 // Instantiate the queue of Runnables
 // as LinkedBlockingQueue
 mThreadQueue = new LinkedBlockingQueue<Runnable>();
 ...
 }
 ...
 }
```

- Once the required parameters are initiated, instantiate a thread pool manager by calling `ThreadPoolExecutor()`. Calling that would create a group of all the threads as the initial pool size and the maximum pool size are the same:

```
private MyManager() {
        . . .
        // Sets the keep alive time
        private static final int KEEP_ALIVE_TIME = 1;
        // Sets the Time Unit to seconds
        private static final TimeUnit KEEP_ALIVE_TIME_UNIT =
TimeUnit.SECONDS;
        // Create a thread pool manager
        mThreadPool = new ThreadPoolExecutor(
                NUMBER_OF_CORES,        // Initial pool size
                NUMBER_OF_CORES,        // Max pool size
                KEEP_ALIVE_TIME,
                KEEP_ALIVE_TIME_UNIT,
                mThreadQueue);
}
```

Running Code on a Thread Pool Thread

Once your thread pool has been created, you need to run your code on this thread pool. To do this, you add the task to the pool's work queue. When a thread becomes available, the `ThreadPoolExecutor` takes a task from the queue and runs it on the thread. The `ThreadPoolExecutor` also allows you to stop the running task in case you find that the task is not required anymore.

In order to start a task on a thread in a particular thread pool, you need to add the runnable in the thread pool's work queue. To add it to the queue you need to pass the Runnable to `ThreadPoolExecutor.execute()`. When an idle thread becomes available, the manager takes the task that has been waiting the longest and runs it on the thread:

```
public class MyManager {
    public void addToQueue(MyTask mTask) {
// Adds the runnable to the queue
mThreadPool.execute(
mTask.getMyRunnable());
. . .
    }
    . . .
}
```

Once the `ThreadPoolExecutor` begins the task defined by a Runnable on a thread, it automatically calls the object's `run()` method.

In order to stop a task, you need to interrupt the task's thread. For this, you need to know which thread to stop. So, you need to save the handle to the current working thread when the task is created, as shown in the following code:

```
class MyRunnable implements Runnable {
    // run method to execute the task
    public void run() {
        /*
         * Save the current Thread in the Task instance.
         */
        mTask.setMyThread(Thread.currentThread());
        ...
    }
    ...
}
```

Now that you know which thread has to be interrupted, call `Thread.interrupt()` to stop that thread. Make sure that the thread has a lock, meaning that it should not be modified outside your app's process. Do that by placing the access in a synchronized block as shown in the following code:

```
public class MyManager {
    public static void stopAll() {
        /*
         * Creates an array of Runnables that is equal to
         * thread pool queue size
         */
        Runnable[] runnableArray = new Runnable[mThreadQueue.size()];
        // Populates the array with the Runnables
        mThreadQueue.toArray(runnableArray);
        // Saves runnable array length
        int runnableArrayLength = runnableArray.length;
        synchronized (mInstance) {
            // Loops through the array of runnable
            for (int index = 0; index < runnableArrayLength; index++) {
                // Gets the current thread
                Thread thread = runnableArray[index].mThread;
                // if the Thread exists, interrupt it
                if (thread!=null) {
                    thread.interrupt();
                }
            }
        }
    }
    ...
}
```

`Thread.interrupt()` stops the thread immediately in most cases, however it is better a check if a thread has already been taken up for an interrupt, as some CPU intensive tasks could slow the interrupt process:

```
/*
 * Checks if a Thread has already been interrupted
 */
if (Thread.interrupted()) {
    return;
}
```

Communicating with the UI Thread

A thread sometimes also needs to communicate with the UI thread, either in between the execution of the thread or at the end of the execution of a thread. Only objects running on the UI thread have access to other objects on that thread. Because tasks that you run on a thread from a thread pool aren't running on your UI thread, they don't have access to UI objects. For example, if you have the task of downloading a large file from a server, then showing the progress of the download would be a good practice. In order to show this progress, your thread must communicate with the UI thread to display the progress as a percentage.

Data from a background thread could communicate with the UI thread using a Handler running on the UI thread. Handler is part of the Android system's framework for managing threads. A Handler object receives messages and runs code to handle the messages.

Handler could be instantiated in the constructor of the class that creates your thread pools. Then connect this handler to the UI thread, instantiating it with the `Handler(Looper)` constructor. This constructor uses a Looper object, which is another part of the Android system's thread management framework, and makes the handler run on the same thread as the Looper:

```
private MyManager() {
...
    // Defines a Handler object that's attached to the UI thread
    mHandler = new Handler(Looper.getMainLooper()) {
        /*
         * handleMessage() defines the operations to perform when
         * the Handler receives a new Message to process.
         */
        @Override
        public void handleMessage(Message message) {
            // Gets the task from the Message object.
            MyTask mTask = (MyTask) message.obj;
```

```
        . . .
      }
   . . .
    }
 }
```

The `handleMessage()` method receives a new message for a thread.

Then, the data has to be moved from a task object running on a background thread to an object on the UI thread. Follow these steps to perform this movement of data:

1. Store data in the task object:
   Store references to the data and the UI object in the task object. For example, in the runnable , once your task gets completed successfully, save a status code, say `TASK_COMPLETE`, in that runnable task:

```
// A Runnable class to perform my task
class MyRunnable implements Runnable {
    . . .
    MyRunnable(MyTask task) {
        mTask = task;
    }
    . . .
    // Runs the code for this task
    public void run() {
    . . .
    // Perform all your tasks here.
    // Once the task is completed save the status task completion
    mTask.saveStatus(TASK_COMPLETE);
    . . .
     }
     . . .
}
```

2. Send status up the object hierarchy (`MyTask` objec):

   Pass the task object and a status code to the object that instantiated the Handler. For this, the runnable class could have another method, which could have access to the next higher object in the hierarchy. The following code shows that the status has been passed to the next higher hierarchy for it to be accessed by the UI thread:

```
public class MyTask {
    ...
    // Gets a handle to the object that creates the thread pools
    mManager = MyManager.getInstance();
    ...
    public void saveStatus(int status) {
    ...
    // Calls the generalized status method
    handleStatus(status);
    }
    ...
    // Passes the status to MyManager
    void handleStatus(int status) {
    /*
     * Passes a handle to this task and the
     * current status to the class that created
     * the thread pools
     */
        mManager.handleStatus(this, status);
    }
    ...
}
```

3. Move data to the UI:

   Send a Message containing the status and the task object to the Handler. The Handler can also move the data to the UI object:

```
public class MyManager {
    ...
    // Handle status messages from tasks
    public void handleStatus(MyTask task, int status) {
        Message mMessage = mHandler.obtainMessage(status, task);
        mMessage.sendToTarget();
    ...
    }
    ...
}
```

Finally, `Handler.handleMessage()` checks the status code for each incoming message. If the status code is `TASK_COMPLETE`, then the task is finished, and any task of displaying on the UI thread could be performed here:

```
private MyManager() {
    ...
        mHandler = new Handler(Looper.getMainLooper()) {
            @Override
            public void handleMessage(Message message) {
                // Gets the task from the incoming Message object.
                MyTask mTask = (MyTask) message.obj;

                ...
                switch (message.what) {
                    ...
                    case TASK_COMPLETE:
                        /*
                         * Perform the task that you need
                         * to perform on the UI thread here
                         */
                        mTask.getMyFinalTaskObject();
                        break;
                    ...
                    default:
                        /*
                         * Pass along other messages from the UI
                         */
                        super.handleMessage(message);
                }
                ...
            }
            ...
        }
        ...
    }
    ...
}
```

Memory optimization

Memory too plays an important role in the performance of an app. The memory optimization standalone does not take part in improving the performance of the app, but it helps in improving performance by helping the network traffic data to reduce considerably, which affects battery consumption by the app.

The technique of memory optimization is done by reducing the amount of data sent or received over a network connection. This reduces the duration of the connection, which conserves battery. This can be done by using the following techniques:

- Compress data, using a compression technique such as GZIP compression:
  Make use of succinct data protocols. The binary serialization formats, such as Protocol Buffers or FlatBuffers, offer a smaller packet size and faster encoding and decoding time, whereas standard data sending techniques like JSON and XML offer human-readability and language-flexibility, but are bandwidth-heavy formats, with high serialization costs in the Android platform.

- Cache files locally:
  Caching is a very important way to reduce the network traffic. The app could avoid downloading the same data again and again by caching the data in the local database. Along with textual data, even the images could be cached. Always cache static resources, including on-demand downloads such as full size images, and cache them for as long as reasonably possible.
  How would you sometimes know which data is cached and which is not? If your app has a lot of static data, then that data has to be cached and the cached data has to be reused. To check if the cached data is the latest data, you could make one network call to check if the various static data in your app are updated to the latest value using date. If some data is updated on the server, then only that data should be fetched.

- Optimize pre-fetch cache size:
  Optimize the amount of network data transfer based on the type of network your device is connected to, such as Wi-Fi, LTE, HSPAP, EDGE, GPRS. Based on these, the amount of data that is pre-fetched could differ.

Treating Battery as part of user's experience

Battery hogging apps usually find only one acknowledgement uninstall.
When you're altering the frequency of your background updates to reduce the effect of those updates on battery life, checking the current battery level and charging state is a good place to start.

The battery-life impact of performing application updates depends on the battery level and charging state of the device. The impact of performing updates while the device is charging over AC is negligible, so in most cases you can maximize your refresh rate whenever the device is connected to a wall charger. Conversely, if the device is discharging, reducing your update rate helps prolong the battery life.

Similarly, you can check the battery charge level, potentially reducing the frequency of or even stopping your updates when the battery charge is nearly exhausted.

Understanding what causes battery drain

When we talk about battery drain we mostly concentrate on these areas:

- Networking
- Wakelocks
- Sensors

This is mostly true, as calls to the server is one of the biggest contributors to draining users battery. Wakelocks, followed by sensors, are the biggest contributors to draining the user's battery life. GPS is one of the most commonly used sensors. Along with these, there are other factors which can be tweaked to improve the user's battery life and lower the app's battery usage. In the next section, we will discuss why and how we can help in saving user's battery by making some changes in the code.

Why Battery Optimization is required?

Most of us may think that providing good UI and a better user experience in the app will be enough for the users. Why should we be bothered about how much battery our app uses? However, most users will think that, in spite of it being a great app, it is not worth keeping an app which drains the battery when they use the app for a short amount of time in a day.

Most likely, they will give bad reviews and uninstall the app. With the bad review, any new users will refrain from even installing the app. So, an app which is battery friendly is more likely to retain users than an app that drains the user's battery.

So, despite what we think, it is one of the most important aspects of app development. Next, we will see some methods which will help in saving a user's battery.

Strategies for battery optimization

Here are some of the methods which we should keep in mind when reducing the power consumption:

- Follow different methodologies till the device is charging:
  This should be the obvious point. We should perform tasks which are heavy on the battery when the device is charging, so this will not count towards draining battery. Unless the task has to be done right away, we can do these tasks when more resources are available and the device is charging. This can be achieved by checking the charging state of the device. Alternatively, in Android 5.0 Lollipop (API 21) `JobScheduler` API was introduced, and this can be used to schedule the Jobs when the conditions are satisfied. The `BatteryManager` can also be used to monitor the battery status.

- Performing batch tasks together:
  There is power cost when we use sensors and threads. If we call these services multiple times, it will cost more than calling them once and using the values multiple times. For example, if we get the users coordinated from the GPS sensor and use this value in multiple places, it will be much more cost effective than getting the user's location multiple times. It is also better to do lots of work in one go instead of doing the same job repeatedly. For example, if we have to update some data on the server which can all be sent at once at a later point, we should send the data in a bulk instead of calling the service multiple times, as calling multiple smaller services is more battery draining than one big call.

- Cache images:
  We should always avoid downloading images from the server multiple times. Instead, we should download the images once and store them in cache which we can use later. For example, if we are displaying a gallery of images it is better to load the images not seen by the user as users have a tendency to scroll through the images more in such types of screen.

- Batch operations to avoid waking a device repeatedly:
  It is very common while developing to load only the data that is required on the screen, but this results in calling the same services repeatedly and making our device move from StandBy to Wake Up mode more often than required. This transition from StandBy to Wake Up drains the device battery. A better approach would be to load all the necessary data that may be required in most section of the app once and store them in a local db, syncing them whenever necessary. This will reduce unnecessary fetching from the server as the data is already present.

- Use Wakelocks and timers sparingly:

  It is very common to use Wakelocks to run some processes at a later time, but this causes the user's device to be woken up more frequently and spend less time sleeping, which drains its battery. You could also forget to release the Wakelocks after the tasks have been completed and hence drain the user's battery.

  For this very reason, wherever when we are using Wakelocks we should use the version of `WakeLock.acquire()` that takes a time-out and always remember to release our WakeLocks. This does not, however, solve the problem of different apps constantly waking up the device, which is where the `JobScheduler` API is extremely useful. This API can batch jobs together for you with other apps, hence avoiding the scenario where different apps are waking up the phone every few minutes.

- Battery drain by sensors:

  The rule for most sensors is fairly straightforward: turn them off as soon as you have the data that you need. Most sensors require you to subscribe or register for updates; once you are done, you should unregister or unsubscribe in order to prevent wasting battery.

  If possible, we can also cache the data from the sensors and use them.

  GPS is one of the most largely used sensors and one of the biggest reasons for the draining of users' batteries. The best way to use this sensor would be to use the user's last known location or request passive location updates if applicable and avoid using the GPS altogether. If you have to use the GPS, determine whether a coarse location is enough and unregister your location listener after coordinates have been received.

  If a fine location is needed, then we must set a timeout for listening for the user's location, such as 30 seconds, after that we must unregister the listener to save battery. If you need constant location updates, then set as large of an update interval as is feasible.

Effective consumption of battery in Zomato

Effective and minimal battery usage has to be performed by any app. An app would be able to do effective consumption of battery by determining the current charge status. Android has a class for determining the current battery status of the app. The `BatteryManager` broadcasts all battery and charging details in a sticky Intent that includes the charging status.

Using this battery manager, Zomato receives the charging status without registering a `BroadcastReceiver` by calling `registerReceiver` and passing in null as the receiver, as shown in the following code:

```
IntentFilter filter = new IntentFilter(Intent.ACTION_BATTERY_CHANGED);
Intent batteryStatus = context.registerReceiver(null, filter);
```

You'll be getting the `batteryStatus` intent, from which you can extract both the current charging status and if the device is being charged. It also determines whether it's charging via USB or AC charger:

```
// Are we charging / charged?
int status = batteryStatus.getIntExtra(BatteryManager.EXTRA_STATUS, -1);
boolean isCharging = status == BatteryManager.BATTERY_STATUS_CHARGING ||
                     status == BatteryManager.BATTERY_STATUS_FULL;

// How are we charging?
int chargePlug = batteryStatus.getIntExtra(BatteryManager.EXTRA_PLUGGED,
-1);
boolean usbCharge = chargePlug == BatteryManager.BATTERY_PLUGGED_USB;
boolean acCharge = chargePlug == BatteryManager.BATTERY_PLUGGED_AC;
```

Zomato makes use of these statuses and accordingly makes changes in code to handle the rate at which the network flows in and out of the app. If the device is connected to an AC charger and you are using the app, then it maximizes the rate of your background updates, but if the device is charging over USB, it reduces the rate of network flow and minimizes it further if the battery is discharging.

Monitoring changes in charging state

It is very important for your app to monitor the changes in the charging state. If the device is currently discharging, and then later kept for charging, it means that there is a change in state and your app must know about this change as soon as it happens, so as to make changes to the refresh rates of the background tasks in your app.

The `BatteryManager` broadcasts an action whenever the device is connected or disconnected from power. Using this, the, app gets the callbacks for the battery state when opened. However, it is also required that it receives the callbacks even when the app is closed and not running for handling background tasks. To receive those updates, register a `BroadcastReceiver` in your manifest to listen for both events by defining the `ACTION_POWER_CONNECTED` and `ACTION_POWER_DISCONNECTED` within an intent filter:

```
<receiver android:name=".BatteryStateReceiver">
  <intent-filter>
    <action android:name="android.intent.action.ACTION_POWER_CONNECTED"/>
    <action
android:name="android.intent.action.ACTION_POWER_DISCONNECTED"/>
  </intent-filter>
</receiver>
```

Then, write the implementation for receiving the updates in the receiver class. The further process of getting the battery state is the same as mentioned above.

```
public class BatteryStateReceiver extends BroadcastReceiver {
    @Override
    public void onReceive(Context context, Intent intent) {
        int status = intent.getIntExtra(BatteryManager.EXTRA_STATUS, -1);
        boolean isCharging = status ==
BatteryManager.BATTERY_STATUS_CHARGING ||
                            status == BatteryManager.BATTERY_STATUS_FULL;

        int chargePlug = intent.getIntExtra(BatteryManager.EXTRA_PLUGGED,
-1);
        boolean usbCharge = chargePlug ==
BatteryManager.BATTERY_PLUGGED_USB;
        boolean acCharge = chargePlug == BatteryManager.BATTERY_PLUGGED_AC;
    }
}
```

Determining the current battery level

A higher level of battery optimization could also be carried out by determining the percentage of battery remaining on the device and accordingly reducing or increasing the number of network tasks in the app.

The current battery charge percentage could be found by extracting the current battery level and scale from the battery status intent:

```
int level = batteryStatus.getIntExtra(BatteryManager.EXTRA_LEVEL, -1);
int scale = batteryStatus.getIntExtra(BatteryManager.EXTRA_SCALE, -1);

float batteryPercentage = level / (float)scale;
```

Using the battery percentage level, Zomato disables all the background updates when the battery is critically low. It also reduces the brightness of the device according to the time of day when the battery is very low. This helps a user use the app and device for more time rather than consuming battery for tasks that won't matter much at the current point if the phone switches off.

Although there are a lot of advantages to battery saving techniques to saving the battery, the same techniques could lead to excessive use of battery if not handled well. Hence, it is necessary to make use of battery monitoring techniques only for significant changes in battery level and it should be handled for only few states of battery level, preferably at low battery levels.

Low battery level states could be handled by using `BatteryLevelReceiver` which is triggered whenever device battery becomes low or exits the low condition by listening for `ACTION_BATTERY_LOW` and `ACTION_BATTERY_OKAY`:

```
<receiver android:name=".BatteryLevelReceiver">
  <intent-filter>
    <action android:name="android.intent.action.BATTERY_LOW"/>
    <action android:name="android.intent.action.BATTERY_OKAY"/>
  </intent-filter>
</receiver>
```

Improving app with battery analyser

An app should focus on preventing battery drain from occurring to improve the performance of the app and the device. In order to reduce the battery usage of an app, the battery usage of the app should be determined. For this purpose, a battery analyzer has to be used to determine how your app uses battery and how performance could be improved.

Battery Stats collects battery data from your device. It creates a dump of all the battery data of a particular selected device using **Android Debug Bridge** (**ADB**) commands. Using these battery stats, the battery usage could be found out using a battery historian which would create a HTML file for viewing the battery stats results in a browser for user viewing.

A graphical representation battery historian of the live Zomato app is shown in the figure below:

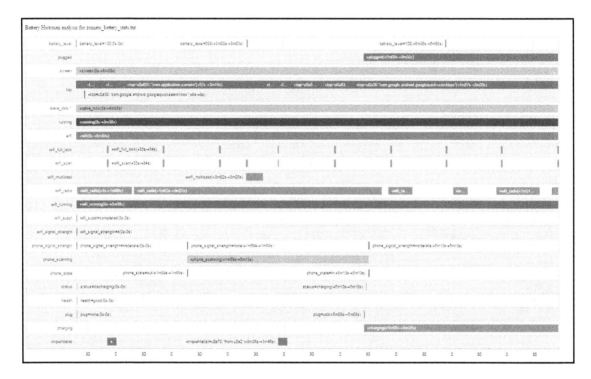

A detailed explanation of the above battery usage elements has been explained in an earlier section of this book.

Summary

In the first section of this chapter, we discussed how performance, impacts the app quality, followed by in ways by which we can target different elements of app performance such as UI, and resources such as the battery. We also discussed the tools that we can use to improve the app performance.

In Chapter 10, *Building Zomato*, we will discuss testing the entire app flow and improving the tests of the app. We will also learn the best practices for testing and supported tools.

10
Building Restaurant finder

This chapter will focus on development segment of the app based on the architecture we discussed in the last segment. Since the UI/UX, architecture is planned in the previous chapters, this chapter will take a deep dive into the core development of the app. Here, you will go through the different screens in the app and will be able to understand how to write the code logic behind implementing the screens in the app.

App sections

Development of each screen of Zomato involves writing of code in two major languages: Java and XML. The code written in XML will mostly involve the UI designs for building the layouts for each screen. It will also be used for writing code that involves styling and theming of the different layouts used in the app, and also other miscellaneous purposes.

In the sections that follow, we will first understand the code to design the layout of the screen and then implement the code logic for the screen. We will walk through each screen starting from the Splash screen and the Login Screen.

Splash, Login, and Signup (including Google and Facebook)

The Splash screen is the first screen of most of the apps. This screen usually has the app logo displayed for a few seconds and then navigates to the next screen. The splash screen can be also used to fetch static data from server at first launch.

Now, we will take a look at the XML layout for designing the splash screen:

```xml
<?xml version="1.0" encoding="utf-8"?>
<RelativeLayout xmlns:android="http://schemas.android.com/apk/res/android"
android:id="@+id/main"
android:layout_width="match_parent"
android:layout_height="match_parent"
android:background="@color/theme_color"
android:gravity="center"
android:orientation="vertical">
<ImageView
android:id="@+id/bgImage"
android:layout_width="wrap_content"
android:layout_height="wrap_content"
android:layout_centerInParent="true"
android:scaleType="fitCenter"
android:src="@drawable/logo_splash" />
</RelativeLayout>
```

The preceding code snippet should be placed in an XML file named `activity_splash.xml`. This file has to be present in the `Zomato\app\src\main\res\layout` folder of your project. All the other layout files should also be present in this same layout folder for a project.

There is `ImageView` that displays the app logo on the splash screen. The `ImageView` is placed within `RelativeLayout`. To display the logo image, it has to be present within the `Zomato\app\src\main\res\drawable` folder.

In Android Studio, the XML layout editor will form the layout and will be displayed as shown:

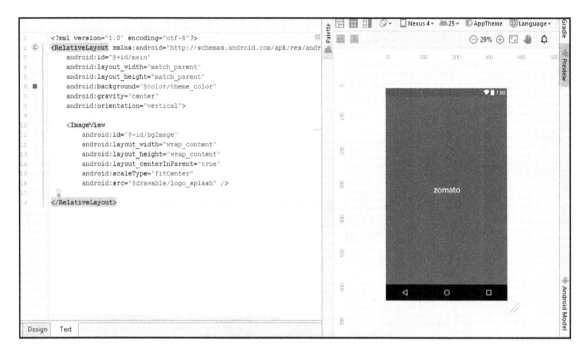

Splash screen layout in Android Studio XML editor

Now, we will look at the Java code to implement the code written in the Splash Screen Activity:

```
/**
 * Splash Activity
 * Starting activity at the beginning of the app
 */
public class SplashActivity extends AppCompatActivity {
private static final String TAG = SplashActivity.class.getSimpleName();
private static final long SPLASH_TIMEOUT = 2300;
private Context context = SplashActivity.this;
private Handler CloseHandler;
//TODO Fonts
private RelativeLayout activity_splash;
private ImageView bgImage;
private Handler handler;
private long startTime = new Date().getTime();
private Runnable CloseRun = new Runnable() {
@Override
```

```
public void run() {
if (SessionPreference.isLoggedIn(context)) {
startActivity(HomeActivity.getCallIntent(context));
finish();
return;
} else {
startActivity(StartActivity.getCallIntent(context));
finish();
return;
}
}
};
@Override
protected void onCreate(Bundle savedInstanceState) {
super.onCreate(savedInstanceState);
setContentView(R.layout.activity_splash);
bgImage = (ImageView) findViewById(R.id.bgImage);
activity_splash = (RelativeLayout) findViewById(R.id.main);
startTime = new Date().getTime();
CloseHandler = new Handler();
tartRunnable();
handler = new Handler();
}
private void StartRunnable() {
CloseHandler.postDelayed(CloseRun, SPLASH_TIMEOUT);
}
@Override
public void onBackPressed() {
try {
CloseHandler.removeCallbacks(CloseRun);
} catch (Exception e) {
e.printStackTrace();
}
super.onBackPressed();
}
@Override
protected void onDestroy() {
super.onDestroy();
try {
Unbinding.unbindDrawables(findViewById(R.id.main));
} catch (Exception e) {
e.printStackTrace();
}
}
}
```

When the app launches, it will start the Splash Activity and execute the code in the onCreate() method. Here, a handler is used to start the next activity after a few seconds. It is shown in the following code snippet:

```
private Runnable CloseRun = new Runnable() {
@Override
public void run() {
if (SessionPreference.isLoggedIn(context)) {
startActivity(HomeActivity.getCallIntent(context));
inish();
return;
} else {
startActivity(StartActivity.getCallIntent(context));
finish();
return;
}
}
};
```

Once the timer executes, it will go to the Login Activity, and if user is already logged in, it will go to the main dashboard.

In order for the Splash Screen to be the first activity to be launched in the app, you need to define it in the AndroidManifest.xml file where all the screens are defined:

```
<activity
android:name=".activity.SplashActivity"
android:label="@string/app_name">
<intent-filter>
<action android:name="android.intent.action.MAIN" />
<category android:name="android.intent.category.LAUNCHER" />
</intent-filter>
</activity>
```

The preceding code shows that the Splash activity has been defined in the Android manifest file, and the following code snippet ensures that it is the first activity to be launched when the app is launched:

```
<intent-filter>
<action android:name="android.intent.action.MAIN" />
<category android:name="android.intent.category.LAUNCHER" />
</intent-filter>
```

The final output screen on the mobile of the splash screen will look like this:

Splash screen layout in Android Studio XML editor

The Signup Flow

From the Splash screen, the user goes to the Login/Signup screen. This screen provides the user with option to Log in/Sign up using their email and password. It also provides users with the option to log in/sign up using their Facebook and/or Google accounts. This screen also has other prominent sections, which we will know about eventually. First, we will look at the layout code of this screen. The layout will be on a similar basis as the splash screen layout, with some additional components:

```
<RelativeLayout
xmlns:android="http://schemas.android.com/apk/res/android"
xmlns:android_ex="http://schemas.android.com/apk/res-auto"
android:layout_width="match_parent"
android:layout_height="match_parent"
ndroid:background="@color/app_bg_color">
<!--Main Screen-->
<RelativeLayout
android:layout_width="match_parent"
```

```
android:layout_height="match_parent">
<ImageView
android:id="@id/image"
android:layout_width="match_parent"
android:layout_height="150dp"
android:scaleType="centerCrop"
android:src="@drawable/im_backdrop" />
<LinearLayout
android:layout_width="match_parent"
android:layout_height="match_parent"
android:layout_below="@id/image"
android:orientation="vertical">
<LinearLayoutandroid:layout_width="match_parent"
android:layout_height="0dp"
android:layout_weight="1"
android:background="@color/white"
android:gravity="center"
android:orientation="vertical"
android:paddingTop="@dimen/dimen_login_logo_margin_view">
<LinearLayout
android:layout_width="match_parent"
android:layout_height="wrap_content"
android:gravity="center">
<ImageView
android:layout_width="wrap_content"
android:layout_height="wrap_content"
android:padding="10dp"
android:src="@drawable/ic_login_1" />
<TextView
style="@style/login_start_info_style"
android:layout_width="wrap_content"
android:layout_height="wrap_content"
android:text="@string/txt_login_1"
android_ex:isHtml="true" />
</LinearLayout>
<LinearLayout
android:layout_width="match_parent"
android:layout_height="wrap_content"
android:gravity="center">
<ImageView
android:layout_width="wrap_content"
android:layout_height="wrap_content"
android:padding="10dp"
android:src="@drawable/ic_login_2" />
<TextView
style="@style/login_start_info_style"
android:layout_width="wrap_content"
android:layout_height="wrap_content"
```

```
android:text="@string/txt_login_2" />
</LinearLayout>
<LinearLayout
android:layout_width="match_parent"
android:layout_height="wrap_content"
android:gravity="center">
<ImageView
android:layout_width="wrap_content"
android:layout_height="wrap_content"
android:padding="10dp"
android:src="@drawable/ic_login_3" />
<TextView
style="@style/login_start_info_style"
android:layout_width="wrap_content"
android:layout_height="wrap_content"
android:text="@string/txt_login_3" />
</LinearLayout>
</LinearLayout>
<LinearLayout
android:layout_width="match_parent"
android:layout_height="wrap_content"
android:orientation="vertical">
<LinearLayout
android:layout_width="match_parent"
android:layout_height="wrap_content"
android:padding="5dp">
<TextView
android:id="@+id/mainSignUp"
style="@style/login_button_style"
android:layout_width="0dp"
android:layout_height="wrap_content"
android:layout_weight="1"
android:onClick="signUpClick"
android:text="Sign Up" />
<TextView
android:id="@+id/mainLogin"
style="@style/login_button_style"
android:layout_width="0dp"
android:layout_height="wrap_content"
android:layout_margin="5dp"
android:layout_weight="1"
android:onClick="logInClick"
android:text="Log in" />
/LinearLayout>
<LinearLayout
android:id="@+id/facebookLogin"
style="@style/facebook_button_style"
android:layout_width="match_parent"
```

```
android:layout_height="wrap_content"
android:onClick="facebookClick">
<ImageView
android:layout_width="wrap_content"
android:layout_height="wrap_content"
android:src="@drawable/com_facebook_button_icon" />
<TextView
android:layout_width="wrap_content"
android:layout_height="wrap_content"
android:padding="5dp"
android:text="Continue with Facebook"
android:textColor="@color/white" />
</LinearLayout>
<LinearLayout
android:id="@+id/sign_in_google"
style="@style/google_button_style"
android:layout_width="match_parent"
android:layout_height="wrap_content"
android:visibility="visible"
android:onClick="googleClick">
<ImageView
android:layout_width="wrap_content"
android:layout_height="wrap_content"
android:src="@drawable/im_google_icon"/>
<TextView
android:layout_width="wrap_content"
android:layout_height="wrap_content"
android:padding="5dp"
android:text="Continue with Google"
android:textColor="@color/black" />
</LinearLayout>
<!-- <com.google.android.gms.common.SignInButton
style="@style/button_style"
android:id="@+id/sign_in_google"
android:layout_width="match_parent"
android:layout_height="wrap_content"
android:visibility="visible"/>-->
<TextView
style="@style/login_footer_style"
android:layout_width="match_parent"
android:layout_height="wrap_content"
android:text="@string/txt_login_start_footer" />
</LinearLayout>
</LinearLayout>
<ImageView
android:id="@+id/logo"
android:layout_width="@dimen/dimen_login_logo"
android:layout_height="@dimen/dimen_login_logo"
```

```
android:layout_below="@id/image"
android:layout_centerHorizontal="true"
android:layout_marginTop="@dimen/dimen_login_logo_margin"android:src="@mipm
ap/logo" />
<TextView
android:layout_width="wrap_content"
android:layout_height="wrap_content"
android:layout_alignParentRight="true"
android:layout_margin="10dp"
android:background="@drawable/tra_white_border"
android:clickable="true"
android:onClick="skipClick"
android:paddingLeft="5dp"
android:paddingRight="5dp"
android:text="SKIP" />
</RelativeLayout>
</RelativeLayout>
```

The preceding layout will give you an output shown in this figure:

Login/Signup Flow screen layout in Android Studio XML editor

We will explain the preceding layout code by splitting it into three sections. The top section is an ImageView where an image is set from the drawable folder. Here, the ImageView is rectangular in shape; hence, the image should also be a rectangular image. The sectional image is shown as follows:

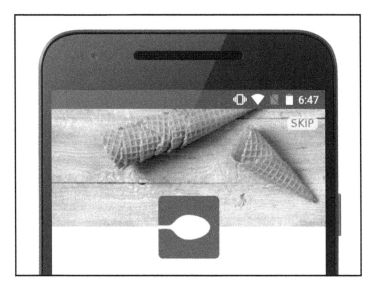

Login/Signup Flow screen's top section with image

Here, an important part to note is that this image should be displayed properly on all the different size devices, and there are two ways to do this. One way is to fit the image exactly within the ImageView bounds, which can be done by fitting the image's width and height to the bound of ImageView using this code:

```
android:scaleType="fitXY"
```

In this case, the image might stretch on some devices with different device dimensions. In order to avoid this stretch, the second option is to crop the image and fit it in the bounds of the ImageView rectangle. There are different ways of cropping this image, but using the centerCrop method for cropping is the best way to crop, because the image fits at least one of the bounds of the ImageView and crops the other bound. For example, the image gets fit width-wise and crops height-wise and fits in the center or it fits height-wise and crops width-wise, and this is handled internally. To do this, the scaleType for the image should be changed to centerCrop:

```
android:scaleType="centerCrop"
```

The next section in the layout is where there are three textual points with an image icon beside each text:

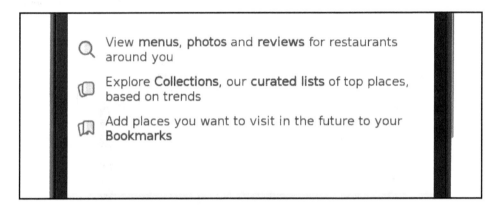

Login/Signup Flow screen's middle section with image and text

This can be done by placing an `ImageView` and `TextView` in a `LinearLayout` with a horizontal orientation, as seen in this code snippet:

```
<LinearLayout
android:layout_width="match_parent"
android:layout_height="wrap_content"
android:gravity="center">
<ImageView
android:layout_width="wrap_content"
android:layout_height="wrap_content"
android:padding="10dp"
android:src="@drawable/im_browse_nearby" />
<TextView
style="@style/login_start_info_style"
android:layout_width="wrap_content"
android:layout_height="wrap_content"
android:text="@string/txt_login_2" />
</LinearLayout>
The TextView has been styled so that one common style can be used for all
the three TextViews. The style includes the TextView's size and color:
<style name="login_start_info_style"><item
name="android:textSize">12dp</item>
<item name="android:textColor">@color/txt_home_title_color</item>
</style>
```

The image icons are three different icons placed in the `drawable` folder. The texts are placed in the `strings.xml` file. All the strings have to be placed in the strings.xml file. The texts here have some of the words in bold. In order to make these bold, you may use HTML tags to make these words bold using the `<b>` tag in the string text:

```
<string name="txt_login_1"><View <b>menus</b>, <b>photos</b> and
<b>reviews</b> for restaurants around you</string>
```

Then, you need to display this text in the HTML format. In order to do that, you may set the text from the Java code in the following manner:

```
login_1_textView.setText(Html.fromHtml(getString(R.string.txt_login_1),
Html.FROM_HTML_MODE_LEGACY));
```

Here, while displaying the text fetched from the `strings.xml` using the `getString` method, it is specified that it is from Html using `Html.fromHtml`.

The next section has the **Sign up**, **Log in**, **Continue with facebook**, and the Continue with Google buttons. The Signup and Login buttons will take you to the **Sign up** and the **Login** screens respectively:

Login/Signup Flow screen's bottom section with login, signup, Facebook, and Google buttons

We will first see what happens when clicked on the `Continue with facebook` button. We will check out how your app is connected to the Facebook API. As Facebook keeps upgrading the way your app connects to it, you need to go the developer's site for Facebook to check out the latest steps to integrate Facebook Login into your app. Check out `https://developers.facebook.com/docs/android` to get a step-by-step process for the same.

By clicking on "Continue with facebook", the Facebook APIs are called to connect the user to their Facebook account. Once connected to Facebook, it responds with an access token on successful login. The connection code is given here:

```
callbackManager = CallbackManager.Factory.create();
LoginManager.getInstance().registerCallback(callbackManager,
new FacebookCallback<LoginResult>() {
@Override
public void onSuccess(LoginResult loginResult) {
// App code
Log.d(TAG, "Get Facebook User Details");
handleFacebookAccessToken(loginResult.getAccessToken());
}
@Override
public void onCancel() {
Log.e(TAG, "Handle Facebook onCancel");
}
@Override
public void onError(FacebookException exception) {
Log.e(TAG, "Handle Facebook onError ");
exception.printStackTrace();
}
});
```

Using the `AccessToken`, fetch user's data like firstname, lastname, email and photo.

******* Code

Later, this data is sent to the Zomato server's database to log in or sign up a user.

On a similar basis, by clicking on `Continue with Google`, the Google APIs are called to connect a user to their Google account. To set up connecting with Google in your app, you require to follow the steps provided at `https://developers.google.com/identity/sign-in/android/start-integrating`.

Once successfully connected to your Google account, it will provide you with the user's data, such as first name, last name, email, and photo. Later, this data is sent to the Zomato server's database to log in or sign up a user.

Clicking on the Login button will take you to to Login Screen for the user to log in to the app using their email and password. We will check how the Login functionality works in detail, but first, let's look at the layout of the login screen:

```
<RelativeLayout xmlns:android="http://schemas.android.com/apk/res/android"
android:layout_width="match_parent"
android:layout_height="match_parent"
android:background="@color/app_bg_color">
<!--Login up-->
<LinearLayout
android:id="@+id/logInLay"
android:layout_width="match_parent"
android:layout_height="match_parent"
android:background="@color/app_bg_color"
android:orientation="vertical">
<!--ToolBar-->
<LinearLayout xmlns:android="http://schemas.android.com/apk/res/android"
xmlns:app="http://schemas.android.com/apk/res-auto"
android:layout_width="match_parent"
android:layout_height="wrap_content"
android:orientation="vertical">
<RelativeLayout xmlns:android="http://schemas.android.com/apk/res/android"
android:layout_width="match_parent"
android:layout_height="wrap_content"
android:background="@color/colorPrimary"
android:gravity="center_vertical"
android:minHeight="?attr/actionBarSize"
android:orientation="horizontal">
<com.androcid.zomato.view.custom.TintableImageView
android:id="@+id/loginClose"
android:layout_width="wrap_content"
android:layout_height="wrap_content"
android:background="@drawable/ripple_white_foreground"
android:clickable="true"
android:onClick="closeClick"
android:padding="10dp"
android:src="@drawable/im_close"
app:tint="@color/close_icon_color" />
<LinearLayout
android:layout_width="match_parent"
android:layout_height="wrap_content"
android:layout_centerInParent="true"
android:orientation="vertical"
android:paddingLeft="8dp"
android:paddingRight="8dp">
<TextView
android:layout_width="match_parent"
android:layout_height="wrap_content"
```

```
    android:gravity="center"
    android:text="Log in"
    android:textColor="@color/white"
    android:textSize="18sp"
    android:textStyle="normal" />
    </LinearLayout>
    </RelativeLayout>
    <View
    android:layout_width="match_parent"
    android:layout_height="4dp"
    android:background="@drawable/shadow_toolbar" />
    </LinearLayout>
    <ScrollView
    android:layout_width="match_parent"
    android:layout_height="match_parent"
    android:fillViewport="true">
    <LinearLayout
    android:layout_width="match_parent"
    android:layout_height="match_parent"
    android:orientation="vertical">
    <LinearLayout
    android:layout_width="match_parent"
    android:layout_height="0dp"
    android:layout_weight="1"
    android:orientation="vertical">
    <LinearLayout
    style="@style/facebook_button_padded_style"
    android:layout_width="match_parent"
    android:layout_height="wrap_content"
    android:onClick="facebookClick">
    <ImageView
    android:layout_width="wrap_content"
    android:layout_height="wrap_content"
    android:src="@drawable/com_facebook_button_icon" />
    <TextView
    android:layout_width="wrap_content"
    android:layout_height="wrap_content"
    android:padding="5dp"
    android:text="Continue with Facebook"
    android:textColor="@color/white" />
    </LinearLayout>
    <LinearLayout
    style="@style/google_button_style"
    android:layout_width="match_parent"
    android:layout_height="wrap_content"
    android:onClick="googleClick">
    <ImageView
    android:layout_width="wrap_content"
```

```
android:layout_height="wrap_content"
android:src="@drawable/im_google_icon" />
<TextView
android:layout_width="wrap_content"
android:layout_height="wrap_content"
android:padding="5dp"
android:text="Continue with Google"
android:textColor="@color/black" />
</LinearLayout>
<TextView
style="@style/login_or_txt_style"
android:layout_width="wrap_content"
android:layout_height="wrap_content"
android:text="@string/txt_login_with_zomato" />
<RelativeLayout
android:layout_width="match_parent"
android:layout_height="wrap_content"
android:padding="10dp">
<TextView
android:id="@+id/logEmailHint"
style="@style/login_hint_txt_style"
android:layout_width="wrap_content"
android:layout_height="wrap_content"
android:text="Email" />
<EditText
android:id="@+id/logEmail"
style="@style/login_edittext_style"
android:layout_width="match_parent"
android:layout_height="wrap_content"
android:layout_below="@id/logEmailHint"
android:layout_toLeftOf="@+id/logEmailCancel"
android:hint="Email or Username"
android:inputType="textEmailAddress" />
<ImageView
android:id="@+id/logEmailLine"
android:layout_width="match_parent"
android:layout_height="1dp"
android:layout_below="@id/logEmail"
android:src="@color/gray_7" />
<ImageView
android:id="@+id/logEmailCancel"
style="@style/login_cancel_button"
android:layout_width="wrap_content"
android:layout_height="wrap_content"
android:layout_alignBottom="@id/logEmail"
android:onClick="cancelClick" />
</RelativeLayout>
<RelativeLayout
```

```
android:layout_width="match_parent"
android:layout_height="wrap_content"
android:padding="10dp">
<TextView
android:id="@+id/logPasswordHint"
style="@style/login_hint_txt_style"
android:layout_width="wrap_content"
android:layout_height="wrap_content"
android:text="Password" />
<EditText
android:id="@+id/logPassword"
style="@style/login_edittext_style"
android:layout_width="match_parent"
android:layout_height="wrap_content"
android:layout_below="@id/logPasswordHint"
android:layout_toLeftOf="@+id/logPasswordCancel"
android:hint="Password"
android:inputType="textPassword" />
<ImageView
android:id="@+id/logPasswordLine"
android:layout_width="match_parent"
android:layout_height="1dp"
android:layout_below="@id/logPassword"
android:src="@color/gray_7" />
<ImageView
android:id="@+id/logPasswordCancel"
style="@style/login_cancel_button"
android:layout_width="wrap_content"
android:layout_height="wrap_content"
android:layout_alignBottom="@id/logPassword"
android:onClick="cancelClick" />
</RelativeLayout>
<TextView
android:id="@+id/logLogin"
style="@style/sign_in_button_style"
android:layout_width="match_parent"
android:layout_height="wrap_content"
android:onClick="logInClick"
android:text="Log in" />
<TextView
style="@style/login_forgot_txt_style"
android:layout_width="match_parent"
android:layout_height="wrap_content"
android:onClick="forgotPasswordClick"
android:text="@string/txt_forgot_password" />
</LinearLayout>
<TextView
style="@style/login_footer_style"
```

```
android:layout_width="match_parent"
android:layout_height="wrap_content"
android:text="@string/txt_login_footer" />
</LinearLayout>
</ScrollView>
</LinearLayout>
</RelativeLayout>
```

The Login screen has two `EditText`: one for taking the user's email and the other for taking input of the user's password. Both are used to take textual input from the user; let's consider the email `EditText` used in the preceding code:

```
<EditText
android:id="@+id/logEmail"
style="@style/login_edittext_style"
android:layout_width="match_parent"
android:layout_height="wrap_content"
android:layout_below="@id/logEmailHint"
android:layout_toLeftOf="@+id/logEmailCancel"
android:hint="Email or Username"
android:inputType="textEmailAddress" />
```

`inputType` defines what kind of input has to be taken from a user. For an email `EditText`, the `inputType` to be mentioned is `textEmailAddress`. This allows the different Android devices to understand that the user will enter an email address, and so help the user by changing the keyboard key positions. For instance, getting the @ key as a new button on keyboard, allowing the user to easily type the email address.

Similarly, to take password input from the user, the inputType has to be changed to `textPassword`, as shown in this snippet:

```
android:inputType="textPassword"
```

Setting this input type will make the `edittext` take hidden dotted password text.

Next we will see the how to set the Login button and make it clickable. We will see the code snippet of the Login button:

```
<TextView
android:id="@+id/logLogin"
style="@style/sign_in_button_style"
android:layout_width="match_parent"
android:layout_height="wrap_content"
android:onClick="logInClick"
android:text="Log in" />
```

In this case, we have used `Textview` as a button for better styling. The button style can be given to get the desired button UI. To make the button clickable, use the `onClick` method. The `onClick` method has to be provided with a text value that will be the name of the function. In this case, we have given the name as `logInClick`. Then, we need to create a method with this name in the Login Activity:

```
public void logInClick(View view) {
if (validateData()) {
String email = logEmail.getText().toString();
String password = logPassword.getText().toString();
loginClick(email, password);
}
}
```

In this method, you need to write what needs to happen when the login button is clicked on.

The first thing that needs to be done when the login button is clicked on is that it should check for validations of email and password. Validations for login will include checking whether the user has entered some email address and password:

```
private boolean validateData() {
if(TextUtils.isEmpty(logEmail.getText().toString())) {
logEmail.setError(getString(R.string.error_field_required));
return false;
}
if(TextUtils.isEmpty(logPassword.getText().toString())) {
logPassword.setError(getString(R.string.error_field_required));
return false;
}
return true;
}
```

Here, the `TextUtils.isEmpty` method checks for the length of the email string and whether the length is greater than zero, then user has entered some text, else it returns false, saying that the value of the string is empty. If the user has entered the email and password, the email and password should be taken and an API call has to be made to the server for log in the user. If the user has not entered an email and/or password, then they have to be shown some error to enter it.

Making an API call to the server will be done by calling a URL and passing the parameters required. This will be done using the REST client Retrofit. We will discuss Retrofit in detail in the next section.

The Login screen will look on a mobile device, as shown:

Login Screen

The Signup Screen is opened after clicking on the Sign up button, which is similar to clicking on the Login button. The signup layout will almost be the same as the Login layout, with an addition of `EditText` to take the user's name. Let's see the layout of Signup screen:

```
<RelativeLayout xmlns:android="http://schemas.android.com/apk/res/android"
android:layout_width="match_parent"
android:layout_height="match_parent"
android:background="@color/app_bg_color">
<!--Sign up-->
<LinearLayout
android:id="@+id/signUpLay"
android:layout_width="match_parent"
android:layout_height="match_parent"
android:background="@color/app_bg_color"
android:orientation="vertical">
<!--ToolBar-->
```

```xml
<LinearLayout xmlns:android="http://schemas.android.com/apk/res/android"
xmlns:app="http://schemas.android.com/apk/res-auto"
android:layout_width="match_parent"
android:layout_height="wrap_content"
android:orientation="vertical">
<RelativeLayout xmlns:android="http://schemas.android.com/apk/res/android"
android:layout_width="match_parent"
android:layout_height="wrap_content"
android:background="@color/colorPrimary"
android:gravity="center_vertical"
android:minHeight="?attr/actionBarSize"
android:orientation="horizontal">
<com.androcid.zomato.view.custom.TintableImageView
android:id="@+id/signupClose"
android:layout_width="wrap_content"
android:layout_height="wrap_content"
android:background="@drawable/ripple_white_foreground"
android:clickable="true"
android:onClick="closeClick"
android:padding="10dp"
android:src="@drawable/im_close"
app:tint="@color/close_icon_color" />
<LinearLayout
android:layout_width="match_parent"
android:layout_height="wrap_content"
android:layout_centerInParent="true"
android:orientation="vertical"
android:paddingLeft="8dp"
android:paddingRight="8dp">
<TextView
android:layout_width="match_parent"
android:layout_height="wrap_content"
android:gravity="center"
android:text="Sign up"
android:textColor="@color/white"
android:textSize="18sp"
android:textStyle="normal" />
</LinearLayout>
</RelativeLayout>
<View
android:layout_width="match_parent"
android:layout_height="4dp"
android:background="@drawable/shadow_toolbar" />
</LinearLayout>
<ScrollView
android:layout_width="match_parent"
android:layout_height="0dp"
android:layout_weight="1"
```

```xml
android:fillViewport="true">
<LinearLayout
android:layout_width="match_parent"
android:layout_height="wrap_content"
android:orientation="vertical">
<LinearLayout
android:layout_width="match_parent"
android:layout_height="0dp"
android:layout_weight="1"
android:orientation="vertical">
<LinearLayout
style="@style/facebook_button_padded_style"
android:layout_width="match_parent"
android:layout_height="wrap_content"
android:onClick="facebookClick">
<ImageView
android:layout_width="wrap_content"
android:layout_height="wrap_content"android:src="@drawable/com_facebook_but
ton_icon" />
<TextView
android:layout_width="wrap_content"
android:layout_height="wrap_content"
android:padding="5dp"
android:text="Continue with Facebook"
android:textColor="@color/white" />
</LinearLayout>
<LinearLayout
style="@style/google_button_style"
android:layout_width="match_parent"
android:layout_height="wrap_content"
android:onClick="googleClick">
<ImageView
android:layout_width="wrap_content"
android:layout_height="wrap_content"
android:src="@drawable/im_google_icon" />
<TextView
android:layout_width="wrap_content"
android:layout_height="wrap_content"
android:padding="5dp"
android:text="Continue with Google"
android:textColor="@color/black" />
</LinearLayout>
<TextView
style="@style/login_or_txt_style"
android:layout_width="wrap_content"
android:layout_height="wrap_content"
android:text="OR SIGN UP USING EMAIL" />
<RelativeLayout
```

```
android:layout_width="match_parent"
android:layout_height="wrap_content"
android:padding="10dp">
<TextView
android:id="@+id/regNameHint"
style="@style/login_hint_txt_style"
android:layout_width="wrap_content"
android:layout_height="wrap_content"
android:text="Name" />
<EditText
android:id="@+id/regName"
style="@style/login_edittext_style"
android:layout_width="match_parent"
android:layout_height="wrap_content"
android:layout_below="@id/regNameHint"
android:layout_toLeftOf="@+id/regNameCancel"
android:hint="Name"
android:inputType="textPersonName" />
<ImageView
android:id="@+id/regNameLine"
android:layout_width="match_parent"
android:layout_height="1dp"
android:layout_below="@id/regName"
android:src="@color/gray_7" />
<ImageView
android:id="@+id/regNameCancel"
style="@style/login_cancel_button"
android:layout_width="wrap_content"
android:layout_height="wrap_content"
android:layout_alignBottom="@id/regName"
android:onClick="cancelClick" />
</RelativeLayout>
<RelativeLayout
android:layout_width="match_parent"
android:layout_height="wrap_content"
android:padding="10dp">
<TextView
android:id="@+id/regEmailHint"
style="@style/login_hint_txt_style"
android:layout_width="wrap_content"
android:layout_height="wrap_content"
android:text="Email" />
<EditText
android:id="@+id/regEmail"
style="@style/login_edittext_style"
android:layout_width="match_parent"
android:layout_height="wrap_content"
android:layout_below="@id/regEmailHint"
```

```
android:layout_toLeftOf="@+id/regEmailCancel"
android:hint="Email"
android:inputType="textEmailAddress" />
<ImageView
android:id="@+id/regEmailLine"
android:layout_width="match_parent"
android:layout_height="1dp"
android:layout_below="@id/regEmail"
android:src="@color/gray_7" />
<ImageView
android:id="@+id/regEmailCancel"
style="@style/login_cancel_button"
android:layout_width="wrap_content"
android:layout_height="wrap_content"
android:layout_alignBottom="@id/regEmail"
android:onClick="cancelClick" />
</RelativeLayout>
<RelativeLayout
android:layout_width="match_parent"
android:layout_height="wrap_content"
android:padding="10dp">
<TextView
android:id="@+id/regPasswordHint"
style="@style/login_hint_txt_style"
android:layout_width="wrap_content"
android:layout_height="wrap_content"
android:text="Password" />
<EditText
android:id="@+id/regPassword"
style="@style/login_edittext_style"
android:layout_width="match_parent"
android:layout_height="wrap_content"
android:layout_below="@id/regPasswordHint"
android:layout_toLeftOf="@+id/regPasswordCancel"
android:hint="Password"
android:inputType="textPassword" />
<ImageView
android:id="@+id/regPasswordLine"
android:layout_width="match_parent"
android:layout_height="1dp"
android:layout_below="@id/regPassword"
android:src="@color/gray_7" />
<ImageView
android:id="@+id/regPasswordCancel"
style="@style/login_cancel_button"
android:layout_width="wrap_content"
android:layout_height="wrap_content"
android:layout_alignBottom="@id/regPassword"
```

```
android:onClick="cancelClick" />
</RelativeLayout>
<TextView
android:id="@+id/regSignUp"
style="@style/sign_in_button_style"
android:layout_width="match_parent"
android:layout_height="wrap_content"
android:onClick="signUpClick"
android:text="Sign Up" />
<TextView
android:id="@+id/regLogin"
style="@style/login_forgot_txt_style"
android:layout_width="match_parent"
android:layout_height="wrap_content"
android:onClick="logInClick"
android:text="@string/txt_already_member" />
</LinearLayout>
<TextView
style="@style/login_footer_style"
android:layout_width="match_parent"
android:layout_height="wrap_content"
android:text="@string/txt_register_footer" />
</LinearLayout>
</ScrollView>
</LinearLayout>
</RelativeLayout>
```

The additional `EditText` for taking user's name has a different `inputType`:

```
<EditText
android:id="@+id/regName"
style="@style/login_edittext_style"
android:layout_width="match_parent"
android:layout_height="wrap_content"
android:layout_below="@id/regNameHint"
android:layout_toLeftOf="@+id/regNameCancel"
android:hint="Name"
android:inputType="textPersonName" />
```

The signup process will go through the same process as the Login flow, but there will be more number of validations done before going on to sign up:

```
private boolean validateData() {
if (TextUtils.isEmpty(regName.getText().toString())) {
regName.setError(getString(R.string.error_field_required));
return false;
}
if (TextUtils.isEmpty(regEmail.getText().toString()) ||
```

```
!Validate.isValidEmail(regEmail.getText().toString())) {
regEmail.setError(getString(R.string.error_field_required));
return false;
}
if (TextUtils.isEmpty(regPassword.getText().toString()) ||
!Validate.isAtleastValidLength(regPassword.getText().toString(), 5)) {
regPassword.setError(getString(R.string.error_field_required));
return false;
}
return true;
}
```

Here, the name validation will be a direct check for an empty string. The email validation will involve an additional validation along with an empty check. It requires checking whether the email entered is a valid email format and not just any random text. For that, you need to pattern match the entered email with a reference pattern:

```
public static boolean isValidEmail(String target) {
if (target.equals("")) {
return false;
} else {
if(android.util.Patterns.EMAIL_ADDRESS.matcher(target).matches())
{
String topLevelDomain = target.substring(target.lastIndexOf(".") + 1);
if(android.util.Patterns.TOP_LEVEL_DOMAIN.matcher(topLevelDomain).matches()
)
{
return true;
}
}
return false;
}
}
```

The Patterns class in Android has a predefined email validator to check whether the email matches a standard email pattern. It also validates if the domain entered is a valid domain.

Once the validation process is complete and all the checks are successful, it goes to do the server API call to sign up the user using Retrofit.

The Signup screen will look on a mobile device, as shown:

Sign up Screen

Discovery Screen

The next screen we will learn is the main dashboard screen or the Discovery Screen. The Discovery screen shows different sections that have the restaurants you may like to visit or restaurants you may like to go out for meal, and many more. Each of these sections scroll horizontally and the fullscreen scrolls vertically. At the top, it also has the toolbar that allows you to select a different location, and also a search button asks you to search through the different places. We will look to implement each of these one by one.

First, we will look at the sections consisting of the restaurants. The main layout where all these have to be placed is inside a `NestedScrollView`. A `NestedScrollView`, in simple terms, is a view that is used to display scrollable content. All the scrolling sections will be placed inside a `NestedScrollView`:

```
<android.support.v4.widget.NestedScrollView
android:layout_width="match_parent"
android:layout_height="0dp"
android:layout_weight="1">
<LinearLayout
android:layout_width="match_parent"
android:layout_height="wrap_content"
android:orientation="vertical">
<!--Browse Nearby-->
<android.support.v7.widget.CardView
android:layout_width="match_parent"
android:layout_height="wrap_content"
android:layout_margin="@dimen/default_layout_margin">
<LinearLayout
android:id="@+id/browseNearby"
android:layout_width="match_parent"
android:layout_height="wrap_content"
android:background="@drawable/place_more_foreground"
android:clickable="true"
android:gravity="center_vertical"
android:padding="6dp">
<ImageView
android:layout_width="wrap_content"
android:layout_height="wrap_content"
android:src="@drawable/ic_browse_nearby" />
<TextView
android:layout_width="0dp"
android:layout_height="wrap_content"
android:layout_weight="1"
android:paddingLeft="10dp"
android:paddingRight="10dp"
android:text="Browse Nearby Places"
android:textColor="@color/txt_home_title_color"
android:textSize="16sp" />
<ImageView
android:layout_width="wrap_content"
android:layout_height="wrap_content"
android:src="@drawable/im_next_right" />
</LinearLayout>
</android.support.v7.widget.CardView>
<!--You might Like-->
<LinearLayout
```

```
    android:id="@+id/mightLike"
    android:layout_width="match_parent"
    android:layout_height="wrap_content"
    android:orientation="vertical">
<TextView
    style="@style/HomeSubTitleTxtStyle"
    android:layout_width="match_parent"
    android:layout_height="wrap_content"
    android:text="@string/txt_might_like" />
<RelativeLayout
    android:layout_width="match_parent"
    android:layout_height="210dp"
    android:gravity="center_vertical">
<android.support.v7.widget.RecyclerView
    android:id="@+id/mightLikeList"
    android:layout_width="match_parent"
    android:layout_height="match_parent" />
</RelativeLayout>
</LinearLayout>
<!--Remaining Items-->
<LinearLayout
    android:layout_width="match_parent"
    android:layout_height="wrap_content"
    android:orientation="vertical">
<TextView
    style="@style/HomeSubTitleTxtStyle"
    android:layout_width="match_parent"
    android:layout_height="wrap_content"
    android:text="@string/txt_might_like" />
<android.support.v7.widget.RecyclerView
    android:id="@+id/allItems"
    android:layout_width="match_parent"
    android:layout_height="wrap_content" />
</LinearLayout>
<LinearLayout
    android:layout_width="match_parent"
    android:layout_height="wrap_content"
    android:orientation="vertical">
<include layout="@layout/layout_zomato_footer"/>
</LinearLayout>
</LinearLayout>
</android.support.v4.widget.NestedScrollView>
```

The static contents are placed in the different layouts. There are a total of four static sections in the `NestedScrollView`.

The first section displays the Browse to Discover button. On clicking, it will take you to the browse places screen. This layout is formed using a `CardView`:

```
<android.support.v7.widget.CardView
android:layout_width="match_parent"
android:layout_height="wrap_content"
android:layout_margin="@dimen/default_layout_margin">
<LinearLayout
android:id="@+id/browseNearby"
android:layout_width="match_parent"
android:layout_height="wrap_content"
android:background="@drawable/place_more_foreground"
android:clickable="true"
android:gravity="center_vertical"
android:padding="6dp">
<ImageView
android:layout_width="wrap_content"
android:layout_height="wrap_content"
android:src="@drawable/ic_browse_nearby" />
<TextView
android:layout_width="0dp"
android:layout_height="wrap_content"
android:layout_weight="1"
android:paddingLeft="10dp"
android:paddingRight="10dp"
android:text="Browse Nearby Places"
android:textColor="@color/txt_home_title_color"
android:textSize="16sp" />
<ImageView
android:layout_width="wrap_content"
android:layout_height="wrap_content"
android:src="@drawable/im_next_right" />
</LinearLayout>
</android.support.v7.widget.CardView>
```

A `CardView` is a widget provided in the Android libraries, which is used to display a view like a card. It has many properties such as elevation and shadow. Within the `CardView`, another layout is placed to design the Browse Nearby places. Designing this layout has already been understood in the previous topics.

The next section shows the code for the horizontal scrolling sections is as follows:

```
<LinearLayout
android:id="@+id/mightLike"
android:layout_width="match_parent"
android:layout_height="wrap_content"
android:orientation="vertical">
<TextView
style="@style/HomeSubTitleTxtStyle"
android:layout_width="match_parent"
android:layout_height="wrap_content"
android:text="@string/txt_might_like" />
<RelativeLayout
android:layout_width="match_parent"
android:layout_height="210dp"
android:gravity="center_vertical">
<android.support.v7.widget.RecyclerView
android:id="@+id/mightLikeList"
android:layout_width="match_parent"
android:layout_height="match_parent" />
</RelativeLayout>
</LinearLayout>
```

This section has horizontal scrolling layout, which is displayed using a `RecyclerView`. The code for `RecyclerView` is this:

```
<android.support.v7.widget.RecyclerView
android:id="@+id/mightLikeList"
android:layout_width="match_parent"
android:layout_height="match_parent" />
```

`RecyclerView` is used to display list of items. The `RecyclerView` items can be placed in the different positions supported. The orientation has to be provided from an `LayoutManager`. In this case, we have used a `LinearLayoutManager` to set the orientation of the list to be horizontal. It has to be set in the Java code by setting the layout manager to the `RecyclerView`:

```
LinearLayoutManager llm
= new LinearLayoutManager(context, LinearLayoutManager.HORIZONTAL, false);
allList.setLayoutManager(llm);
```

After that, the next section has a `RecyclerView`, which has the remaining sections placed within it:

```
<LinearLayout
android:layout_width="match_parent"
android:layout_height="wrap_content"
```

```
android:orientation="vertical">
<TextView
style="@style/HomeSubTitleTxtStyle"
android:layout_width="match_parent"
android:layout_height="wrap_content"
android:text="@string/txt_might_like" />
<android.support.v7.widget.RecyclerView
android:id="@+id/allItems"
android:layout_width="match_parent"
android:layout_height="wrap_content" />
</LinearLayout>
The RecyclerView can be added in your Java code, as shown:
First, declare your List, custom adapter, and RecyclerView:
List<PlaceDisplayItem> allList;
PlaceVerticalAdapter allAdapter;
RecyclerView allItems;
Then initialize each of them.
allList = new ArrayList<>();
allAdapter = new PlaceVerticalAdapter(context, allList);
allItems = (RecyclerView) findViewById(R.id.allItems);
```

The next step is to set up the Layout Manager. Here, we will use a `GridLayoutManager` with vertical orientation:

```
GridLayoutManager llm = new GridLayoutManager(this, 3);
llm.setOrientation(GridLayoutManager.VERTICAL);
```

The Grid will be divided into three columns so that three restaurants fit in horizontally. So, the grid will have at least three columns, and if the number of restaurants is more than three, the fourth restaurant will be displayed in the next row. The next figure shows it more clearly:

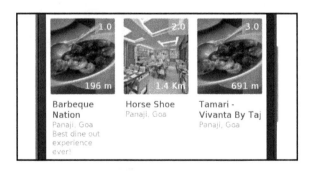

GridLayoutManager with three columns

Now, there will be a header before each of the horizontal layouts. These are not grids but a single list item. However, we have used a Grid Layout with three columns. To show the header layout as one item, we need to span the three columns into one; this can be done by defining `setSpanSizeLookup` for the Layout Manager:

```
llm.setSpanSizeLookup(new GridLayoutManager.SpanSizeLookup() {
@Override
public int getSpanSize(int position) {
switch (allAdapter.getItemViewType(position)) {
case PlaceVerticalAdapter.TYPE_HEADER:
return 3;
case PlaceVerticalAdapter.TYPE_ITEM:
return 1;
case PlaceVerticalAdapter.TYPE_MORE:
return 3;
default:
return -1;
}
}
});
```

`setSpanSizeLookup` says that if the type of view to be displayed is a header layout, span three columns of the grid to one. Here's an illustration of the same:

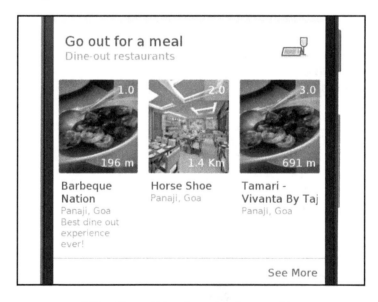

GridLayoutManager with three columns and span for one type of view

Now, let's look at how the different views are displayed from the Java code custom adapter. We have used PlaceVerticalAdapter as the custom adapter where the header view and the item restaurant views are differentiated:

```
@Override
public ViewHolder onCreateViewHolder(ViewGroup viewGroup, int viewType) {
View itemView = null;
if (viewType == TYPE_ITEM) {'itemView =
LayoutInflater.from(viewGroup.getContext()).inflate(R.layout.item_place_ver
tical, viewGroup, false);
} else if (viewType == TYPE_MORE) {
itemView =
LayoutInflater.from(viewGroup.getContext()).inflate(R.layout.item_place_mor
e, viewGroup, false);
} else if (viewType == TYPE_HEADER) {
itemView =
LayoutInflater.from(viewGroup.getContext()).inflate(R.layout.item_place_hea
der, viewGroup, false);
}
return new ViewHolder(itemView);
}
```

The different layouts are placed in three different XML layout files and are inflated as a view using the `LayoutInflater`. Once the layouts are inflated, the different views in the adapter view have to be initialized. They have been initialized in the `ViewHolder`:

```
public class ViewHolder extends RecyclerView.ViewHolder {
ImageView image;
TextView name;
TextView location;
TextView description;
TextView rating;
TextView distance;
public ViewHolder(View itemView) {
super(itemView);
image = (ImageView) itemView.findViewById(R.id.image);
name = (TextView) itemView.findViewById(R.id.name);
location = (TextView) itemView.findViewById(R.id.location);
description = (TextView) itemView.findViewById(R.id.description);
rating = (TextView) itemView.findViewById(R.id.rating);
distance = (TextView) itemView.findViewById(R.id.distance);
}
}
```

In the adapter, the respective views will be displayed based on the `viewType` that is mentioned in the list. Accordingly, the code has to be written to handle the display in the adapter based on the view type:

```
@Override
public void onBindViewHolder(final ViewHolder holder, final int position) {
PlaceDisplayItem displayItem = list.get(position);
if (displayItem.getType() == TYPE_ITEM) {
RestaurantItem item = displayItem.getRestaurantItem();
//TODO EXTRA
String name = item.getName() != null ? item.getName() : "";
String description = item.getDescription() != null ? item.getDescription()
: "";
String location = item.getLocation() != null ? item.getLocation() : "";
holder.name.setText(name);
holder.location.setText(location);
holder.description.setText(description);
holder.rating.setText(CommonFunctions.formatRating(item.getRating()));
holder.distance.setText(CommonFunctions.formatDistance(item.getDistance()))
;
if (!CommonFunctions.checkNull(item.getImage()).equals("")) {
Picasso.with(context)
.load(RetroInterface.IMAGE_URL+item.getImage())
.resize(200,200)
.placeholder(R.drawable.placeholder_200)
.error(R.drawable.placeholder_200)
.into(holder.image);
}
holder.itemView.setOnClickListener(new View.OnClickListener() {
@Override
public void onClick(View view) {
if (clickListener != null) {
clickListener.onItemClickListener(view, position);
}
}
});
} else {
if (displayItem.getType() == TYPE_HEADER) {
MealTypeItem item = displayItem.getMealTypeItem();
holder.name.setText(item.getName());
holder.description.setText(item.getDescription());
}
}
}
```

Once the layout is ready and the data fetched from the server is loaded, the view will look the following way in a mobile device:

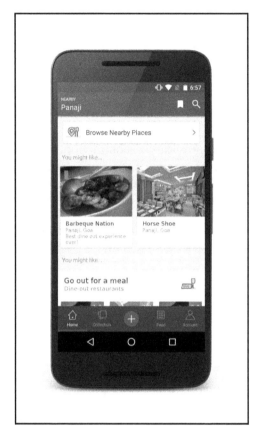

Discovery Screen

Database

When data is fetched from the server, it needs to be saved to the local database for a seamless user experience. The local database used is one provided by Google, known as Room. Now, let's look how we integrate room into our code in detail.

Room

Development and description of this section, in detail, including code snippets of how it is used in Zomato.

Room is a part of Android Architecture Components, which consists of three components:

1. Room
2. LiveData
3. ViewModel

Room is a persistence library that provides an abstraction layer over the existing SQLite database. Room thus increases the security of the database, making it easier to access and also makes it easier to set up and access the new database. All the commands are now annotated, except the SELECT command that works with @Query.

To add room to our app, first we need to add the dependencies in the build.gradle file. First, we need to add the following to our project level build.gradle file:

```
buildscript {
repositories {
maven { url 'https://maven.google.com' }
...
}
}
...
...
allprojects {
repositories {
maven { url 'https://maven.google.com' }
...
...
}
}
```

Next, we need to add the following dependencies to our app level build.gradle file:

```
compile 'android.arch.persistence.room:runtime:1.0.0-alpha1'
compile 'android.arch.lifecycle:extensions:1.0.0-alpha1'
annotationProcessor 'android.arch.persistence.room:compiler:1.0.0-alpha1'
```

After the following dependencies are added and gradle is synced. we are ready to use Room in the app.

Let's now see how Room can be implemented in the app--using an example of searching a location by its name.

Here, we enter the name of a place we want to set as our location. We make a server call to get the list. This list is then stored in the database with the help of room.

This helps to quickly fetch possible places from the local Sqlite database instead of waiting for the server to respond.

First, let's create Entity that will hold the data we want to store in a table. In room, instead of creating DatabaseHelper, we add annotation to the model class itself to determine its primary key:

```
@Entity
public class UserLocation {
@PrimaryKey(autoGenerate = true)
@SerializedName(Constant.ID)
int id;
@SerializedName(Constant.NAME)
String name;
@SerializedName(Constant.LATITUDE)
float latitude;
@SerializedName(Constant.LONGITUDE)
float longitude;
public UserLocation(int id, String name, float latitude, float longitude) {
this.id = id;
this.name = name;
this.latitude = latitude;
this.longitude = longitude;
}
public int getId() {
return id;
}
public String getName() {
return name;
}
public float getLatitude() {
return latitude;
}
public float getLongitude() {
return longitude;
}
public void setId(int id) {
this.id = id;
}
public void setName(String name) {
this.name = name;
```

```
    }
    public void setLatitude(float latitude) {
    this.latitude = latitude;
    }
    public void setLongitude(float longitude) {
    this.longitude = longitude;
    }
    }
```

In the preceding code snippet, the class name also has the `@Entity` annotation, which represents that it is a model that will be saved in the Sqlite database, and the class name will be used as the table name. If we want to use a table name different from the class name, we have to specify with the table name such as `@Entity(tableName = "user_location")`.

The next one is `@PrimaryKey(autoGenerate = true)`. This represents that the variable is a primary key, and if not set, it is to be autoincremented, just like in a normal database.

If we want to add indices and unique column check in the table, we need to add the indices along with the Entity annotation, as follows:

```
    @Entity (indices = {@Index("name"), @Index(value = {"name"})})
```

If the name of the column is different from the variable name, we can specify by setting the `@ColumnInfo` annotation to that field as shown:

```
    @ColumnInfo(name = "user_name")
    String name;
```

Now that we have created an entity, let's create a `Dao`.

The Dao is an interface class that contains all the various types of query operations that can be carried on in the table, that is, Insert, Delete, Select, and Update. To represent an interface is a Dao interface, we specify the `@Dao` annotation to the class name. Here's the Dao interface and how it is used:

```
    @Dao
    public interface UserLocationDao {
    @Query("select * from UserLocation")
    LiveData<List<UserLocation>> getAllUserLocations();
    @Query("select * from UserLocation where name like :name order by
    name")
    LiveData<List<UserLocation>> getUserLocationsByName(String name);
    @Insert(onConflict = REPLACE)
    void addUserLocations(List<UserLocation> userLocations);
    @Delete
    void deleteUserLocation(UserLocation userLocation);
    }
```

The @Insert annotation automatically insert the data in the database without us having to write insert queries.

Similarly, we can delete data using the @Delete annotation.

To select, we use the @Query annotation and write the logic, which is to be used to select the data just like in a normal SQlite database.

Here, we also have the LiveData; this keeps observing the database of any changes in the data and automatically callbacks/informs the activity of the changes, due to which we do not have to write separate code to check for changes in the table.

Next, let's create a database class that will contain all the entities and their corresponding Dao classes.

For a database, we create an abstract class and add the @Database annotation with the list of all the entity classes that are to be present in the database.

Here's an example of a database class:

```
@Database(entities = {UserLocation.class}, version = 1)
public abstract class AppDatabase extends RoomDatabase {
private static AppDatabase INSTANCE;
public static AppDatabase getDatabase(Context context) {
if (INSTANCE == null) {
INSTANCE = Room.databaseBuilder(context.getApplicationContext(),
AppDatabase.class, "zomato_room_db")
.build();
}
return INSTANCE;
}
public static void destroyInstance() {
INSTANCE = null;
}
public abstract UserLocationDao getUserLocationDao();
}
```

Here, as we have only one entity class, it is added in the entity list in the database annotation--@Database(entities = {UserLocation.class}, version = 1).

The version represents the version of the database. After any changes are done to the entity class or any new entity classes are added, we need to increase this value to reflect the changes.

To access the various `Dao` methods, we use a `viewmodel` that is used in the activities as a link between the activity and the Database class. The `viewmodel` consists of the methods that will be used by the activities. The `viewmodel` must extend `AndroidViewModel` so as to follow the room life cycle.

Here's the `Viewmodel` that is used in our example:

```
public class UserLocationViewModel extends AndroidViewModel {
private AppDatabase appDatabase;
public UserLocationViewModel(Application application) {
super(application);
appDatabase = AppDatabase.getDatabase(this.getApplication());
}
public LiveData<List<UserLocation>> getUserLocationsByName(String name){
return appDatabase.getUserLocationDao().getUserLocationsByName(name);
}
public void addUserLocations(final List<UserLocation> userLocations) {
new Thread(new Runnable() {
@Override
public void run() {
appDatabase.getUserLocationDao().addUserLocations(userLocations);
}
}).start();
}
}
```

Here, we first initialize the database in the constructor of the `Viewmodel`. Next, we will write the various methods that are used by the activity.

The `addUserLocations` method is used to add the location to the local database, where as `getUserLocationsByName` is used to fetch the list of locations.

Now, let's see how room will be used in the activity.

The room life cycle can only be used in activity/fragment.

The activity/fragment must implement the `LifecycleRegistryOwner` as it controls the life cycle of the room objects.

Here's the implementation:

```
public class SelectLocationActivity extends
extends AppCompatActivity implements LifecycleRegistryOwner{
private final LifecycleRegistry mRegistry = new LifecycleRegistry(this);
@Override
public LifecycleRegistry getLifecycle() {
return mRegistry;
```

```
    }
  }
```

The preceding code helps in maintaining the life cycle of the room objects.

Now, let's see how we can use room to get the list of addresses after searching.

Here, we first initialize the `viewmodel` so that we can get an instance of the database and its corresponding entity.

To get the instance of the `viewmodel`, we use the `ViewModelProviders` class. It uses the instance of the activity to get the `viewmodel`.

Here's a sample code from our example:

1. Global instance of the `viewmodel`:

   ```
   UserLocationViewModel userLocationViewModel;
   ```

2. Initializing the `viewmodel` with the help of the `ViewModelProviders` class:

   ```
   userLocationViewModel=
   ViewModelProviders.of(this).get(UserLocationViewModel.class);
   ```

After the view model has been initialized, we can use it to fetch and insert the `userlocation` items directly into the table of the Entity.

First, we make a server call to load the list of possible places that the user is searching for. When we get the result instead of directly showing them to the user, we can insert them into the table. As room uses `Livedata` to constantly observe the database for any changes, if new/updated entries are made into the database, they are automatically fetched by room callbacks.

Firstly, lets add those entries to our database. To add the entries, we make use of the `addUserLocations(final List<UserLocation> userLocations)` function of the `UserLocationViewModel` class.

Here's how we use the function:

```
userLocationViewModel.addUserLocations(userLocationResponse.getUserLocation
s());
```

In the preceding code sample, `userLocationResponse` is the response that we get from the Retrofit that contains the list of all the corresponding user locations that the user is searching for.

Next, to constantly check/call the live data to check for any changes in the database, we make an instance of the `LiveData` class with `UserLocation` Entity:

```
LiveData<List<UserLocation>> liveData;
if (liveData != null) {
liveData.removeObservers(this);
}
liveData = userLocationViewModel.getUserLocationsByName("%" + search +
"%");
liveData.observe(this, new Observer<List<UserLocation>>() {
@Override
public void onChanged(@Nullable List<UserLocation> serviceItems) {
userLocations = serviceItems;
if (!(search.equals(""))) {
refreshList();
}
}
});
```

In the preceding code sample, we are creating an instance of `LiveData` of `UseLocation`. Here, we are always listening for locations whose name contains the search parameter.

The `liveData.observe` function observes the database for any data that matches the condition and returns the list in its `onChanged` method. After the list is returned, we can show the list to the user by setting it to the adapter of the `recyclerview`.

Summary

The focus in this chapter was to understand the core techniques of coding the different components and screens of the Zomato app by yourself. After reading these topics, you understood what are the components required to develop certain sections on a screen. Once you get a hold of these components, they can be reused in other screens with similar requirements.

11
Backend Service

Firebase is a cloud-based **backend-as-a-service** (**BaaS**) service provided by Google that provides a structural way to save your data very efficiently and also retrieve it at much faster speeds. It acts like a complete backend database solution for your web or app. It is very robust and handy to use and has features that make your app experience better in various ways.

Firebase has grown to be a unified app platform for Android, iOS, and Mobile Web development. Not only does it help to develop faster, but it also has inbuilt services that help you improve app quality, acquire and engage users, and monetize apps. Firebase has many features inbuilt which are very useful in a complete app development cycle. What makes Firebase handy is that it does not need any server side configurations. Everything gets handled from your app. Also it has a real time feature, meaning that what is updated in one place gets updated everywhere else at real time. This makes the app experience really wonderful.

The entire feature list provided by Firebase is shown in the image below. It provides you with a single place to set up and manage services of your apps. Firebase provides you with 15 technologies that help you develop, grow, and earn from your mobile apps:

1. Develop

    1. Backend services

        1.1 Real-time database

        1.2 Authentication

        1.3 Hosting

        1.4 Storage

1.5 Cloud messaging

1.6 Remote configuration

2. App quality services

2.1. Test Lab for Android

2.2. Crash reporting

2. Grow

1. Acquisition

1.1. Dynamic links

1.2. Invites

1.3. Adwords

2. Re-engagement

2.1. Notifications

2.2. App indexing

3. Earn

1. In-App ADs

1.1. Admob

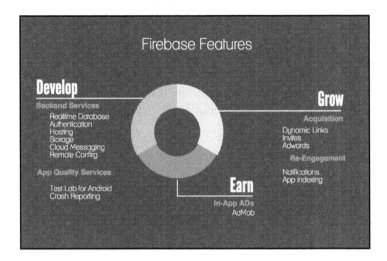

Firebase features

Let us now walk through each of the services that we would be using in our app.

Realtime Database

The Firebase Realtime Database is a NoSQL cloud-hosted database. The data is stored as JSON and it allows syncing of data across all the clients in real time. No matter which platform you are building on, using Firebase, all your clients share one realtime database instance. Firebase uses a data synchronization mechanism with which, every time the data changes, any connected device can receive new updates within no time.

This is how the Firebase uses realtime sync, rather than just a typical HTTP request:

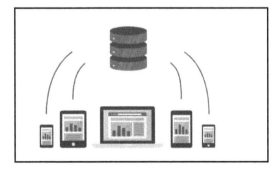

Realtime Sync of Data across several devices

One of the biggest pains for developers is to ensure data remains available, even when the app is offline. Firebase-built apps allow apps to remain responsive when your device goes offline. This is possible as Firebase Realtime Database SDK maintains your data to disk, ensuring that it can be available while offline. It synchronizes the changes onto your device which were missed when your device was offline. It also automatically facilitates merging of any conflicts that might arise while syncing fresh content from the current server state.

Firebase allows expression-based rules which are known as Firebase Realtime Database Security Rules. Using these rules, developers can define the structure for the data and when this data can be read or written. This structure is simple and using the declarative rule language you can not only structure the data but also define security rules. Using the security rules you can secure your data stores. By default, read and write access to your database is restricted, so only authenticated users can read or write data.

How to write a database structure

Firebase Database is based on NoSQL, which means there are no tables or records. With every entry of new data set, the JSON tree gets updated with a new entry as a node with an associated key. You can create and define your own keys, but they must be UTF-8 encoded. The other specifications include a maximum of 768 bytes and the key cannot contain ., $, #, [,], /, or ASCII control characters 0-31 or 127.

Let us take an example to see what this structure looks like. Consider in our app we are maintaining a contact list of friends. A typical user profile is located at a path, such as /users/$uid. The database entry for the user jsouza would look something like this:

```
{
    "users": {
            "jsouza": {
            "name": "John Souza",
            "contacts": { "shanep": true },
        },
        "shanep": { ... },
        "raverp": { ... }
    }
}
```

Here, jsouza is the user John Souza's uid. So, to fetch his details the path would be /users/jsouza. It would fetch all details of John Souza within this node.

When you look at the nested loop, one might be tempted to include nesting data in the database. No doubt that is possible as Firebase Realtime Database allows nesting data up to 32 levels deep, which might be treated like the default structure. But imagine the case wherein you have to fetch data at a location in your database and then it has to retrieve all of its child nodes, when you might require only a little data from that node.

Let us consider the same code above, to understand this situation well.

If we are trying to get a user's name, we will have to retrieve data at `/users/$uid`, but along with the user's name we will also get contacts and any other nodes that are present at this level which are not currently required. Retrieving all of this data will consume time and the user's mobile internet data. So, in order to fetch only the data which we require, we have to change the structure of the database, as shown below:

```
{
"users": {
"jsouza": {
    "uId": "jsouza",
"name": "John Souza"
},
"shanep": { ... },
"raverp": { ... }
},
"contacts": {
"Jsouza": {
    "shanep": true
},
"shanep": { ... },
"raverp": { ... }
}
    }
```

Now, in the above structure we have separated the user details section from the user contacts section. So, when we want to retrieve the user details we can get it from `/users/$uid` node without any unnecessary data. Also, if we want to retrieve contacts, we can call `/contacts/$uid`.

Add security to data structure

One thing that might need an observation here is that security rules cascade--which means that, if you grant read or write privileges to a user on any node, you automatically grant that user read or write privileges on all child nodes. If you ask to read a node which has read permission, Firebase will return the entire node and all of its children. This means that Firebase won't go down parsing through the node based on nested security. The same thing applies with write actions. If you're allowed to write to a node, you're allowed to overwrite everything. Looking at these points it might look like the cascading security rule is a problem, but if you structure data according to the privileges that you want to grant, all will be fine.

The following is an example about how we can write a security rule based on the above data structure:

```
{
  "rules": {
      "users":{
"$uid": {
  ".read": "auth!=null && (data.child('uId').val()==auth.uid)",
  ".write": "auth != null && $uid === auth.uid"
}
    },
    "contacts":{
"$uid": {
  ".read": "auth != null",
  ".write": "auth != null && $uid === auth.uid"
}
    }
  }
}
```

auth means Authentication for a user. **data** means data present at that node.

Now, based on the rules written above, only authenticated users can perform the read and write operations in the database. If a user is not an authenticated user, he will not be able to read or write.

Now, in the user node, a user can read only his own details and does not have access to other users' details, as we are checking this from:

```
(data.child('uId').val() == auth.uid),
```

Here, if ID, auth, and uid is the same as the data we are reading, then read is allowed. Similarly, while writing in the user node, user can only write into his own node and cannot change other users, details as we are comparing the node key value `$uid` with the `auth.uid` value.

Now, in the contact node, a user can see all other user contacts but can only write in his own contacts.

The Firebase team recommends using Flatten data structures as one of the best practices. If the data is instead split into separate paths, it can be efficiently downloaded in separate calls, as it is needed. Breaking your data up into its component parts enables you to query just the data that is needed. You can avoid making join allowing the server to be responsible for duplicating data appropriately.

Firebase database rules have a JavaScript-like syntax and come in four types:

- `.read`
- `.write`
- `.validate`
- `.indexOn`

Type	Description
`.read`	Describes if and when data is allowed to be read by users.
`.write`	Describes if and when data is allowed to be written.
`.validate`	Defines what a correctly formatted value will look like. It also checks whether it has child attributes, and the data type.
`.indexOn`	Specifies a child to index to support ordering and querying.

The Firebase team recently released a security rule generator named Bolt. This allows developers to review the rules that it creates. You can check the following link to explore this tool: `https://github.com/firebase/bolt`. Now, we'll look at how easy it is to integrate it into an Android app.

Please follow the steps below to start the new project. Go to Firebase console: `https://console.firebase.google.com/` . Please provide the Firebase name for your project. Note that, when you create a project, it means that you have access to the container of features such as database, user management, and remote config across your apps. Here are steps for creating a new Firebase app:

1. First, open the Firebase console : `https://console.firebase.google.com/`:

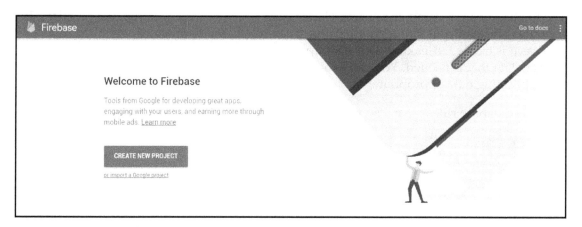

2. Next, click on **CREATE NEW PROJECT.**
3. After entering the project name and selecting the country, click **Create Project** and your new Firebase app will be ready.
4. After creating the new project, you will see the Firebase Dashboard for your app. On the left side of the browser you will see the key areas of the Firebase features:

Firebase App Dashboard

5. Here, click on the **Add Firebase to your Android app**. This is to add Firebase to the Android section of your app:

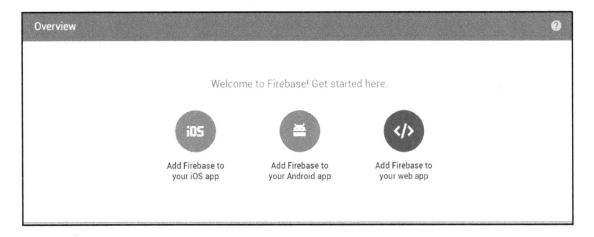

6. Next, you will be asked to enter the details of the app:

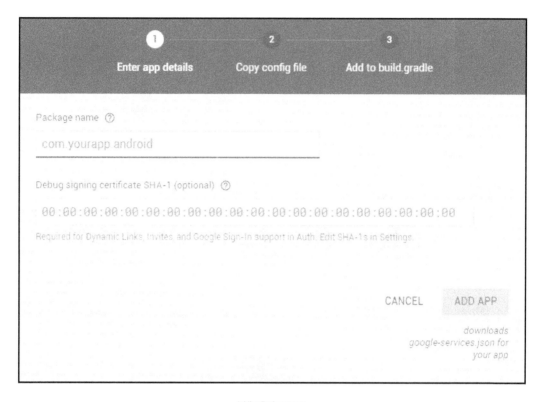

Adding Package name

Here we can see two fields: package name and SHA-1 certificate of your keystore. While entering the package name it should be the same as the package name in the `AndroidManifest.xml` file in your app.

Now the second part requires us to generate a SHA-1 certificate. To generate the signing-certificate fingerprint, follow the steps below:

1. First, open your command prompt.
2. Now, as we are in development, we will use the `debug.keystore` to generate the signing-certificate fingerprint.
3. For the `debug.keystore` the default alias is `androiddebugkey` and store password used is `android`.

4. Now to get the signing-certificate fingerprint, from `debug.keystore` we run the following command:

```
keytool -list -v -keystore "C:\Users\%your
name%\.android\debug.keystore" -alias androiddebugkey -
storepass android -keypass android
```

5. This will generate the signing-certificate fingerprint which will be used to create the credentials.
6. When the build is about to go into production we will use the live `keystore/jks` file to generate the signing-certificate fingerprint.

This will create the credential file.

7. After both of these details have been filled, click on **Add app**. This will generate the `google-services.json` file:

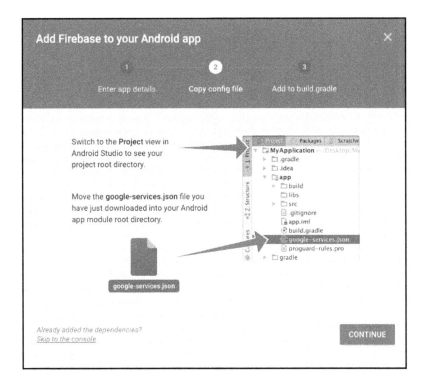

Download JSON file

8. Move the `google-services.json` file you just downloaded into your Android app module root directory.

9. Now, we need to add dependencies in the `build.gradle` file of the app module:

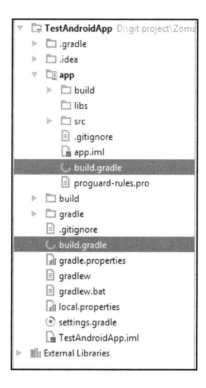

Dependencies to build.gradle

10. First, we'll add rules in the root level `build.gradle` file, to include the google-services plugin as follows:

```
buildscript {
// ...
dependencies
{
    // ...
    classpath 'com.google.gms:google-services:3.0.0'
  }
}
```

11. Then, in your app's Gradle file (usually the `app/build.gradle`), we need to add the apply plugin line to enable Gradle Plugin as follows:

```
apply plugin: 'com.android.application'
android {
 // ...
}
dependencies {
   //All the apps dependencies are written here
   compile 'com.google.firebase:firebase-core:10.0.1'
}
// Add this at the bottom of the file
apply plugin: 'com.google.gms.google-services'
```

Firebase Cloud Messaging

Firebase Cloud Messaging (**FCM**), formerly known as Google Cloud Messaging, is a revised version of the cross-platform messaging solution that empowers you to send notifications at no cost. In the app, these services will be used to notify users such as in the case of new offers or comments on restaurants feedback. Firebase inherits GCM's core infrastructure but it simplifies client-side development.

In Google Cloud Messaging, developers had to write their own registration or subscription retry logic, which now gets ruled out. Simply by writing a few lines of code, FCM can be integrated into the app. It contains a server that is responsible for assigning an identifier token to each device that is subscribed to send and receive notifications. This also ensures that messages are sent and received by a particular device.

The following process takes place until the sending or receiving messages is initiated:

1. When the app is installed, the devices, say A or B, are asked for a token by sending a request to Firebase Cloud Messaging.
2. The Firebase Cloud Messaging then generates and returns a token to identify each of the devices. Please note that in the following cases this might lead to a change in the registration token that you must have generated:
    * The app deletes Instance ID
    * The app is restored on a new device
    * The app is uninstalled/reinstalled
    * The app's data is cleared

3. The developer can save this token on the server and assign this token to the specific user, if needed.
4. You can now use either the Firebase console or build logic on your service using SDK to send messages to devices.

One of the key advantages of using FCM is that the Firebase console has a feature, Firebase Notifications, like Facebook's Parse, before it was shut down.

Let us take a look at the notification section on the Firebase console. First, head to the Firebase console URL and click on the **Notification** option in the left menu panel. For the first time, you will be greeted with the welcome message helping you to understand more about this notification section. Passing through this you will see the actual messaging section for configuration. Click on **New Message** and you will see the following section as shown below:

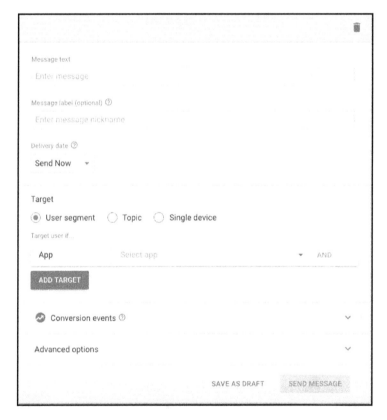

Create Message Section

Message text defines what text gets displayed in the notification. **Message label** is an option field. **Delivery date** is either sending it right away or scheduling it one month in advance. If you are scheduling the message one month in advance, you can also set the specific time and, most importantly, the time zone of the recipient. When **Time zone** is set to **Recipient time zone**, the message will be delivered to users based on their device's time zone settings:

Setting Delivery date

The next section is the **Target**. The target is divided into three parts:

- **User segment**: A selection of apps to choose from to package their applications. You can also filter user groups, languages, and versions too. Setting up to target multiple applications to deliver is also possible:

- **Topic**: Topic of work is to be delivered to the user which allows them to subscribe to that topic. Topic messaging supports unlimited topics and subscriptions for each app. Take a case like a news app, wherein you have to notify the user depending on the topic of preference, say politics, sports, and so on. In this case, setting customized topic messaging could set the right tone for messaging depending on users. Topic messages are optimized for throughput rather than latency. Avoid using topic messaging if you wish to send messages to multiple devices per user. You can opt for device group messaging in those cases.

- **Single device**: Knowing the FCM registration token, you can send notification to a specific device:

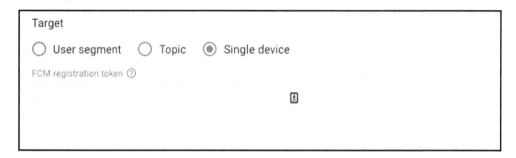

The console also allows an option of conversion tracking. Enable it to capture the key events to evaluate notification effectiveness. The actions, like sent and opened, are provided by default:

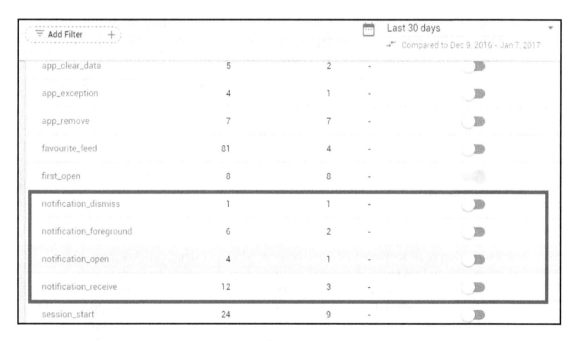

From the above screen, we can see few events that are captured by default, for sending a notification from the Notification tab. These events are captured and stored automatically each time a user interacts with the notification sent from the Notification tab.

But these events are not yet marked for conversion, which can be identified from the switch button. For now, only `first_open` is marked for conversion which is set by default. If other keys are to be made for conversion they can be made from this screen.

After the key has been marked for conversion, all the events which are captured can be seen in the `ATTRIBUTION` tab under the `CONVERSION EVENTS` tab:

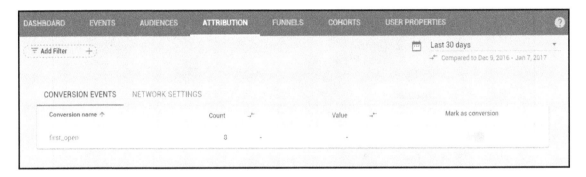

The events that are captured after making the key as marked for conversion will be shown here.

If you wish to add optional events, you can set them up too, using the steps below:

1. In Firebase Analytics, click the **Events** tab then click **Network Settings**.
2. Click the **Selector** menu then click **Enable conversion**.
3. Once an event has been enabled as a conversion, it is available in Attribution | | Conversion Events.
4. Attribution reporting begins for that event at the time you enable it as a conversion.

Using the **Advanced options**, you can allow further customization to the messages you send to the devices:

Here are the fields under the **Advanced options** section:

1. **Title** is generally shown to end users as the notification title. **Custom data** is the key/value pairs that will be delivered with the message to your app.
2. **Priority** is either grouped as High or Normal. By default, the priority of messaging is Normal. Normal priority messages won't open network connections on a sleeping device, and their delivery may be delayed ensuring conservation of the battery. In the case of High priority, FCM delivers the messages immediately. This also makes sure that FCM service will wake a sleeping device when possible and open a network connection to your app server.
3. **Sound** indicates a sound to play when the device receives a notification. Typically, a sound file is used.

4. The **Expires** section defines how long the messages should be kept for redelivery. The maximum expiry period is four weeks after the first delivery attempt. By default, the messages are sent instantly, but there could be cases whereby the device could be off or offline. In such circumstances, FCM might intentionally delay messages to prevent an app from consuming excessive resources that might have impact on battery life. Parameter `time_to_live` allows us to specify the maximum lifespan of a message. It is supported in both HTTP and XMPP. The value of this parameter must be of a duration from 0-2,419,200 seconds. This value corresponds to the maximum period time for which FCM stores and tries to deliver the message. By default, the maximum period is four weeks.

So far, we have handled the setting up of FCM for sending messages. In the section below, we will discuss how to receive the messages. Firebase notifications behave differently depending on whether the notification is triggered in the foreground or background state. The table below explains the two states and their callback actions:

State	Notification	Data	Both
Foreground	onMessageReceived	onMessageReceived	onMessageReceived
Background	System tray	onMessageReceived	Notification as System Tray data

With FCM, we can send two types of messages to the client.

Notification messages, sometimes thought of as display messages. These messages are directly displayed on the user devices without any processing on the client app. These messages have a predefined set of user-visible keys.

To send Notification messages we use the Notification tab in the Firebase console, which has been discussed above. If the app is not in the foreground, it is directly displayed without any processing from the app, otherwise if it processed by the notification service in the `onMessageReceived` method where it is processed and notification is displayed.

Data messages, which are handled by the client app. These messages are sent from the server using the FCM server API. For apps in both the foreground and the background, the data message is received by the app in the `onMessageReceived` method.

The following is a small snippet to show how the `onMessageReceived` handles the FCM message:

```
@Override
public void onMessageReceived(RemoteMessage remoteMessage) {
    // TODO(developer): Handle FCM messages here.
    Log.d(TAG, "From: " + remoteMessage.getFrom());
    // Check if message contains a data payload.
```

```
    if (remoteMessage.getData().size() > 0) {
        Log.d(TAG, "Message data payload: " + remoteMessage.getData());
    }
    // Check if message contains a notification payload.
    if (remoteMessage.getNotification() != null) {
        Log.d(TAG,"Message Notification Body: " +
remoteMessage.getNotification().getBody());
    }

    // Also if you intend on generating your own notifications as a result
of a received FCM
    // message, here is where that should be initiated. See sendNotification
method below.
    }
```

In the app, we would also be using group messaging, for which the obvious choice of course in FCM would be device group messaging. In this case, app servers can send a single message to multiple instances of an app running on devices belonging to a group. The strategy of distributing the message here is that all devices in a group share a common notification key, which is the token that FCM uses. The limit on the data payload is 4KB when sending to devices such as Android except in the case of iOS where the limit is 2KB.

Before sending the messages to the device group, we need to set it up in the FCM notification console:

1. Obtain the registration token for each device you want to add into the group.
2. In the case of managing groups on the app's server, send a POST request that provides a name for the group and a list of registration tokens for the devices.
3. Create the notification_key, which identifies the device group by mapping a particular group to all of the group's associated registration tokens. The maximum number of members allowed for a notification_key is 20.

To create a group, send a request to https://android.googleapis.com/gcm/notification, as shown below:

https://android.googleapis.com/gcm/notification

```
Content-Type:application/json
Authorization:key=API_KEY
project_id:SENDER_ID
{
    "operation": "create",
    "notification_key_name": "appUser-Chris",
    "registration_ids": ["id1", "id2", "id3", "id4", "id5", "id6"]
}
```

Both the `SENDER_KEY` and `API_KEY` can be found in the cloud messaging tab in the Settings section:

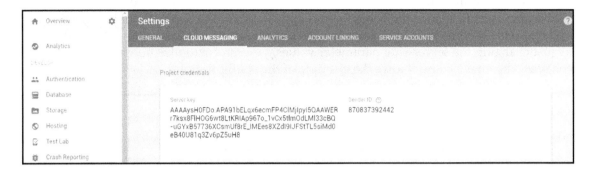

The response for the above call will be a notification key, with which we can send notification to this newly formed group:

```
{   "notification_key": "ART91bGHXQTB...9QgnYOURPwm0I3lmyqzk2TXQ" }
```

Now, in order to send a FCM message to this group we use the following:

`https://fcm.googleapis.com/fcm/send`

```
Content-Type:application/json
Authorization:key=API_KEY

{
  "to": "aUniqueKey",
  "data": {
    "hello": "This is a Firebase Cloud Messaging Device Group Message!",
   }
}
```

The unique key here can be either a topic, a device token of a user, a multiple device token, or a notification key.

Remote configuration

One more important feature that is powered by Firebase is remote configuration. This allows app users to change the behavior and appearance of the app without the app being updated. This is made possible by creating in-app default values that control this behavior. By just changing the server-side parameter values, you can customize how the app looks or behaves. The image below shows the example of the configurations:

Now, let us discuss how we can add remote configuration to our app.

To add remote configuration into the android app, first we have to add the following line in the dependency section of the app level `build.gradle` file:

```
compile 'com.google.firebase:firebase-config:10.0.1'
```

After the app, has synced, we can how use the `Config` object which will help us to use the remote configurations.

Next, let's create sample configurations on the Firebase Remote Configuration console which will be used in the app:

After you have added the configuration, they will not be available in the app until they are published. To publish the changes click on PUBLISH CHANGES and they will be available in the app to use:

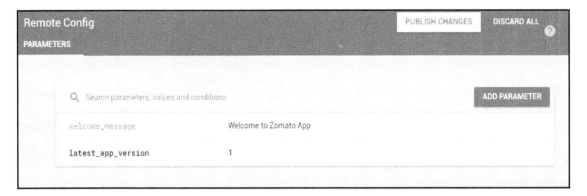

Now, in the app, create an XML file which will have all the default values of the remote configuration. If the remote configurations have not yet loaded the values, then the default values will be displayed instead. Store these XML files in the res/xml folder.

Here's a quick view of what the default value XML will look like:

```xml
<?xml version="1.0" encoding="utf-8"?>
<!-- START xml_defaults -->
<defaultsMap>
    <entry>
        <key>welcome_message</key>
        <value>Welcome to Your App</value>
    </entry>
    <entry>
        <key>latest_app_version</key>
        <value>1</value>
    </entry>
</defaultsMap>
<!-- END xml_defaults -->
```

Now, to use these values in the app, first we will initialize an instance of
`FirebaseRemoteConfig`:

```
mFirebaseRemoteConfig = FirebaseRemoteConfig.getInstance();

FirebaseRemoteConfigSettings configSettings = new
FirebaseRemoteConfigSettings.Builder()
        .setDeveloperModeEnabled(BuildConfig.DEBUG)
        .build();
mFirebaseRemoteConfig.setConfigSettings(configSettings);
```

Then we will set the default values to the configurations using the XML created before:

```
mFirebaseRemoteConfig.setDefaults(R.xml.remote_config_defaults);
```

Now, to fetch the configurations from the server, we need to call the `fetch()` method of
the remote configurations. Use the updated values into the app.

The following is a code sample to show how the fetch method is used:

```
// cacheExpirationSeconds is set to cacheExpiration here, indicating that
any previously
// fetched and cached config would be considered expired because it would
have been fetched
// more than cacheExpiration seconds ago. Thus the next fetch would go to
the server unless
// throttling is in progress. The default expiration duration is 43200 (12
hours).
mFirebaseRemoteConfig.fetch(cacheExpiration)
        .addOnCompleteListener(this, new OnCompleteListener<Void>() {
            @Override
            public void onComplete(@NonNull Task<Void> task) {
                if (task.isSuccessful()) {
                    Toast.makeText(MainActivity.this, "Fetch Succeeded",
                        Toast.LENGTH_SHORT).show();

                    // Once the config is successfully fetched it must be
activated before newly fetched
                    // values are returned.
                    mFirebaseRemoteConfig.activateFetched();
                } else {
                    Toast.makeText(MainActivity.this, "Fetch Failed",
                        Toast.LENGTH_SHORT).show();
                }
                displayWelcomeMessage();
            }
        });
```

The `displayWelcomeMessage()` method is called to set the values of the remote configurations.

Now, if we want to retrieve the values from the remote configurations we use the following calls:

Call	Return type
`getBoolean(String key)`	Returns a boolean value corresponding to the given key.
`getByteArray(String key)`	Returns a byte array value corresponding to the given key.
`getDouble(String key)`	Returns a double value corresponding to the given key.
`getLong(String key)`	Returns a long value corresponding to the given key.
`getString(String key)`	Returns a string value corresponding to the given key.

For more information regarding remote configuration methods, visit `https://firebase.google.com/docs/reference/android/com/google/firebase/remoteconfig/FirebaseRemoteConfig`.

For example, if we want to retrieve the `welcome_message` from the remote configuration, we make the following call:

```
String welcomeMessage = mFirebaseRemoteConfig.getString("welcome_message");
```

Here, `welcome_message` is the constant key where the message is stored and we call the `getString` method as we know the value stored in the remote configuration corresponding to it is a string value.

This feature can be best used when you want to force a user to update the app. You can simply set the values, as shown in the table below:

Parameter Key	Default Value
`force_update_required`	False (or True)
`force_update_new_version`	1.0.1
`force_update_app_url`	< URL of the All>

Depending on these values, the app will behave and force the user to update the app.

Authentication

Firebase Console allows app developers to securely identify a user's identity and securely save user data in the cloud and provide a personalized experience for the user. The Firebase Authentication SDK provides methods that support authentication using passwords and popular login providers such as Google, Facebook, Twitter, and GitHub. Since it all happens under the Firebase cloud, this service integrates with other Firebase services and leverage industry standards like OAuth 2.0 and OpenID Connect, so that interaction with storage is seamless. In the next section we will discuss more about the storage.

Storage

Firebase also supports built-in capabilities for app developers who wish to store and serve contents such as photos, videos, or any other user-generated content. The Firebase is backed by Google Cloud Storage. Uploads and downloads take place regardless of network quality. Uploads and downloads are robust which means that it resumes from where they stopped, ensuring saving of time and bandwidth of the user. Currently, the storage enables storing of static files only. This storage operates on a pay-as-you-go model, which means that there is no need to migrate from Firebase Storage to cloud storage or any other provider; Firebase Storage scales automatically.

Summary

In the beginning of the chapter, we discussed Firebase's features: develop, grow, and earn. We then ggive insights on the setting of Firebase console for the project. This was followed by explaining features of backend, including Firebase Cloud Messaging and its setup. Finally, we discussed other key features such as authentication and storage. In the next section, we will discuss how Firebase can help developers to bring the best of app quality.

12
App Quality Service

One of the most awaited features released under Firebase at the Google I/O 2016 was crash reporting in the beta stage. You can not only analyze the app crashes, but also understand the crash behavioral pattern. This helps developers to understand the crash and find the fixtures that can be deployed. To date, there have been several tools such as Crashlytics, HockeyApp, Instabug, and many more that help us receive crash reports using a console. There is a crash reporting tool for every occasion out there; then what's so special about Firebase Crash Reporting? In this chapter we will discuss the features of Firebase Crash Reporting.

Firebase Crash Analytics works with the new Google Play Services 9.0. Please follow the steps below to integrate Firebase Crash Analysis tool into the app:

1. If you haven't set up Firebase Project, set it up by visiting `http://firebase.google.com`. Since we have already created the setup, we can skip this step.

2. Next, include the following lines to your root-level `build.gradle` file:

```
buildscript {
    //...
    dependencies {
    // ...
    classpath 'com.google.gms:google-services:3.0.0'
    }
}
```

3. Add a dependency in your `build.gradle` file using the following command:

```
compile 'com.google.firebase:firebase-crash:10.0.1'
```

4. To capture the crash, add a call to the static report method in the main activity:

```
FirebaseCrash.report(new Exception("Demo Crash Marker"));
```

You can confirm if logging is enabled by checking the ADB Logs or Android Studio Logs. There will be a message confirming that Crash Reporting is enabled, suggesting that the setup has been completed. Firebase also allows you to log custom events in your error reports and optionally the Logcat. If you want to track a log, but do not want the Logcat output, you can pass a string as the argument, as shown below. If you want to create Logcat output, you must also supply the log level and a tag:

```
FirebaseCrash.log("Activity Initiated");
```

It takes around few minutes for the crash reports to appear on the console dashboard, as shwon figure shown below:

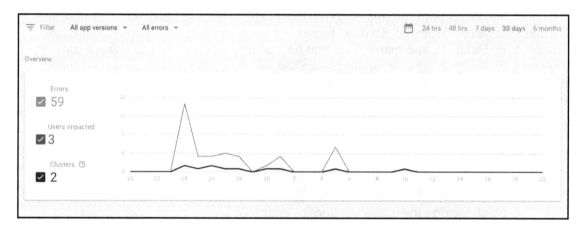

Firebase Crash Reporting Console

As seen in the above image, Firebase Console helps you provide crash details including key features like what kind of errors: Fatal or Nonfatal; and their occurrence pattern along with versions. The graph also indicates the number of users who have been impacted by this crash. The timeline helps to judge the pattern frequency.

From the dashboard shown above, you'll notice that there is something called `Clusters`. This section helps developers by grouping exceptions with similar stack traces:

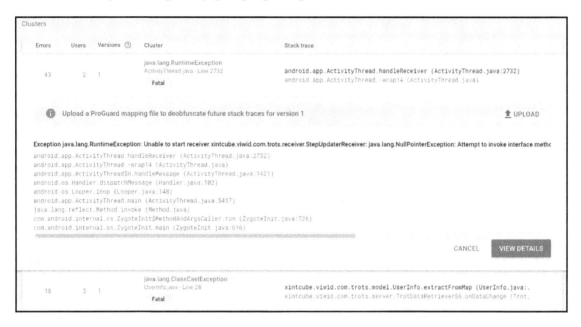

Unlike many other crash reporting tools, which allow one line to initialize crash reporting all through the app, Firebase doesn't enable such a utility. To enable handling of your uncaught exceptions, consider adding the following code block in your main application:

```
public void uncaughtException(Thread thread, Throwable ex)
{
        FirebaseCrash.report(ex);
}
```

Firebase Crash Analytics also allows to deobfuscate Proguard labels. We would be having the final build with ProGuard, so we will need a `mapping.txt`, which gets generated at the path below:

```
<project root>/<module name>/build/outputs/mapping/<build type>/<appname> -
proguard-mapping.txt
```

Take a look at the screenshot below to learn more about the **Upload mapping files** section:

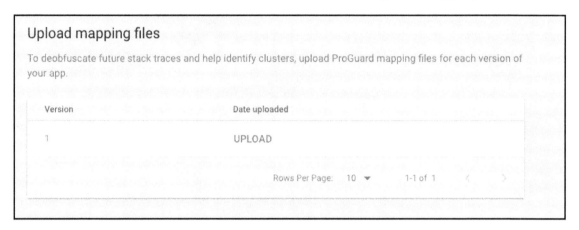

Uploading mapping files in the Firebase Crash Analytics section allows you to see deobfuscated stack traces in the Crash Reporting interface. While testing, you can set up Proguard for debug build types and then build with `./gradlew` assembleDebug as shown below:

```
debug {
    minifyEnabled true
    proguardFiles getDefaultProguardFile('proguard-android.txt'),
      'proguard-rules.pro'
}
```

Since this feature is in beta, we can expect more updates from Google in the near future. But one of the key features it misses is to ensure marking the bugs are fixed. Some of the other features missing or dependencies are:

1. Searching through the crashes becomes difficult, as the only information we get is the location of the crash.
2. There is no grouping of the crashes under classes so we can find numerous crashes that occurred from a single activity:

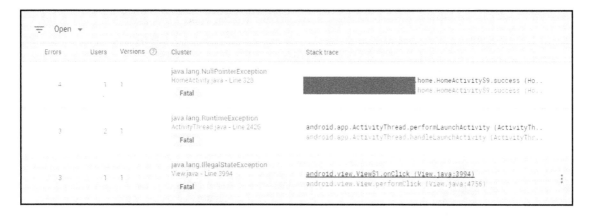

3. Dependencies on Google Play Services on the device.
4. ProGuard/DexGuard mapping files have to be uploaded manually.
5. Unable to implant a listener in the session just after a crash has occurred.

In fact, since it is in beta, we can expect a few more misses too. But we admire one feature the most: Integration with Firebase Analytics, which allows you to create a group of users that experienced troubles when using the app. This feature can then be clubbed with a notification system to notify users.

Firebase Test Lab

Growth of your app's user base depends on several factors and one of the crucial factors is the quality of your application. According to Google, most of the apps given a one star rating is directly related to app crashes and bugs in the app.

For many developers, it is challenging to find and resolve these bugs prior to releasing to the market. As the Android ecosystem evolves, it becomes more challenging to adhere to the quality of the app. Manually testing the app becomes more complex as the user base increases; accessing devices that are unavailable in your country also becomes difficult. Setting a pre-testing facility for testing is an expensive affair to begin with, and is an ever evolving process in terms of continual maintenance.

To help developers with seamless testing, Google has introduced Firebase Test Lab, which is a cloud-based infrastructure for testing Android apps. This is an automated platform, the same as what Google uses to test its own products. With easy steps, you can launch your tests on Google's actual devices to test the quality of your apps. Firebase Test Cloud allows you to select from a variety of device manufacturers and models, device configurations, and different Android versions. Currently, this is only available for Blaze plan users on Firebase. To learn more about the pricing, please check the following link: `https://firebase.` `google.com/pricing/`.

Automation involves writing test cases and, if you have written these tests using Espresso, UI Automator 2.0, or Robotium, you can begin running those tests on the Firebase Test Cloud's hosted devices. Alternatively, you can use Espresso's Test Recorder tool to record the test cases rather than writing them. All you have to do is launch the app in recording mode and the test recorder will observe and remember your interactions. Post completion of the recording, the tool generates test code in Espresso that duplicates those interactions. Uploading these to Firebase Test Cloud will allow you to test recorded scenarios.

Now, we will discuss the steps to be taken while running these tests:

1. To access the Firebase Test Lab open the Test Lab tab in the Firebase app console.
2. Here, we will see two options: Robo test and instrumental test.
3. First, in Robo test we require the debug APK which can be found in `app/build/outputs/apk/`.

Upload this APK, as shown below:

4. After the APK is loaded, Click CONTINUE. Here, you will find the options to test the APK in various physical and virtual devices and Android versions. Select which devices and the Android version you want to test the APK against and click **Start the test**. After a couple of minutes you will see a full report of where the app failed, what tests where performed, along with screenshots, warning messages, and a video of the test performed.
5. Similarly, for instrumental tests, we require the debug and the test APK which needs to be uploaded:

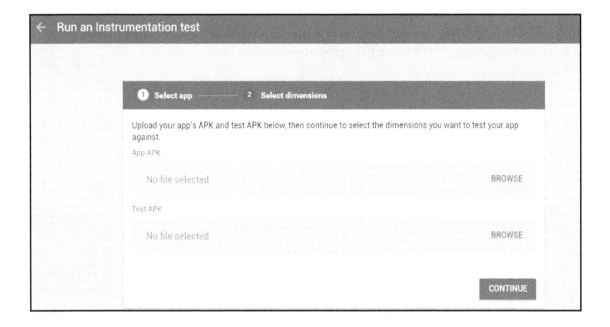

6. After the two APKs have been uploaded, the next steps are the same as that of the Robo test.

Summary

Many developers will agree that buggy and unresponsive apps lead to uninstalling of the apps. But it is also the fact that testing on all the devices is a point of concern. Thus, it is important to learn and gather information from the end users to bring the best of quality back to the user. In the first part of this chapter, we detailed our how Firebase Crash Analytics can be used to understand the buggy areas of the app. Using these reports, developers can rework the buggy sections of the app before they ship new updates to the users. In the last part of the chapter, we discuss how Firebase allows users to test the app using Test Lab.

In Chapter 20, *Grow Up*, we will discuss how we can use Firebase Grow techniques to ensure that we engage more users using the app and also tap.

13
Grow Up

Acquiring and engaging users are two of the most essential components that ensure the success of an app. Most developers find it hard to acquire new users, which is one of the keys to making the app reach millions. Equally important is how you make the user engage with the app, so that the app is never out of focus.

Let us take an example of e-commerce apps which allow you several notifications, such as holiday offers, coupon discounts, and many more. These are teasers for the user to use the app again and probably make a purchase thereafter.

In this section, we will cover how two of these key components can be used using Firebase services.

Dynamic links

A few years back, URLs were merely a trigger to take people to open web pages. As we move towards mobile computing, links have evolved as per the trend. Today, they allow you to go to specific content or a specific section within the app. This is similar to a concept which most refer to as **deep linking**. For example, say if you received a link from a friend and clicking the link can open the app, or if the **Try our app** button on a website could not only take users to your app, but provide a way to specific content within the app for which the app was installed. Not only does it engage users, it also personalizes the entire app environment. With just one URL, you can not only send users right into the app, but also to a specific section within the app.

In addition, Dynamic Links work across app installs: if a user opens a Dynamic Link, and doesn't possess the app, the user will be taken to the app install page. Post installation, your app starts and can access the link. These links work across several mediums such as email, web, and social media referrals to ensure an increase in user acquisitions and retention. The links can be configured to provide the best possible user experience. Dynamic Links help developers to understand which initiatives and content drive growth. This is made possible by Firebase's analytic console that allows you to gather insights on which links drive installations or app use. You could also use referrer tracking to track growth channels.

One of the most promising examples of the Dynamic Links use cases is Google Maps. If you search any location on the maps, you will able to see the data as given in the image below:

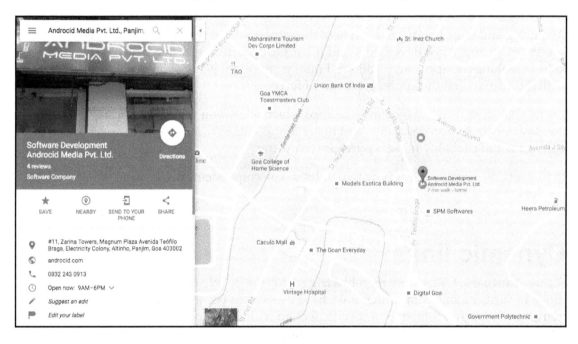

Google Maps Send to your phone feature

Clicking the option **Send to your Phone** will show up several options along with the devices registered with Google. As an example, we have used **Send as Email** option. Once this option is clicked, the email is sent and you will see the content of the email as shown below:

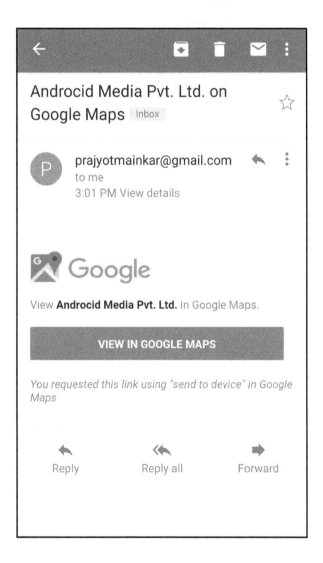

1. Clicking on the option 'View In Google Maps' will open the location in Google maps, and the marker would be pointing at the location you searched on the web. This is a great asset for travelers:

Google Maps integration

Thus far, Branch Inc. is a lone player in the app deep linking space, and the company was quick enough to have a *How we are better* comparison table as published here: `https://blog.branch.io/firebase-dynamic-links-vs-branch-links-a-comparison`:

Features	Branch Links	Firebase Links
String-built, Long links via Query Parameters	Yes	Yes
Google App Indexing Support	Yes	Yes
Single SDK	Yes	No
Rich attribution analytics	Yes	No
Web to app tools	Yes	No
Integrations with marketing channels/platforms	Yes	No
Support for over 6000 deep linking edge cases	Yes	No
Support for cross platform development tools	Yes	No
Industry-leading, SLA-backed technical support	Yes	No

As discussed earlier, Dynamic Links also help you to convert mobile web users to native app users. With minimal effort, you can add a feature for a user by which, with just a click of a link on the mobile web, the user is taken to the corresponding page in your app. It is no matter if they have to go to the App Store or Google Play store to install it first.

Take a look at the following example of a use case, where a click on **View in the Amazon app** would take the user to that context in the app. If the app doesn't exist, the user will first be diverted to the respective store to install and then it will take them to the context:

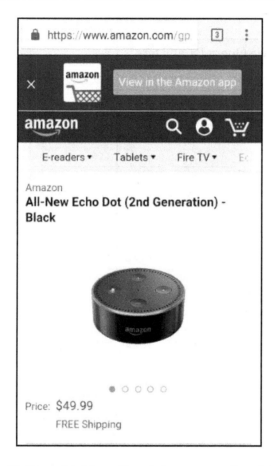

If you are a first timer with Deep Linking, Google has an excellent kit here: https://developer.android.com/training/app-indexing/deep-linking.html#adding-filters

Let's move the focus to the Firebase console now, to generate the Dynamic Links:

1. Add a dependency to the `build.gradle` file and compile `com.google.firebase:firebase-invites:10.0.1`

2. In the Firebase console, open the Dynamic Links section. You will see a section similar to the screenshot below:

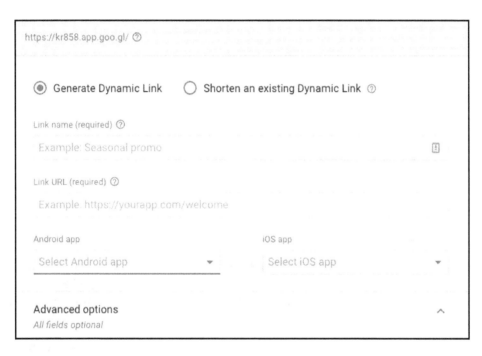

If you observe closely, the project's Dynamic Links domain looks like `appcode_app.goo.gl`. You can also create links manually by adding custom parameters to the URL.

3. Next, click on **New Dynamic Link** and ensure that Generate Dynamic Link is selected. Provide the Name and URL and then select the Android App. The link is a well-formatted URL and defines the link your app will open. You could also specify it to be a link to a your app's content, or a URL displaying a specific welcome screen. The package name should be the package name of the Android app to use to open the link.

4. Firebase also allows you to shorten the dynamic link using the option **Shorten an existing Dynamic Link**.

5. Once the **Android app** is selected, three optional sections are seen:

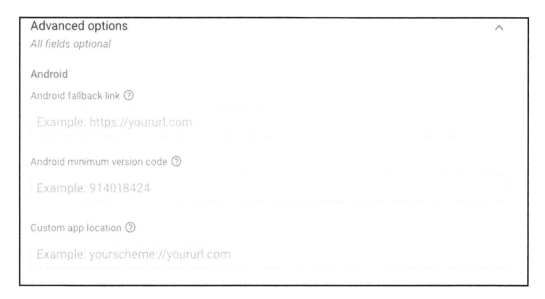

Android fallback link is a link that is visited if the app is not installed or if it's installed but does not meet the minimum version on an Android device. This is defined by the version code, which has the minimum value version of your app that can open the link. The Custom app location overrides the Fallback link, if specified explicitly.

After the link is generated, Firebase Console also allows you to use the analytics to understand the traction:

Dynamic Links provide the best experience across different platforms. Not only does it allow us to engage already existing users, it also allows us to send potential users to any specific location within your app. This makes it possible to survive the install process and ensure users see just the right content when they are boarded.

Let us now check how we can make the app's data deep-linkable. If you have already done the app deep linking, this process might be familiar to you:

1. Start setting up Firebase and the Dynamic Link SDK as explained above. This will allow Firebase to enable passing of data about the Dynamic Link after the app installation.

2. Next, set up *Open in app* links to your web pages. This section will help users to move from the mobile web to the native app, holding the context of the same data. On each page of your website, dynamically generate a Dynamic Link. The link parameter can be marked as the URL of the page it's on. The link might look as follows:

```
    <a
href="https://yourapp.goo.gl/?link=https://yourapp.com/content?item%3D2345&
apn=co
        m.your.app&ibi=com.your.app">View in Your App</a>
```

3. Finally, open the linked content in the app, when the link is clicked. This is made simple by Dynamic Links SDK. On Android, you use the `getInvitation()` method to get data from the Dynamic Link:

```
AppInvite.AppInviteApi.getInvitation(mGoogleApiClient, this,
false).setResultCallback(/* ... */);
```

This can be followed by a callback action, in which you can get the data passed in the Dynamic Links link parameter by calling the `getDeepLink()` method:

```
String link = AppInviteReferral.getDeepLink(intent);
```

Similarly, sharing content from your app with your friends is one of the ways to growth hack app downloads. Not only it will allow new users on board, it will also re-engage existing users. With Dynamic Links, you can create a great user-to-user sharing experience. For example: users who receive content recommendations from their friends can click a link, which can then take them to the shared content in your app. This link can be shared across platforms and sharing is even possible whether or not their friends have your app installed.

To set this up, the only change to the above steps is to configure a `Share` button, which will generate Dynamic Links to be send to your friends using the app of your user's choice. In Android, the Share button starts an activity with the `ACTION_SEND` intent:

```
Intent sendIntent = new Intent();
String text = "Please check this link for 20% food coupon: " +
myDynamicLink;
sendIntent.setAction(Intent.ACTION_SEND);
sendIntent.putExtra(Intent.EXTRA_TEXT, text);
sendIntent.setType("text/plain");
startActivity(sendIntent);
```

Finally, you need to receive the link that's passed to your app, so that you can display the content. This is possible using the `getInvitation()` method:

```
AppInvite.AppInviteApi.getInvitation(mGoogleApiClient, this,
false).setResultCallback(/* ... */);
```

After that, in the callback, you can get the data passed in the Dynamic Link's `LINK` parameter by calling the `getDeepLink()` method:

```
String link_to_send = AppInviteReferral.getDeepLink(intent);
```

App indexing

Ever tried searching flights tickets from Google Search on mobile? The search results would include listings which are similar to the one below:

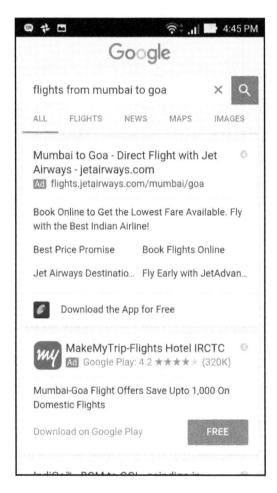

It shows a list of apps that might help you book tickets online. In fact, Google takes this search to another level by showing apps that you have on your device and which can help you plan. In this case, we had Cleartrip app installed and it showed an option **Open On Cleartrip.com**:

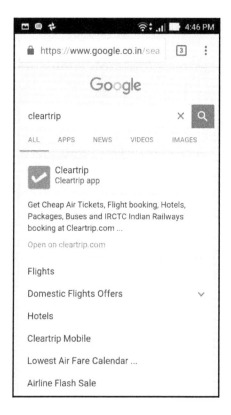

In short, if the app is installed when users search for related content, they will launch the app directly from the search results. Android apps support HTTP URLs and use association to verify the relationship between an app and its website. Once this association is verified, Google search indexes URLs that work for both, your site as well as your app, right from the search results.

Take a look at some of the App indexing options provided by Google for App developers:

Type of App Indexing	Description
Search Results	Displays and promotes the app in search results.
App Installs	App Install Card is displayed next to your website card. This helps users to discover your app.
Auto Complete	Helps users to see the app pages they have visited as suggested results on the Google app.
Now On Tap	Allows Now on tap's results to be showcased to the app users.

With the help of the App Indexing API, you can index user actions in your app. To know how to set up this API in your code, please follow the steps below:

Add the following dependency to the `build.gradle` file:

```
compile 'com.google.android.gms:play-services-appindexing:10.0.1'
```

Import the following classes into the project:

```
import com.google.android.gms.appindexing.Action;
import com.google.android.gms.appindexing.AppIndex;
import com.google.android.gms.common.api.GoogleApiClient;
```

Next, add the App Indexing API calls to your project class. It asks for Title, Description, URL, and type of relevant activities and builds the Action Object. You can add the snippet, as shown in the example below:

```
protected void onCreate(Bundle savedInstanceState) {
    mClient = new
GoogleApiClient.Builder(this).addApi(AppIndex.API).build();
    mUrl = "http://yourcloneapp.com/food/goa-foods";
    mTitle = "Goa Foods";
    mDescription = "Check out the latest article on Goa Foods";
}
```

You can also refer to the link below to learn more about these actions:

```
https://developers.google.com/android/reference/com/google/android/gms/
appindexing/Action#constant-summary
```

Finally, indicate the activity for initialization. Call the `AppIndexApi.end()` method after the activity completes, and disconnects your client.

Admob

In this section, we will discuss what AdMob is, as well as the guidelines of using Admob in an app. AdMob by Google helps you to monetize the app through in-app advertisements. The ads can be displayed in various formats like banner ads, interstitial ads, native ads, or video ads.

Before you can display ads in the app, you will need to create an AdMob account and activate one or more ad unit IDs. These IDs are used in the app where the ad is to be displayed.

Now, let's get started with adding AdMob in android.

The best way to use AdMob is with Firebase, but it is also available as a standalone for those who don't want to use it with Firebase. Firebase provides analytics which can be used to monetize the app more intelligently by seeing the user's behavior and the type of ads the user likes. In the following explanation we will be describing how we can implement AdMob with Firebase.

 You are not allowed to click on your own live ads during development of testing. It may lead to suspension of your AdMob account.

If you already have your AdMob account, link it to your Firebase app from the Firebase console:

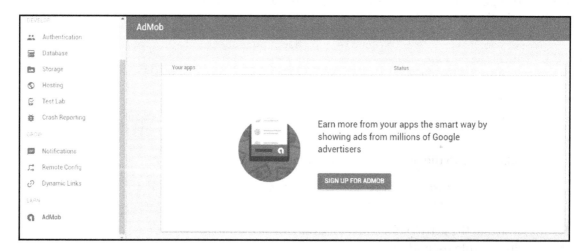

To start ads in Android, first we add the dependencies in the app level gradle file and sync the gradle file from the `Sync Now` option:

```
compile 'com.google.firebase:firebase-ads:10.0.1'
```

After the syncing is complete, `Ad` objects will be available which can be used in your code to display the ads. An `Ad Unit ID` is a unique identifier, given to an ad that needs to be displayed in the app. Ads can be displayed at different sections of the app and each ad should have a different Ad Unit ID.

For example, if we are displaying the ads in two sections of the app, then we need to have two ads, each with its own `Ad Unit Id`. Keep all the `Ad Unit Ids` in the `string.xml` file, so that we can have all the ids in one place. In case we have to change the ad id, we could manage it faster in one place rather than opening the activities where the ads are present.

Now, let us discuss some guidelines that are to be followed while displaying ads in the app:

- **Think about the user experience while placing ads**:
  We should always consider the flow of our app when deciding where to place our ads. The best place for the ads be placed is where the users are expected to be less engaged with the app, such as when user is redirected to a new activity.

- **Do not force users to click the ad**:
  We should not use phrases such as `click this ad` or any other similar phrases. We should not give any compensation or other incentives to user for clicking ads. Giving incentives to users in any way to click on links and/or non-AdMob ads is prohibited.

- **Reserve ad space during loading of app pages**:
  A fixed space needs to be dedicated to display an ad when a screen in the app is displayed. Sometimes, ads may not load at the same time as your app content due to bad internet connectivity. In this case, we have to ensure that the ads do not cover or shift the content of the app, to prevent accidental clicks.

- **Avoid placing ads on the screens without any content**:
  Before implementing any ads, you should first consider user experience and the type of interaction users may have with your app. Ads should not be placed on screens with no content (for example, thank you, log in, exit, error pages, and so on). These screens are the ones that the user sees upon starting the app, while he is about to exit the app, or after performing a specific action on the screen. Ads that are the main focus on these types of screens can confuse users into thinking that the ads are actual part of the app, so we should avoid placing ads on such screens. We should also avoid placing ads on an app screen when users do not have their attention on the screen.

- **Refresh ads at proper intervals**:
  It is recommend that ads should persist for 60 seconds or longer, depending on the functionality of the app, as this provides the best performance for both advertisers and publishers. If the app is automatically refreshing the ads, make sure that the ad requests are not made when the screen is off. Also, if users navigate to and from pages with ads in an app over a short period of time, a new ad request should not be made sooner than the recommended 60 second rate.
- **Ensure the right ad format for the right screen**:
  Make sure you use the right type of ad for the screen mode - landscape or portrait. For instance, when we are placing a portrait ad when the app is in landscape mode it may impact the performance of the ad. In these cases, we should utilize smart banners to get the most appropriate ads for your apps.

Banner Ads

Banner ads are ads that cover a portion of the screen. To implement the banner ad we have to add the view in the XML of the activity:

```
<com.google.android.gms.ads.AdView
    android:id="@+id/adView"
    android:layout_width="wrap_content"
    android:layout_height="wrap_content"
    android:layout_alignParentBottom="true"
    android:layout_centerHorizontal="true"
    ads:adSize="BANNER"
    ads:adUnitId="@string/banner_ad_unit_id" />
```

Here, `adSize` represents the size of the ad that we want to display and the `adUnitId` is the ad ID that is to be displayed.

The various sizes that are supported by the banner ads are as follows:

Size	Description	AdSize Constant
320x50	Standard Banner	`BANNER`
320x100	Large Banner	`LARGE_BANNER`
300x250	IAB Medium Rectangle	`MEDIUM_RECTANGLE`
468x60	IAB Full-Size Banner	`FULL_BANNER`
728x90	IAB Leaderboard	`LEADERBOARD`
Screen width x 32|50|90	Smart Banner	`SMART_BANNER`

The `FULL_BANNER` and `LEADERBOARD` are only supported in tablet devices, whereas others are supported in both tablets and phones.

The size of the ad can also be changed from the code, using the following code:

```
AdView adView = new AdView(this);
adView.setAdSize(AdSize.SMART_BANNER);
```

Here, we have set the size of the ad to Smart Banner.

Smart Banners are ad units that render banner ads on any screen size and in either orientation. Smart Banners `smartly` detect the width of the phone and its current orientation, so as to make the ad view for that size.

Ad lifecycle event callbacks

Now, let us discuss the ad lifecycle event callbacks. The `ad` object provides a listener to get the status of various states of the ad. We can add a callback listener for the ad by using `AdView.setAdListener()`. The various callbacks that are available from these listeners are as follows:

```
public abstract class AdListener {
    public void onAdLoaded();
    public void onAdFailedToLoad(int errorCode);
    public void onAdOpened();
    public void onAdClosed();
    public void onAdLeftApplication();
}
```

`onAdLoaded()` is called when an ad is ready to be displayed.

`onAdFailedToLoad(int errorCode)` is called when an ad request failed; it also returns the reason why the request failed. The error code usually is one of the following:

Error Code	Description
ERROR_CODE_INTERNAL_ERROR	Something happened internally, like, an invalid response was received from the ad server while trying to get the ad.
ERROR_CODE_INVALID_REQUEST	The ad request was invalid; this usually occurs when the ad unit ID was incorrect.
ERROR_CODE_NETWORK_ERROR	The ad request was unsuccessful due to network connectivity.
ERROR_CODE_NO_FILL	The ad request was successful, but no ad was returned due to lack of ad inventory.

`onAdOpened()` is called when an ad opens an overlay that covers the screen.

`onAdClosed()` is called when the user is about to return to the application after clicking on the close button of the ad.

The `onAdLeftApplication()` is called when an ad leaves the application (for example, to go to the browser).

Now we know how to display the ads, let's discuss some guidelines that are to be followed while we are displaying banner ads in the app.

Discouraged banner implementations

Here are some examples of poor banner ad implementations that cause invalid activity, due to the proximity of the ad to app clickable elements:

- **Avoid placing ads near Interactive Elements**:
  Placing the banner ads very close to the interactive elements is one of the biggest causes of accidental clicks. We must try to place the ads in places with less user interactivity on the screen to avoid accidental clicks. Some of the interactive elements that cause such types of accidents are buttons, such as a `next` button or a custom app menu bar interactive content like a text chat box, or an image in an image gallery.

- **Refrain from placing ads between app items**:
This type of of placement when the ad is placed between various interactive elements. Users are likely to come across this banner ad multiple times with a higher level of engagement with the app. So, they are more likely to click on the banner ads accidentally.
- **Ads should not overlap the app content**:
Banner ads should not float or hover over app content. If an app has a scrolling view, banner ads should be placed over the content. Banner ads should not move as a user scrolls through the content, as users may try to click on a section of the view but may accidentally click on the banner ad.

Such banner ad placement can put your app or your account at risk if too many accidental clicks occur, so it is recommend to avoid such an implementation.

Recommended banner implementations

- Separate the ad from the interactive elements:
Separating the banner ad from app interactive elements helps reduce user confusion and accidental clicks. It is important to provide some space/buffer between ads and clickable elements to avoid accidental clicks.
- Separate the ad from app content using a border:
Banner ads that remain fixed on the screen as the user scrolls through the content can be placed either at top or bottom of the screen, as long as there is a separator/border between the ad and the interactive elements. It's recommended that the border should be non-clickable.
- Reserve a fixed space for the ad:
Sometimes it may take time for the banner ads to load on the screen. So, to handle the delay in the display of an ad even after the content has been loaded, a fixed area where the ad is to be displayed should be kept so that whenever the ad gets displayed it does not affect the other content of the screen.

Interstitial Ads

Interstitial ads are ads which occupy the full screen of the device.

The following are the steps involved in implementing an interstitial ad through your code. First, we have to create an instance of the interstitial ad:

```
private InterstitialAd mInterstitialAd;
```

Then, we initialize the ad in the onCreate method of the activity:

```
@Override
protected void onCreate(Bundle savedInstanceState) {
   super.onCreate(savedInstanceState);
   setContentView(R.layout.activity_interstitial_ad);
   ...
   // Create the InterstitialAd and set the adUnitId (defined in
values/strings.xml).
   mInterstitialAd = newInterstitialAd();
   loadInterstitial();
}


private InterstitialAd newInterstitialAd() {
   InterstitialAd interstitialAd = new InterstitialAd(this);
   //Set the ID of Ad
   interstitialAd.setAdUnitId(getString(R.string.interstitial_ad_unit_id));
   interstitialAd.setAdListener(new AdListener() {
       @Override
       public void onAdLoaded() {
//Button Used to Display the AD
          mNextLevelButton.setEnabled(true);
       }

       @Override
       public void onAdFailedToLoad(int errorCode) {
//Button Used to Display the AD
          mNextLevelButton.setEnabled(true);
       }

       @Override
       public void onAdClosed() {
          // Proceed to the next level.
          goToNextLevel();
       }
   });
   return interstitialAd;
}
```

```
private void loadInterstitial() {
    // Disable the next level button and load the ad.
    mNextLevelButton.setEnabled(false);

    AdRequest adRequest = new AdRequest.Builder()
            .setRequestAgent("android_studio:ad_template").build();
    mInterstitialAd.loadAd(adRequest);
}

private void goToNextLevel() {
    // Show the next level and reload the ad to prepare for the level after.
    mLevelTextView.setText("Level " + (++mLevel));
    mInterstitialAd = newInterstitialAd();
    loadInterstitial();
}
```

Here, we load the ad, but it is not displayed until a user does some specific interaction with the app. In the above case, until they click on the mNextLevelButton.

When the user clicks on the **Next level** button, the ad is displayed:

```
mNextLevelButton.setOnClickListener(new View.OnClickListener() {
    @Override
    public void onClick(View view) {
        showInterstitial();
    }
});

private void showInterstitial() {
 // Show the ad if it's ready. Otherwise toast and reload the ad.
    if (mInterstitialAd != null && mInterstitialAd.isLoaded()) {
        mInterstitialAd.show();
    } else {
        Toast.makeText(this, "Ad did not load", Toast.LENGTH_SHORT).show();
        goToNextLevel();
    }
}
```

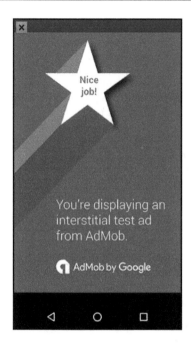

The call `mInterstitialAd.show()` should not be made in the `onAdLoaded()` callback of the ad listener. As the `onAdLoaded()` is an asynchronous method, there is no control on when the `onAdLoaded()` callback would happen. This would be called when the loading of the ad gets completed. Now, if the `show()` method is called on this callback, the display of the ad would be dependent on the asynchronous loading of the ad instead of the app state, which can be when the user is in the middle of another interaction with the app. This can result in policy violations due to accidental clicks.

Instead, we recommend loading the ad earlier in the lifecycle of the application, then polling `interstitial.isLoaded()` to see if the ad is ready to be shown. If it isn't ready, we recommend moving to the next state in the application.

Here are some questions that one should ask while implementing the interstitial ad:

- How will the user engage with the app when the ad is shown?
- Will the user be surprised by the interstitial ad?
- Is it the right time to show an interstitial ad?

Interstitial ads have certain guidelines while implementing them in the app. Here are some of the key points:

Discouraged interstitial implementations

On app launch or app exit:

- Avoid showing an interstitial ad when the user launches the app or when the user is exiting the app. The best place to use interstitial ads is between the screens of the app's content. Ads should not be placed when the app is running in the background or outside the app's environment.

Here are some examples describing when an interstitial ad should not be shown:

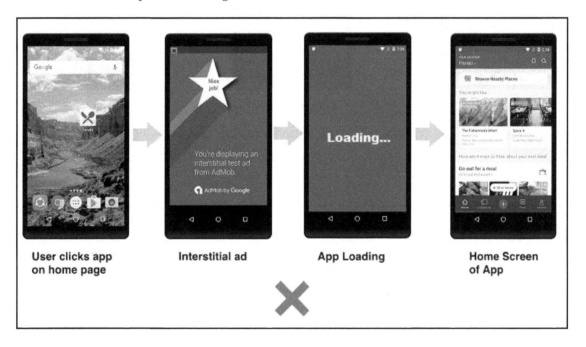

| User clicks app on home page | Interstitial ad | App Loading | Home Screen of App |

In the preceding example shown, the user is shown an interstitial ad immediately after he has launched the app; the normal loading occurs after the ad is closed. Another situation is when the user tries to exit the app:

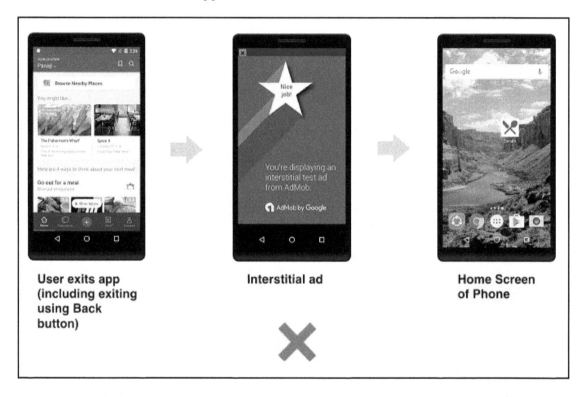

| User exits app (including exiting using Back button) | Interstitial ad | Home Screen of Phone |

When the user is exiting the app, avoid showing the interstitial ads. Not only does it impact the user's experience, it might impact its revisit changes too. Assuming that you still want to use the ad, here is an alternative approach:

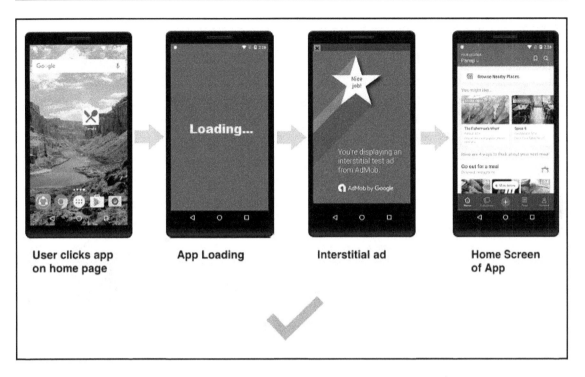

User clicks app on home page → App Loading → Interstitial ad → Home Screen of App

In this case, the user will see a screen of the app indicating that the app has launched and is loading the details, during which an ad is displayed.

- **Ads shown repeatedly**:
  It is a bad practice to display an ad to a user too frequently, as there could be a possibility that he clicks on the ads rather than actually experiencing the ad. We should not display an ad to a user frequently, as there are chances that the user may accidently click an ad.

Some of the implementations of this types are as follows:

1. Avoid showing ads after each app interaction:

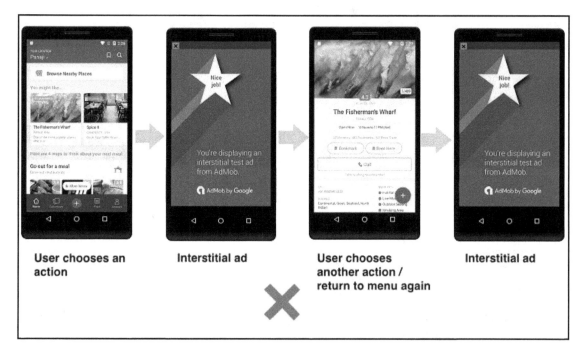

| User chooses an action | Interstitial ad | User chooses another action / return to menu again | Interstitial ad |

Here, the user sees an interstitial ad after every interaction with app.

2. Placing back to back ads:

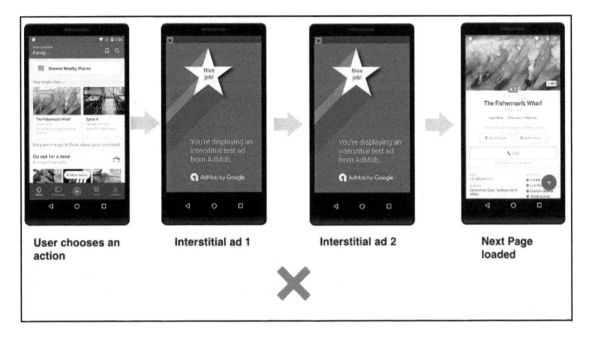

| User chooses an action | Interstitial ad 1 | Interstitial ad 2 | Next Page loaded |

Here, the user sees two or more interstitial ads after performing an action. This might confuse the user into thinking it is a part of the app and can cause an accidental click.

A simple way to avoid these cases is to keep track of when the last interstitial ad was displayed and not show the user ads too often. Show ads only after the user has completed a series of actions or at the end of the stage.

Ads shown unexpectedly:
Don't show the interstitial ad suddenly while the user is performing an action, as this may often frustrate the user. The user should see the ads at logical breaks within our app, such as when the user is about to complete a particular sequence of tasks, to make sure that the user does not get surprised by the ad.

A common issue is that, even though you may intend for the ad to load in between page content, the ad itself appears shortly after a new page of content has loaded due to carrier latency. To prevent this from happening, it is recommend that you preload the interstitial ad in advance and show the ad when the user performs an action.

Here are some examples showing the unexpected launch of interstitial ads:

1. Showing an ad after the app has been loaded:

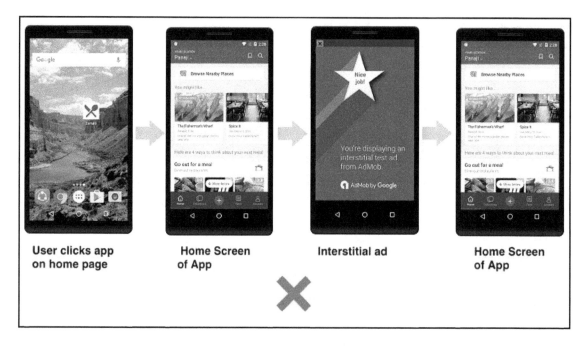

| User clicks app on home page | Home Screen of App | Interstitial ad | Home Screen of App |

Here, the user sees the ad after the app has been launched and content has been displayed without any user interaction. This can lead to accidental clicks if the user was about to perform an action.

2. Showing an ad after they have performed the action but content has already loaded:

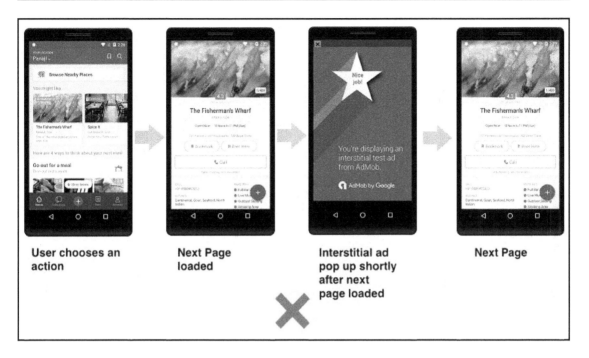

User chooses an action

Next Page loaded

Interstitial ad pop up shortly after next page loaded

Next Page

Here, after the user has performed an action on the home screen, they see the second screen but, shortly afterwards, an ad is displayed.

In both of the above cases, the interstitial ad is displayed without an interaction from the user, due to which the user may be surprised while performing an action in the app, leading to accidental clicks.

Now we will show an example of how the above cases can be solved:

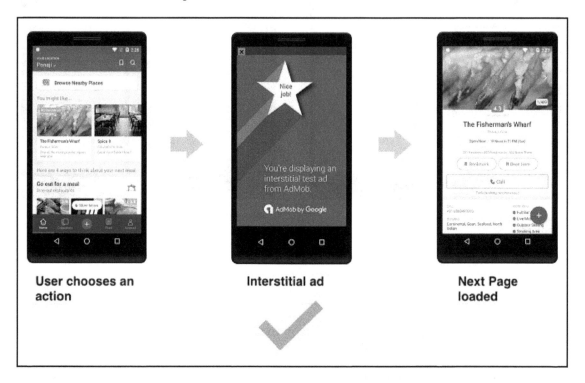

| User chooses an action | Interstitial ad | Next Page loaded |

As shown in the above example, we are displaying the interstitial ad on the user's interaction with the app and not without. As the user is not surprised by the display or ad, this prevents accidental clicks. The user is able to follow the natural flow of the app after he has closed the ad.

Interstitial ad implementations

- How to place an ad in your app:
An interstitial ad could be placed between two tasks. It should be placed at a point where the user's first task gets completed and they are about to start with another.
For example, if your app has an order section involved, then an interstitial ad could be shown to the user after the order process gets successfully completed and they are about to go back to the products list page. It is recommended that the interstitial ads appear before the page break, rather than after the page break. In the case of a game app, the ad could be placed between the levels or stages of a game, as a level or stage provides a break from the app. Using an interstitial ad at a proper break point encourages a user to evaluate the ad instead of just ignoring it.
A page break usually ends by asking the user to click on a **Continue** or **Next** button, or a similar kind of button. Hence, it is important to show the interstitial ad before that button to avoid accidental clicks. It will make a user see or click the ad genuinely.

Some apps asks users to click on **Continue** buttons to proceed to the next pages. In such apps, interstitial ads could be shown at places while the processing takes place. For example, while the next page is being loaded, the ad could be shown alongside the loader. Here, a user will avoid clicking on it accidentally.

Summary

In this chapter, we first discussed how Deep Linking can help to acquire and engage users. This topic was followed by discussion on how app indexing can help users to visit the specific content within the app from a webpage. This allows users to receive an in-app content experience based on the searches made on Google. In the last section, we discussed how developers can use AdMob to monetize their apps.

14
Testing

Mobile App testing needs a careful process of implementation. Starting small, this process can progress into several large forms of execution. As per the Qualcomm Band Tracker, battery life is something people look for in a phone, and, on average, 11 apps are installed on a smartphone. Your app has to undergo serious testing to be among the top 11.

In this chapter, we will highlight some of the major testing techniques to be followed in the development process.

Testing Mechanisms (Functionality , Performance , Security , and Compatibility)

Testing is an important part of the software development life cycle. A good strategy for software testing is the designing of software test cases into a series of steps that need to be well planned.

The strategy should include the steps to be taken, the effort, time, and resources that would be required. A proper plan needs to be laid down with test case designs, rules, stages, time estimation, complexity evaluation, milestones for verification, reporting, and progress reporting.

Software testing has goals that vary, depending on factors such as, type of project, magnitude of the project, and so on. But, some of the major goals that remain unified across any testing plan are mentioned here:

1. Finding defects which may be created by the programmer while developing the software.
2. To avoid any unwanted behavior when the product has been deployed.

3. To make sure that the final product is as per the business and user requirements and specifications.

4. To gain the confidence of the customers by providing them with a quality product.

Software Testing Life Cycle (STLC)

The Software Testing Life Cycle covers the entire process that defines various phases of software testing. It has certain objectives and phases that can also be illustrated by the following diagram:

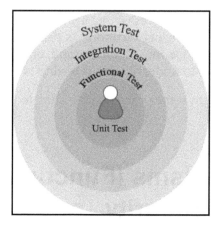

Testing Cycle

The Software Testing Life Cycle proceeds outward. The process flow goes out from a developer to a tester. Hence, the basic and the first tests have to be performed by the developer who codes a section of the functionality, and then it proceeds outward toward the tester. Given below are some of the key testing mechanisms:

- **Unit testing:** In unit testing, the testing techniques are used to detect errors in a software's individual component. They are instant test cases, which are performed, mostly by the developer, on completion of a section or component that could function independently.

- **Functional testing:** Functional testing includes the testing of the actual functionality of a components for any issues. It also involves validation testing of the user inputs at various places.

- **Integration testing:** Once the unit and functional tests of the individual components are a success, all these sections have to be integrated. Upon integration, there might be errors which could come up. Hence, the integration testing becomes a necessity. It focuses on issues associated with verification and program construction as components begin interacting with one another.
- **System testing:** System testing involves the overall system elements properly. It checks that the overall system function and performance has been achieved. It performs the full testing and also considers the user experience.

Many software errors are eliminated before testing begins by conducting effective technical reviews. Different testing techniques are appropriate at different points in time. The developer of the software conducts testing and may be assisted by independent test groups for large projects. Testing and debugging are different activities. Debugging must be accommodated in any testing strategy.

Organizing for Software Testing

- Specify and highlight the product requirement in clear format before testing begins
- Specify testing objectives explicitly
- Identify categories of users for the software and develop a profile for each
- Prepare the Test Plan and focus on rapid cycle testing
- Use effective formal reviews as a filter prior to testing
- Conduct formal technical reviews to assess the test strategy and test cases
- Focus on continuous improvements to work on better test cases

Integration Testing

When giving the in depths about the integration testing, the testers should strive to identify critical modules having the following requirements.

Top-down integration testing

The top-down integration technique tests the modules at a lower hierarchy that are not yet integrated in the main code. The lower modules are simulated and are called stubs. The preceding modules are integrated and tested, although the lower modules are not complete:

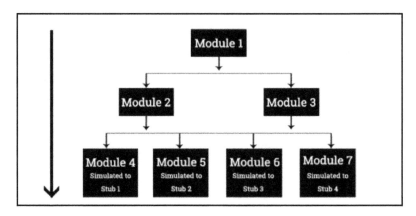

Top Down integration Testing

The preceding figure shows that the module 1, 2, and 3 are individually completed and tested. Module 4, 5, 6, and 7 are not completed or tested. The top level modules 1, 2, and 3 are integrated and tested. The module 2 needs integration of modules 2, 4, and 5. Hence, the modules 4 and 5 are simulated to stubs and then integrated. Similarly, the modules 3, 6, and 7 are integrated.

As the top-down integration gives a complete product before its completion, it gives the overall idea of how the final product would look. Also, it could be used for demonstration purpose. It could also help find any top level bugs in the product and could be rectified earlier.

Bottom-up integration testing

The bottom-up integration testing is completing and testing the complete lower-level modules, and then integrating the lower modules with the higher modules and testing the integrated module:

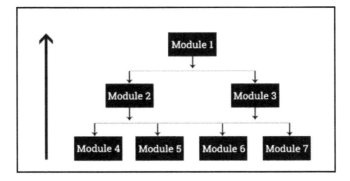

Bottom Up integration Testing

The preceding figure shows the bottom-up integration testing flow. Here, the lower-level modules 4, 5, 6, and 7 are tested and integrated with the higher-level modules and then tested. For instance, the modules 4, 5, and 2 are completed, unit tested, and integrated and then again tested after integration. It is similar for modules 6, 7, and 3. Then later, the modules 2, 3, and 1 are integrated and tested.

Regression testing

Regression testing is testing the existing software that has been tested previously again, after changes are made in same or some other modules, in order to find errors or bugs that occur in the existing software.

Regression testing helps verifying if the existing module works correctly after integrating a new one. It ensures that it does not error the existing working of a module and the existing functionality is maintained.

Smoke testing

Smoke tests are performed on a build which is integrated to verify that the functionalities it performs are as expected. It is also known as Build Verification Testing, which ensures that the important functions of the build work correctly.

Acceptance Testing

Acceptance testing is making sure that the software works correctly for intended users in his or her normal work environment. At times, the software might work well at the development environment because of suitable conditions. But, it might not work well or as expected when deployed at the client environment. Hence, the Alpha and Beta tests play an important role to make sure the product works correctly in both environments.

Alpha test

The test of the complete software is tested by customer under the supervision of the developer at the developer's site. We will be discussing this in detail when we talk more about the Google Play Developer Console in Section 7.

Beta test

The test of the complete software is tested by the customer at his or her own site without the developer being present. Google provides an option to run several Beta tests on the Google Play, which we will be discussing in depth in Section 7.

Performance Testing

Performance testing is the process of determining the speed or effectiveness of a device. This process can involve quantitative tests, such as measuring the response time at which an app functions. Qualitative attributes such as reliability, scalability, and interoperability may also be evaluated.

Performance testing can verify that a system meets the specifications claimed by its manufacturer or vendor. The process can compare two or more devices in terms of parameters such as speed, data transfer rate, bandwidth, throughput, efficiency, or reliability.

Android Studio has an in-built tool to monitor the performance of the app. The Monitor section in the Android Studio, which is already mentioned in the Chapter 2, *Exploring Android Studio Developer Tools*, is a tool that could be used to test the performance of the app at the developer level. It gives you how much memory is consumed by the app, and if it frees up space upon usage of the memory. Along with memory, it also allows you to monitor the network usage.

The performance testing has to be also carried out, by testing your app across different devices with different device specifications. Testing of the app on a device with lower memory is the best way to test your app for performance.

Security Testing

Security testing is one very important testing if your app contains sensitive data. It is required that your app is completely secured over the network when you send any sensitive data like a user's bank details across the network. Also, it is required that no sensitive data is saved onto the device, and if saved it should be correctly encrypted.

An app that is not security tested could be vulnerable to attacks and the sensitive user data could be compromised. Hence, various security testing mechanisms need to be followed to make sure that your app is secured.

Compatibility Testing

Compatibility testing is testing your app across different devices. The app should be displaying the data correctly across all these devices. It plays a very important role when scalability is of utmost importance.

Compatibility across devices has many different classes. The testing on the devices must satisfy conditions across devices like:

1. **Screen Size**: Your app must be displayed properly across different device sizes, like a small phone, a normal size phone, or a tablet device.
2. **Screen Resolution**: The app must display data and images across the devices with different resolutions. The most important test is image as different sizes of same image are required on different resolution devices.
3. **OS**: The app should be functional across all the Android versions that are mentioned to be supported by your app. There are different functionalities that happen across different versions of Android. For example, additional permissions are required on the latest versions of Android devices.
4. **Orientation**: If your app is functional in both portrait as well as landscape then, the tests need to be performed to check if the app displays correctly in both portrait and landscape mode. Also, a test needs to be made when the transition between landscape mode to portrait mode and vice versa takes place.

5. **Hardware Accessibility**: Not all devices have all the hardware installed into them. Hence, it is required to test on devices that do not support hardware, and you are using it in your app. For example, if your app is making use of the mobile camera, but a device is not having a camera, then the app might crash.

Automating User Interface Tests

User interface (**UI**) testing makes sure that the functional requirements and various features of the app are working correctly. UI testing could be made using a human tester to test all the cases of UI manually, and make sure that the app UIs function correctly as expected. This will make sure that the test cases are checked and verified, but it would involve a lot of time testing these cases one by one. Also, the human intervention for testing could mean, they could miss out some critical complex tests. Hence, a much better approach to test the UI components is automating the test cases by writing code snippets. The automated test approach ensures that the tests are more reliable and efficient.

Android Studio has made a provision to write the UI test cases in code. The project has a folder (`src/androidTest/java`) to write the automated test cases. After writing the test cases in the Java class file, you need to run the test file on the target device. The app would be running in the test mode and would work based on the test code that has been written. Complex test scenarios could also be performed using the UI testing frameworks and cannot be used to simulate user interactions on the target app.

UI test cases could depend on its own single app or it could depend on other multiple apps:

1. **UI tests that depend on a single app**: This test case depends on a single app, that is, the app you are currently testing; it allows you to check if the correct output is returned directly. Here, how the app acts or if it responds as expected needs to be verified, when a user action is performed or the user inputs some data. You will get the response of this test case directly and can fix it without any other dependencies. Espresso is one of the UI testing frameworks, which will allow you to simulate user actions.

2. **UI tests that depend on multiple apps**: This UI test case, as it says, depends on multiple apps, where the correct behavior of the app depend on interactions between the current app and other user or system apps. For instance, if your app makes needs some pictures from the device, then it needs to access the gallery app. For that, your app has to ask permission and use the app, and fetch the gallery files required. UI Automator allows you to create test cases for multiple app test cases.

Testing UI for a single app

Testing UI within a single app helps us ensure that the users will not encounter any problems when using the app. We should always create a UI test case for each of the sections of the app so that we can test them regularly to see the app is functioning correctly, even after some changes are made in the app.

Testing App using Espresso in Android Studio

Espresso is a testing framework that is used to write test cases which can simulate user actions on an app. It is provided by Android Testing Support Library and has APIs that can be used in your code for simulation as per your needs. The Espresso tests can run on devices running Android 2.3.3 (API level 10) and higher.

Espresso has a lot of advantages. It particularly does the synchronization of simulated actions with the UI automatically, of the app that you are testing. Espresso can also know if the main thread is active or in an idle state. This makes Espresso time independent, that is, it will allow to run your test app sequences at the required time. This improves the reliability of the test cases and also relieves you from having to add any timing workarounds, such as `Thread.sleep()` in your test code.

Setting up Espresso in Android Studio

Before we start building the UI test cases with Espresso, we have to add the dependencies into the build.gradle file of the app module as follows:

```
dependencies {
// Other dependencies ...
androidTestCompile 'com.android.support.test.espresso:espresso-core:2.2.2'
}
```

Once the gradle file is successfully synced, we can now start writing the Espresso test class.

Create an Espresso Test Class

First, we need to create a Java class in order to create an Espresso test case:

1. The `onView()` method could be used to find the UI component that you want to test in the activity. It is to be used to find the UI component to test in case of an `AdapterView`. For example, a sign-in Button or any button in the activity.

2. `ViewInteraction.perform()` or `DataInteraction.perform()` can be used to simulate a specific user interaction to perform on that UI component. For example, clicking on the sign-in button could be simulated by the `perform()` method. Multiple actions on the same UI component can be sequentially performed using a comma-separated list in the method argument.

3. The steps above can be repeated to simulate a user flow across multiple activities in the app.

4. The `ViewAssertions` method checks if the UI reflects the expected state or behavior, after these user interactions are performed.

The following code snippet shows how your test class may invoke this basic workflow:

```
ViewInteraction linearLayout = onView(
allOf(withId(R.id.browseNearby), isDisplayed()));
linearLayout.perform(click());
```

In the preceding snippet, we found a view with the `R.id.browseNearby` ID. First, check if it is displayed in the current view or not. If it is present, we performed the click on that view.

If the view was not present and we had performed the click on this view, it would have thrown a `NoMatchingViewException`.

Specifying a View Matcher

You can specify a view matcher using the following approaches. The calling methods in the ViewMatchers class is as follows:

1. If you want to find a view with the text that is given, we can use the `withText()` to get the view. It can be used as shown in the following example:
   `onView(withText("Submit"));`

2. Similarly, you can call `withId()` and provide the resource ID (`R.id`) of the view, as shown in the following example: `onView(withId(R.id.button_submit));`

Android resource IDs are not always unique. Two ID names may be the same. Hence, in this case if a resource ID is used by more than one view, Espresso throws an AmbiguousViewMatcherException. Check `https://developer.android.com/reference/android/support/test/espresso/AmbiguousViewMatcherException.html` to know about `AmbiguousViewMatcherException`.

The Hamcrest Matchers class has a method `allOf()`, which can be used to combine multiple matchers, such as `containsString()` and `instanceOf()` to find the correct view. This allows us to filter the match results more and gets the view with more accuracy, as shown in the following example:

```
onView(allOf(withId(R.id.button_signin), withText("Submit")));
```

The not keyword can be used to filter views that don't correspond to the matcher as follows:

```
onView(allOf(withId(R.id.button_signin), not(withText("Save"))));
```

Once you import the Hamcrest Matchers class in your test class, you'll be able to use all of these methods of that class. To import the class use the import the `org.hamcrest.Matchers` package.

To improve the performance of an Espresso test case, we have to specify minimal matching information to find a view. For example, if a view can be easily identifiable by its description, we do not need to specify more details such as the type of view we are looking for.

Performing Actions

When we are running test cases, it becomes very common to perform user interaction on some views such as typing text in an edit text, clicking on a button, and so on. Espresso has provided `ViewInteraction.perform()` or `DataInteraction.perform()` methods, which are used to simulate such user interactions with the app's UI. These methods take one or more `ViewAction` objects as arguments. After the actions have been provided, Espresso then fires these actions in a sequence to the one that is provided. Espresso executes them in the main thread itself so as to simulate real action.

The ViewActions class also has a list of methods which can be used to perform certain actions. The methods specifies such actions as follows:

- `ViewActions.click()`: This clicks on the view.
- `ViewActions.typeText()`: This clicks on a view and enters a specified string.
- `ViewActions.scrollTo()`: This scrolls the view. The target view must be subclassed from ScrollView and the value of its `android:visibilityproperty` must be `VISIBLE`. For views that extend AdapterView (for example, ListView), the `onData()` method takes care of scrolling for you.
- `ViewActions.pressKey()`: This performs a key press using a specified keycode.
- `ViewActions.clearText()`: This clears the text in the target view.

If the target view is inside a ScrollView, perform the `ViewActions.scrollTo()` action first to display the view in the screen before other proceeding with other actions. The `ViewActions.scrollTo()` action will have no effect if the view is already displayed. An example code with the preceding mentioned capabilities are as follows:

```
@LargeTest
@RunWith(AndroidJUnit4.class)
public class SplashActivityTest {
@Rule
public ActivityTestRule<SplashActivity> mActivityTestRule = new
ActivityTestRule<>(SplashActivity.class);
@Test
public void splashActivityTest() {
// Added a sleep statement to match the app's execution delay.
try {
Thread.sleep(10000);
} catch (InterruptedException e) {
e.printStackTrace();
}
ViewInteraction appCompatTextView = onView(
allOf(withText("SKIP"), isDisplayed()));
appCompatTextView.perform(click());
try {
Thread.sleep(10000);
} catch (InterruptedException e) {
e.printStackTrace();
}
ViewInteraction linearLayout = onView(
allOf(withId(R.id.browseNearby), isDisplayed()));
linearLayout.perform(click());
// Added a sleep statement to match the app's execution delay.
try {
Thread.sleep(10000);
} catch (InterruptedException e) {
e.printStackTrace();
}
ViewInteraction tintableImageView = onView(
allOf(withClassName(is("com.androcid.zomato.view.custom.TintableImageV
ew")), isDisplayed()));
tintableImageView.perform(click());
// Added a sleep statement to match the app's execution delay.
try {
Thread.sleep(10000);
} catch (InterruptedException e) {
e.printStackTrace();
}
ViewInteraction linearLayout2 = onView(
```

```
allOf(withId(R.id.bottom_menu_collection),
withParent(withId(R.id.bottomBar)),
isDisplayed()));
linearLayout2.perform(click());
// Added a sleep statement to match the app's execution delay.
try {
Thread.sleep(10000);
} catch (InterruptedException e) {
e.printStackTrace();
}
ViewInteraction linearLayout3 = onView(
allOf(withId(R.id.bottom_menu_feed),
withParent(withId(R.id.bottomBar)),
isDisplayed()));
linearLayout3.perform(click());
// Added a sleep statement to match the app's execution delay.
try {
Thread.sleep(10000);
} catch (InterruptedException e) {
e.printStackTrace();
}
ViewInteraction linearLayout4 = onView(
allOf(withId(R.id.bottom_menu_account),
withParent(withId(R.id.bottomBar)),
isDisplayed()));
linearLayout4.perform(click());
}
}
```

In the preceding example, we are traversing within the app performing clicks, which will lead the users to a new screen with each click. If the view is not found at any of the instances, then the test case will fail.

The flow of the screens is as shown in the following figure:

Test your activities in isolation with Espresso Intents

Espresso Intents helps us to validate intents sent out by an app. With Espresso Intents, you can test an app, activity, or service in isolation by capturing outgoing intents, stubbing the result, and sending it back to the component under test.

To begin testing with Espresso Intents, you need to add the following line to your app's build.gradle file:

```
dependencies {
androidTestCompile 'com.android.support.test.espresso:espresso-
intents:2.2.2'
}
```

To test an intent, you need to create an instance of the `IntentsTestRule` class, which is very similar to the `ActivityTestRule` class. The `IntentsTestRule` class initializes Espresso Intents before each test, terminates the host activity, and releases Espresso Intents after each test.

Testing WebViews with Espresso Web

Espresso Web allows you to test WebView components contained within an activity. It uses the WebDriver API to inspect and control the behavior of a WebView.

To begin testing with Espresso Web, you need to add the following line to your app's build.gradle file:

```
dependencies {
// Other dependencies ...
androidTestCompile 'com.android.support.test.espresso:espresso-web:2.2.2'
}
```

When creating a test using Espresso Web, you need to enable JavaScript on the `WebView` when you instantiate the `ActivityTestRule` object to test the activity. In the tests, you can select HTML elements displayed in the `WebView` and simulate user interactions, such as entering text into a `textbox` and then clicking on a button. After the actions are completed, you can then verify that the results on the Web page match the results that you expect.

Verifying Results

To verify/check whether the final result of the UI we can use the `ViewInteraction.check()` or `DataInteraction.check()` method, to compare them with some expected state.

We have to pass in a `ViewAssertion` object as the argument. If the assertion fails, Espresso throws `AssertionFailedError`.

The `ViewAssertions` class provides a list of helper methods for specifying common assertions. The assertions you can use include:

- `doesNotExist`: This asserts that there is no view matching the specified criteria in the current view hierarchy.
- `matches`: This asserts that the specified view exists in the current view hierarchy and its state matches some given Hamcrest matcher.
- `selectedDescendentsMatch`: This asserts that the specified children views for a parent view exist, and their state matches some given Hamcrest matcher.

The following is a simple example of how the test can be written to use the preceding conditions:

```
@LargeTest
@RunWith(AndroidJUnit4.class)
public class SimpleIntentTest {
private static final String MESSAGE = "St Inez";
/* Instantiate an IntentsTestRule object. */
@Rule
public IntentsTestRule<HomeActivity> mIntentsRule =
```

```
new IntentsTestRule<>(HomeActivity.class);@Test
public void verifyMessageSentToMessageActivity() {
ViewInteraction appCompatTextView2 = onView(
allOf(withId(R.id.subtitle), withText("NEARBY"), isDisplayed()));
appCompatTextView2.perform(click());
// Types a message into a EditText element.
onView(withId(R.id.searchText))
.perform(typeText(MESSAGE), closeSoftKeyboard());
onView(withId(R.id.submit)).perform(click());
// Verifies that the DisplayMessageActivity received an intent
// with the correct package name and message.
// Check that the text was changed.
onView(withId(R.id.subtitle))
.check(matches(withText(MESSAGE)));
}
}
```

Testing UI for Multiple Apps

It is very rare that your app will not make use of some other apps in your phone or some of the system apps present on your device. Hence, testing of such cases where your app has to open another app, make use of that app, and come back, involves some more serious testing. These test cases have to verify that the interactions happening across the other apps are as expected.

When your app has interactions with other apps, it has to first call the other app from your app, open the other app, and see if that app displays the expected behavior, that your app wants it to do, and finally get the response from that other app, if required. If there is a response that is returned from the other app, then it has to be verified and checked if it is as expected by your app.

There could be two examples that I would give. The first in which your app does not require any response back, and the second in which the response is required. An example of a case where a response is required is when your app needs to use another app, such as camera or gallery. We shall take an example of gallery app. Here, your app will require to open the gallery, view all the gallery images, files, videos, and so on, as per your requirement, and then use one or multiple images, files, and so on from gallery into your app and display.

Another example is mail app that lets the user enter a subject, message, and recipients, and launch the mail sending screen and send the mail to all recipients and then returns control to the original app.

Such UI tests which involve using of multiple apps could be done using the UI Automator testing framework provided by the Android Testing Support Library. The UI Automator APIs allows you to interact with visible elements on a device, regardless of which Activity is in focus. The test case can check a specific UI component by using descriptors such as the text displayed. UI Automator tests can run on devices running Android 4.3 (API level 18) or higher.

The UI Automator testing framework is an instrumentation-based API and works with theAndroidJUnitRunner test runner.

Set Up the UI Automator

To setup the UI Automator we have to add the dependency in the build.gradle file of the app module:

```
dependencies {
androidTestCompile 'com.android.support.test.uiautomator:uiautomator-
v18:2.1.1'
}
```

To optimize your UI Automator testing, you should first inspect the target app's UI components and ensure that they are accessible. These optimization tips are described in the next two sections.

Inspecting the UI on a device

We have to make sure that all the UI components, which we are going to be testing are visible on the device. We also make sure that the UI Automator can access these UI components. In order to check that, add the contentDescription line in your XML code:

```
android:contentDescription
```

This line makes sure that the UI components to be tested will have some visible texts for all the labels.

We can use the uiautomatorviewer tool, which provides a visual interface that can be used to inspect the hierarchy of the layout and the properties of a view in the UI components that are visible on the device. For example, you can create a UI selector that matches a specific visible property:

1. To launch the uiautomatorviewer tool:
2. Open your app on an actual device.

3. Then, connect that device to your development machine.
4. Open a terminal window and navigate to the `<android-sdk>/tools/` directory.

Run the tool with this command: $ `uiautomatorviewer`

To view the UI properties for your application:

1. Click on the Device Screenshot button.in the `uiautomatorviewer` interface.
2. Then, hover over the snapshot in the left-hand panel to see the UI components identified by the `uiautomatorviewer` tool. The properties are listed in the lower right-hand panel and the layout hierarchy in the upper right-hand panel.
3. Optionally, click on the Toggle NAF Nodes button to see UI components that are non-accessible to the UI Automator. Only limited information may be available for these components.

Ensuring your Activity is accessible

Make sure that your activities are accessible to the UI Automator test framework. When the Android accessibility features are present or have been used in your app, the UI Automator works, and performs best. For instance, using View, or a subclass of View from the SDK or Support Library, there is no need to separately implement accessibility support.

But, many apps have custom UI elements to provide a better UI for their app. For such kind of apps, the UI Automator would not provide automatic accessibility. You need to explicitly add accessibility for such UI components in the app.
If your app contains instances of a subclass of View that isn't from the SDK or Support Library, you have to make sure that you add accessibility features to these elements by completing the following steps:

1. Create a concrete class that extends `ExploreByTouchHelper`.
2. Associate an instance of your new class with a specific custom UI element by calling `setAccessibilityDelegate()`.

The following code snippet shows a test which would be getting an instance of UI Device and simulate the press of the Home Button on the device:

```
@RunWith(AndroidJUnit4.class)
@SdkSuppress(minSdkVersion = 18)
public class ChangeTextBehaviorTest {
private static final String BASIC_SAMPLE_PACKAGE
= "com.androcid.zomato";
private static final int LAUNCH_TIMEOUT = 5000;
```

```
private static final String STRING_TO_BE_TYPED = "UiAutomator";
private UiDevice mDevice;
@Before
public void startMainActivityFromHomeScreen() {
// Initialize UiDevice instance
mDevice =
UiDevice.getInstance(InstrumentationRegistry.getInstrumentation());
// Start from the home screen
mDevice.pressHome();
// Wait for launcher
final String launcherPackage = mDevice.getLauncherPackageName();
Assert.assertThat(launcherPackage, CoreMatchers.notNullValue());
mDevice.wait(Until.hasObject(By.pkg(launcherPackage).depth(0)),
LAUNCH_TIMEOUT);
// Launch the app
Context context = InstrumentationRegistry.getContext();
final Intent intent = context.getPackageManager()
.getLaunchIntentForPackage(BASIC_SAMPLE_PACKAGE);
// Clear out any previous instances
intent.addFlags(Intent.FLAG_ACTIVITY_CLEAR_TASK);
context.startActivity(intent);
// Wait for the app to appear
Device.wait(Until.hasObject(By.pkg(BASIC_SAMPLE_PACKAGE).depth(0)),
LAUNCH_TIMEOUT);
}
}
```

The preceding example code would work only on devices with Android API level 18 and higher. To make sure that this condition is satisfied, the following line in the code does that for you:

```
@SdkSuppress(minSdkVersion = 18)
```

This is as required by the UI Automator framework.

The `findObject()` method is used to retrieve `UiObject` which represents a view that matches a given selector criteria.

We can reuse the instances of UiObject that have been created in other parts of testing, as needed.

Note that the UI Automator test framework searches the current display for a match every time your test uses a `UiObject` instance to click on a UI element or query a property.

The following snippet shows how your test might construct `UiObject` instances that represent a Skip button in an app:

```
UiObject skipButton = mDevice.findObject(new UiSelector()
.text("SKIP").className("android.widget.TextView"));
// Simulate a user-click on the OK button, if found.
try {
if (skipButton.exists() && skipButton.isEnabled()) {
skipButton.click();
}
} catch (UiObjectNotFoundException e) {
e.printStackTrace();
}
```

Selector Specification

The UiSelector class has multiple UI elements that can be used to display the UI components in an app. It has a query for each element in the displayed UI on the target device. Using these matching elements, we can identify each of the UI components. If more than one element if found that is matching, the element if selected which is first found by the class in the layout file.

Multiple UI Selector properties could be chained together to find the correct UI component in the layout. Even after using all the multiple properties, if the UI component is not found, then a `UiAutomatorObjectNotFoundException` exception is thrown by the class which could be used to handle error cases.

The `childSelector()` method is used to nest multiple UiSelector instances. For instance, if you need to find a `ListView` component from the layout in a currently displayed UI, then you would need to use multiple properties to find that component as seen in the code here:

```
UiObject appItem = new UiObject(new UiSelector()
.className("android.widget.ListView")
.instance(1)
.childSelector(new UiSelector()
.text("Apps")));
```

Using a Resource ID instead of using a text element or content Descriptor proves to be more helpful when specifying a selector. The resource ID has to be used wherever possible, as they have many advantages:

- Not all elements have a text element (for example, icons in a toolbar).
- Text selectors can lead to test failures if there are some minor changes to the UI, but using resource ID would not affect any changes.

- Using a resource ID could be used across multiple languages but a text element may not scale across different languages.
- Also, your text selectors may not match translated strings.
- It can be useful to specify the object state in your selector criteria.

The `checked()` method: If you want to select a list of all checked elements so that you can uncheck them, call this method with the argument set to true.

Performing Actions

The UiObject class has multiple methods, which could be used to perform user interactions on the UI component.
The methods of the class are as follows:

- `click()`: This clicks on the center of the visible bounds of the UI element.
- `dragTo()`: This drags this object to arbitrary coordinates.
- `setText()`: This sets the text in an editable field, after clearing the field's content. Conversely, the `clearTextField()` method clears the existing text in an editable field.
- `swipeUp()`: This performs the swipe up action on UiObject. Similarly, the `swipeDown()`, `swipeLeft()`, and `swipeRight()` methods perform corresponding actions.

Tools and Techniques: Espresso and Monkeyrunner

Testing becomes an important part of the development life cycle. As seen, automation testing becomes an important component of the cycle. Hence, it is a necessary to have good automation testing tools.

There are many tools that can be used for automation testing for the UI in Android.

Espresso, Monkeyrunner, and Robotium are some of them.

Robotium

Robotium is an open source library that extends JUnit. It has many methods that can be used for Android UI testing. It provides powerful and robust automatic black-box test cases for Android apps (native and hybrid) and web testing. With Robotium, you can write function, system, and acceptance test scenarios, and test applications where the source code is available.

Robotium recorder is a tool which helps in writing robotium test classes. It can record all the user interactions that have been made by the user on the app and create a test class, which can be used to perform the test.

To start writing the test classes with Robotium, we first have to add the dependencies into the `build.gradle` file:

```
dependencies {
androidTestCompile 'com.jayway.android.robotium:robotium-solo:5.6.3'
}
```

After the dependencies have been synced with the app, we can start writing the test classes.

Here is a basic example of Robotium:

```
public class RobotiumTest1 extends
ActivityInstrumentationTestCase2<SplashActivity> {
private Solo solo;
public RobotiumTest1() {
super(SplashActivity.class);
}
public void setUp() throws Exception {
super.setUp();
solo = new Solo(getInstrumentation());
getActivity();
}
@Override
public void tearDown() throws Exception {
solo.finishOpenedActivities();
super.tearDown();
}
public void testRun() {
//Wait for activity: 'com.androcid.zomato.activity.SplashActivity'
solo.waitForActivity(com.androcid.zomato.activity.SplashActivity.class,
2000);
//Wait for activity: 'com.androcid.zomato.activity.login.StartActivity'
assertTrue("com.androcid.zomato.activity.login.StartActivity is not
found!",
solo.waitForActivity(com.androcid.zomato.activity.login.StartActivity.class
```

```
));
//Click on SKIP
solo.clickOnText(java.util.regex.Pattern.quote("SKIP"));
//Wait for activity: 'com.androcid.zomato.activity.HomeActivity'
assertTrue("com.androcid.zomato.activity.HomeActivity is not found!",
solo.waitForActivity(com.androcid.zomato.activity.HomeActivity.class));
//Click on NEARBY St Inez, Panaji, Goa
solo.clickOnText(java.util.regex.Pattern.quote("NEARBY"));
//Wait for activity: 'com.androcid.zomato.activity.SelectLocationActivity'
assertTrue("com.androcid.zomato.activity.SelectLocationActivity is not
found!",
solo.waitForActivity(com.androcid.zomato.activity.SelectLocationActivity.cl
ass));
//Click on Empty Text View
solo.clickOnView(solo.getView(com.androcid.zomato.R.id.searchText));
//Enter the text: 'pa'
solo.clearEditText((android.widget.EditText)
solo.getView(com.androcid.zomato.R.id.searchText));
solo.enterText((android.widget.EditText)
solo.getView(com.androcid.zomato.R.id.searchText), "pa");
//Click on Collection
solo.clickOnView(solo.getView(com.androcid.zomato.view.custom.TintableImage
View.class, 1));
Timeout.setSmallTimeout(5000);
//Click on Collection
solo.clickOnView(solo.getView(com.androcid.zomato.R.id.bottom_menu_collecti
on));
//Wait for activity:
'com.androcid.zomato.activity.collection.CollectionActivity'
assertTrue("com.androcid.zomato.activity.collection.CollectionActivity is
not found!",
solo.waitForActivity(com.androcid.zomato.activity.collection.CollectionActi
vity.class));
//Set default small timeout to 14750 milliseconds
Timeout.setSmallTimeout(14750);
//Click on Feed
solo.clickOnView(solo.getView(com.androcid.zomato.R.id.bottom_menu_feed,
1));
//Wait for activity: 'com.androcid.zomato.activity.FeedActivity'
assertTrue("com.androcid.zomato.activity.FeedActivity is not found!",
solo.waitForActivity(com.androcid.zomato.activity.FeedActivity.class));
//Click on Account
solo.clickOnView(solo.getView(com.androcid.zomato.R.id.bottom_menu_account,
1));
//Wait for activity:
'com.androcid.zomato.activity.AccountActivity'assertTrue("com.androcid.zoma
to.activity.AccountActivity is not found!",
solo.waitForActivity(com.androcid.zomato.activity.AccountActivity.class));
```

```
//Click on Home
solo.clickOnView(solo.getView(com.androcid.zomato.R.id.bottom_menu_home,
1));
//Click on RelativeLayout Barbeque Nation Panaji, Goa Best dine out
experience ever!
solo.clickInRecyclerView(0, 0);
//Wait for activity: 'com.androcid.zomato.activity.PlaceDetailActivity'
assertTrue("com.androcid.zomato.activity.PlaceDetailActivity is not
found!",
solo.waitForActivity(com.androcid.zomato.activity.PlaceDetailActivity.class
));
}
}
```

The UI Animator

The UI Animator is a tool that can be used to test the Android app. The UI animator framework allows you to test the UI of your native Android apps on one or more devices. Another advantage of uiautomator is that it runs JUnit test cases with special privileges, which means test cases can span across different processes. It also provides five different classes for developers to use, including:

- com.android.uiautomator.core.UiCollection;
- com.android.uiautomator.core.UiDevice;
- com.android.uiautomator.core.UiObject;
- com.android.uiautomator.core.UiScrollable;
- com.android.uiautomator.core.UiSelector

The UI Animator only works on Android devices with API level 16 or higher. Another downside of uiautomator is that it doesn't support webview, with no way to directly access Android objects.

To start using the UI Animator for testing, we must first add the following dependencies into the build.gradle file:

```
dependencies {
androidTestCompile 'com.android.support.test.uiautomator:uiautomator-
v18:2.1.1'
}
A basic example of the use of the UI animator is given here:
@RunWith(AndroidJUnit4.class)
@SdkSuppress(minSdkVersion = 18)
public class UIAnimatorTest {private static final String
```

```
BASIC_SAMPLE_PACKAGE= "com.androcid.zomato";
private static final int LAUNCH_TIMEOUT = 5000;
private static final String STRING_TO_BE_TYPED = "UiAutomator";
private UiDevice mDevice;
@Before
public void startMainActivityFromHomeScreen() {
// Initialize UiDevice instance
mDevice =
UiDevice.getInstance(InstrumentationRegistry.getInstrumentation());
// Start from the home screen
mDevice.pressHome();
// Wait for launcher
final String launcherPackage = mDevice.getLauncherPackageName();
Assert.assertThat(launcherPackage, CoreMatchers.notNullValue());
mDevice.wait(Until.hasObject(By.pkg(launcherPackage).depth(0)),
LAUNCH_TIMEOUT);
// Launch the app
Context context = InstrumentationRegistry.getContext();
final Intent intent =
context.getPackageManager().getLaunchIntentForPackage(BASIC_SAMPLE_PACKAGE)
;
// Clear out any previous instances
intent.addFlags(Intent.FLAG_ACTIVITY_CLEAR_TASK);
context.startActivity(intent);
// Wait for the app to appear
mDevice.wait(Until.hasObject(By.pkg(BASIC_SAMPLE_PACKAGE).depth(0)),
LAUNCH_TIMEOUT);
}
@Test
public void checkPreconditions() {
assertThat(mDevice, notNullValue());
}
@Test
public void testChangeText_sameActivity() {
UiObject skipButton = mDevice.findObject(new UiSelector()
.text("SKIP").className("android.widget.TextView"));
// Simulate a user-click on the OK button, if found.
try {
if (skipButton.exists() && skipButton.isEnabled()) {
skipButton.click();
}
} catch (UiObjectNotFoundException e) {
e.printStackTrace();
}
}
@Test
public void testChangeText_newActivity() {
// Type text and then press the button.
```

```
mDevice.findObject(By.res(BASIC_SAMPLE_PACKAGE, "editTextUserInput"))
.setText(STRING_TO_BE_TYPED);
mDevice.findObject(By.res(BASIC_SAMPLE_PACKAGE, "activityChangeTextBtn"))
.click();
// Verify the test is displayed in the Ui
UiObject2 changedText = mDevice
.wait(Until.findObject(By.res(BASIC_SAMPLE_PACKAGE, "show_text_view")),
500 /* wait 500ms */);
assertThat(changedText.getText(), is(equalTo(STRING_TO_BE_TYPED)));
}
}
```

From the preceding test class, we demonstrated how we can check whether the UI that was intended to be used exists or is enabled using the `.exists()` and `.isEnabled()` methods, and we performed actions on the view using the `.click()` method.

Espresso

Espresso is a testing framework that has many APIs that can be used to perform UI testing of Android apps. With the latest 2.0 release, it has now become a part of the Android Support Repository, which makes it easier to create automated testing support for your project. It is supported from the API level 8 and above. It's quite reliable, synchronizing with the UI thread, and it's fast because there is no need for any sleeps (tests run on same millisecond when an app becomes idle).

To add Espresso in the app, we have to add the following dependencies into the app module's build.gradle file:

```
dependencies {
androidTestCompile 'com.android.support.test.espresso:espresso-core:2.2.2'
}
Here is a simple example of how to write the Test classes with Espresso:
@LargeTest
@RunWith(AndroidJUnit4.class)
public class SplashActivityTest {
@Rule
public ActivityTestRule<SplashActivity> mActivityTestRule = new
ActivityTestRule<>(SplashActivity.class);
@Test
public void splashActivityTest() {
// Added a sleep statement to match the app's execution delay.
// The recommended way to handle such scenarios is to use Espresso idling
resources:
//
https://google.github.io/android-testing-support-library/docs/espresso/idli
```

```
ng-resource/index.html
try {
Thread.sleep(10000);
} catch (InterruptedException e) {
e.printStackTrace();
}
ViewInteraction appCompatTextView = onView(
allOf(withText("SKIP"), isDisplayed()));
appCompatTextView.perform(click());
// Added a sleep statement to match the app's execution delay.
try {
Thread.sleep(10000);
} catch (InterruptedException e) {
e.printStackTrace();
}
ViewInteraction linearLayout = onView(
allOf(withId(R.id.browseNearby), isDisplayed()));
linearLayout.perform(click());
// Added a sleep statement to match the app's execution delay.
try {
Thread.sleep(10000);
} catch (InterruptedException e) {
e.printStackTrace();
}
ViewInteraction tintableImageView = onView(
allOf(withClassName(is("com.androcid.zomato.view.custom.TintableImageV
ew")), isDisplayed()));
tintableImageView.perform(click());
// Added a sleep statement to match the app's execution delay.
try {
Thread.sleep(10000);
} catch (InterruptedException e) {
e.printStackTrace();
}
ViewInteraction linearLayout2 = onView(
allOf(withId(R.id.bottom_menu_collection),
withParent(withId(R.id.bottomBar)),
isDisplayed()));
linearLayout2.perform(click());
// Added a sleep statement to match the app's execution delay.
try {
Thread.sleep(10000);
} catch (InterruptedException e) {
e.printStackTrace();
}
ViewInteraction linearLayout3 = onView(
allOf(withId(R.id.bottom_menu_feed),
withParent(withId(R.id.bottomBar)),
```

```
isDisplayed()));
linearLayout3.perform(click());
// Added a sleep statement to match the app's execution delay.
try {
Thread.sleep(10000);
} catch (InterruptedException e) {
e.printStackTrace();
}
ViewInteraction linearLayout4 = onView(
allOf(withId(R.id.bottom_menu_account),
withParent(withId(R.id.bottomBar)),
isDisplayed()));
linearLayout4.perform(click());
}
@LargeTest
@RunWith(AndroidJUnit4.class)
public class SimpleIntentTest {
private static final String MESSAGE = "St Inez";
/* Instantiate an IntentsTestRule object. */
@Rule
public IntentsTestRule<HomeActivity> mIntentsRule =
new IntentsTestRule<>(HomeActivity.class);
@Test
public void verifyMessageSentToMessageActivity() {
ViewInteraction appCompatTextView2 = onView(
allOf(withId(R.id.subtitle), withText("NEARBY"), isDisplayed()));
appCompatTextView2.perform(click());
// Types a message into a EditText element.
onView(withId(R.id.searchText))
.perform(typeText(MESSAGE), closeSoftKeyboard());
//onView(withId(R.id.submit)).perform(click());
// Verifies that the DisplayMessageActivity received an intent
// with the correct package name and message.
// Check that the text was changed.
onView(withId(R.id.subtitle))
.check(matches(withText(MESSAGE)));
}
}
}
```

Monkeyrunner

Monkeyrunner is a testing tool that has been designed to test applications on devices at a functional level and also for running unit test cases. This framework has been designed in Python so that all the cases have to be written in Python; the framework can control the Android device or an Android Emulator by writing codes in Python. It does not require the Android code to control the device.

Monkeyrunner has its APIs, which could be used to install an Android app on a device and take user input. It could also take the screenshot of the device and save the screenshots in its workstation.

In order to run the monkeyrunner, it has a tool which is also known as the monkey tool. The monkey tool runs in an adb shell directly on the device or emulator and generates pseudo-random streams of user and system events. The monkeyrunner tool controls devices and emulators from a workstation by sending specific commands and events from an API.

The monkeyrunner tool provides the following features for Android testing:

- **Multiple device control:** The Monkeyrunner API can run across multiple devices at the same time. The same test cases could be tested on multiple emulators or devices that are connected when test cases are running. The devices have to be attached physically at once but the code has to connect each device separately and then run the test at once on all devices.
- **Functional testing:** The Monkeyrunner can do an automated test of an entire Android application. The inputs could be provided, while testing using keystrokes or touch events. Then, monkeyrunner will provide you with screenshots of the results.
- **Regression testing:** The Monkeyrunner can do the regression testing in an automated fashion by comparing the resulting screenshots of a test case with some reference screenshots that are correct.
- **Extensible automation:** The Monkeyrunner can be used for controlling any Android device using the extensive range of APIs that are provided by the Monkeyrunner API toolkit. It can also be called from the standard Python OS and subprocess modules to call Android tools in turn, such as Android Debug Bridge. Your own classes can also be added to the monkeyrunner API.

An implementation of Python that uses the Java programming language, Jython, allows the monkeyrunner API to interact with the Android framework. In Jython, the Python syntax itself can be used to access constants, classes, and methods of the API.

An example code sample of a Jython program is shown here:

```
from com.android.monkeyrunner
 import MonkeyRunner, MonkeyDevice

device = MonkeyRunner.waitForConnection()

device.installPackage('ZomatoProject/bin/Zomato.apk')

package = 'com.android.zomato'

activity = 'com.android.zomato.MainActivity'

runComponent = package + '/' + activity

device.startActivity(component=runComponent)

result = device.takeSnapshot()

result.writeToFile('ZomatoProject/screenshot1.png','png')
```

The preceding Python program connects to an Android device, installs the apk, and then takes a screenshot of the device and saves.

First it waits for a connection to the device using the following:

```
device = MonkeyRunner.waitForConnection()
```

Then, it installs the Zomato apk as follows:

```
device.installPackage('ZomatoProject/bin/Zomato.apk')
```

This is the activity which needs to start. It appends the package with the activity and starts that component:

```
activity = 'com.android.zomato.MainActivity'
 runComponent = package + '/' + activity
 device.startActivity(component=runComponent)
```

Here, it takes a snapshot of the device: `result = device.takeSnapshot()`

It then saves it in a file in the workstation:
`result.writeToFile('ZomatoProject/screenshot1.png','png')`

- **Monkeyrunner API:** The Monkeyrunner API is contained in three modules in the package com.android.monkeyrunner.
- **MonkeyRunner:** The MonkeyRunner class has utility methods for running monkeyrunner programs. It has methods for connecting monkeyrunner to a device or emulator and for creating UIs for a monkeyrunner program.
- **MonkeyDevice:** This MonkeyDevice is the actual representation class of a device or an emulator. It has methods for installing and uninstalling packages, starting an activity, sending keyboard or touch events to an application and running test packages.
- **MonkeyImage:** This MonkeyImage class is used to take the screen capture image. It has methods for capturing screens, converting bitmap images to various formats, comparing two MonkeyImage objects, and writing an image to a file.
- **Access monkeyrunner classes:** All the classes from the MonkeyRunner APIs have to be imported into the code manually. The monkeyrunner tool does not import these modules automatically. To import a module using the Python from statement:

```
from com.android.monkeyrunner import <module>
```

Here, `<module>` is the classname you want to import. You can import more than one module in the same from statement by separating the module names with commas.

- **Running monkeyrunner:** The `MonkeyRunner` programs can be run from a file, or interactively by entering `monkeyrunner` statements. The `monkeyrunner` tool is found in the tools/subdirectory of your SDK directory.

The syntax of the monkeyrunner command is as follows:

```
monkeyrunner -plugin <plugin_jar><program_filename><program_options>
```

Supported on	Robotium	UI Animator	Espresso
Android	Yes	Yes	Yes
iOS	No	No	No
Scripting Language	Java	Java	Java
Creation Tools	Robotium Recorder	UI Animator Viewer	Espresso Test Recorder
Supported API levels	All	16 and greater	8 and greater

Summary

We started the section leaning about how the testing is done in Android Apps and glancing through some of the general concepts of testing. These topics were followed by several Android development testing support tools that allow us to test Android apps more effectively, including UI Animator, Espresso, and Monkeyrunner.

Moving ahead, we will be discussing some the performance strategies that can be implemented in the Android app. Some of the key elements under consideration will be memory, battery, and data optimization.

Mobile App testing needs a careful process of implementation. Starting small, this process can progress into several large forms of execution. As per the Qualcomm Band Tracker, battery life is something people look for in a phone, and on an average, 11 apps are installed on a smartphone. Your app has to undergo serious testing to be among the top 11.

In this chapter, we will highlight some of the major testing techniques to be followed in the development process.

15
Preparing for Google Play

When you are ready to release your application, you will need to configure, build, and test a release version of your application. The configuration task is simple; it involves basic code clean up and code modification tasks that may optimize the app. The build process is similar to the debug process, which can be accomplished by Java SE Development and Android SDK tools. Finally, the testing of the app in a real-world condition will ensure that the build functions as expected against the cases.

In the preceding section, we described several techniques to test the app. At this moment, we have the app that has already undergone testing. However, before we distribute this Android application, we need to prepare it for release. In this chapter, we will take a look at release preparation.

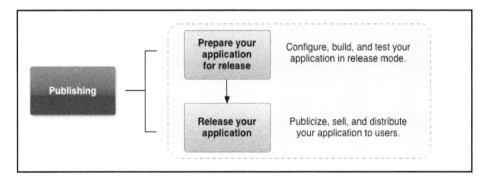

The publishing process (Source: Google)

Once we are done, we will need to prepare the application for the final release. In this process, we will generate a signed APK file, which can be used to distribute the app directly to the user, or can be published and distributed through an application marketplace, such as Google Play and Amazon Store.

Versioning Your App

Versioning of the app is a critical course of the app release, as it maintains information on app upgrades and maintenance strategy. When users install the app, it provides information on details of the version and what this particular version has to offer. This also applies for users who install updates of an app that is installed on their devices. Services through which you will publish your app will also need to display the version to users. The publishing service may also check the app version to determine compatibility and perform the upgrade/downgrade action accordingly. Since the Android System does not use app version information to enforce restrictions on upgrading, downgrading, or the compatibility of third party apps, the developer has to configure this setting. Using the `minSDKVersion` setting, you can allow an app to specify the minimum system API with which the app is compatible.

[PACKT] Defining the app version directly in the `<manifest>` element, the version values in the Gradle build file will override the settings in the manifest. Removing these version values from `<manifest>` will allow greater flexibility and potential overwriting when the manifest files are merged during the build process. Defining version settings in the Gradle build file instead helps to manage the build variations better.

You can define the values for the version settings in the Gradle build files. These values are then merged into the app's manifest file during the build process. Two settings are available, and you have to set both their values:

1. `versionCode`: An integer used as an internal version number. This just indicates that there is a new version of the app available other than the previous one, and this number is not shown to the user. Typically, the first version of the app is set as 1 and gets increments for subsequent releases. The greatest value Google Play allows for `versionCode` is `2100000000`.

2. `versionName`: A string value, which is typically the version number shown to the users. This can be defined as a raw string or a reference to a string resource.

   ```
   android {
   ...
   defaultConfig {
   ...
   versionCode 2
   versionName "1.1"
   }
   ```

In the preceding snippet, the `defaultConfig` block has two values, `versionCode` and `versionName`. `versionCode`'s value indicates that the current APK contains the second release of the app, and the `versionName` value of 1.1 indicates that it will appear to the users as version 1.1 after they install or upgrade it.

Now that we have set the `versionCode` and `versionName`, we can proceed to generate the build. In the next section, we will learn about generating a signed APK.

Generating a signed APK

The Android ecosystem requires that app APKs be digitally signed with a certificate before they can be installed on Android devices. Only after generating a signed APK, can we upload the APK on Google Play for people to install. This section will explain how to generate a signed APK using Android Studio. This section will also cover creating and storing your certifications. Android Studio allows you to manually generate the signed APKs, either one at a time or for multiple build variants at once.

Perform the following steps to generate the build using a manual sign procedure:

1. In Android Studio, click on **Build** | **Generate Signed APK** from the menu.
2. In the next section, select the **Module** you would like to release and click on **Next**:

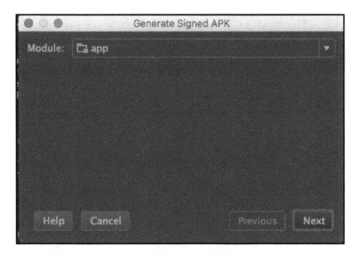

Selecting a build module

3. If you already have the Key store generated, you may proceed to select the **Choose existing** button and select the key from the specific path. Then, enter the Key store password, Key alias, and **Key password**. If you do not have the key, click on the **Create New** button:

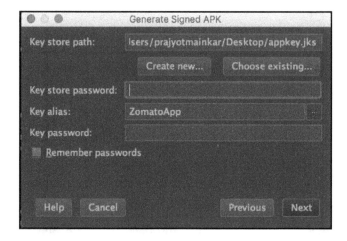

Generate signed APK

4. When you click on the **Create New** button, you will note the following option:

The New Key Store key generation

Key store path is the path where you want your key store to be generated. Ensure that the password is secure enough to protect the key. **Alias** is a name indicator of your key store. The **Validity** should be set in years and defines the period for which the key is valid. For example, selecting 25 years makes the key valid for 25 years, and you can sign app updates with the same key throughout the span of that period.

5. On the **Generate Signed APK** Wizard window, select a keystore and private key and enter the passwords for both.

6. Finally, set the APK generation folder along with the type of the build: **release** or **debug**:

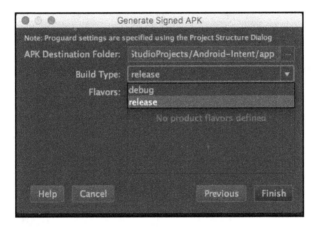

The generate signed APK final step

The following is a screenshot of the APK generation folder for Android Studio 2.3.3 (Windows):

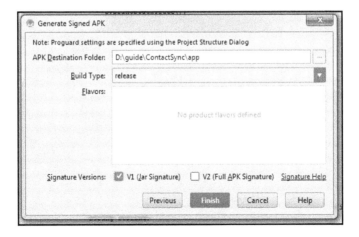

7. When the process is completed, the APK will be generated in the destination path you selected in the preceding step. This APK will be a *ready-to-publish* APK on publishing channels such as Google Play. In case you are making any changes to the app in the near future, the APK should be signed with the same certification throughout the lifespan of your app:

```
4:12:37 PM Executing tasks: [:app:assembleRelease]
4:13:09 PM Gradle build finished in 31s 737ms
4:13:09 PM Generate Signed APK
           APK(s) generated successfully.
           Reveal in Finder
```

The generate signed APK confirmation in Log

So far, we have discussed how to manually process the signed APK. In the next segment, we will discuss how to preconfigure the automatic generation of the signed APK.

Preconfiguring to automatically Sign Your APK

Android Studio allows you to configure your project in such a way that you can sign your release APK automatically during the build process, by creating a signing configuration and assigning it to your release build type. To create a signing configuration and assign it to your release build type, follow these steps:

1. In the Project window, right-click on your app and click on **Open Module Settings**:

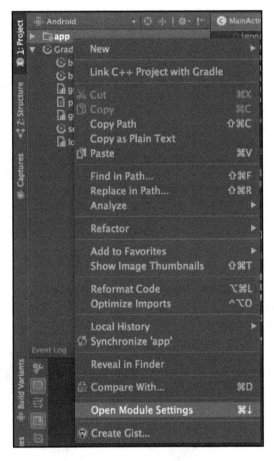

Pre Configuration of Automatic Signing Procedure

2. On the **Project Structure** window, under **Modules** in the left panel, select the module you would like to sign:

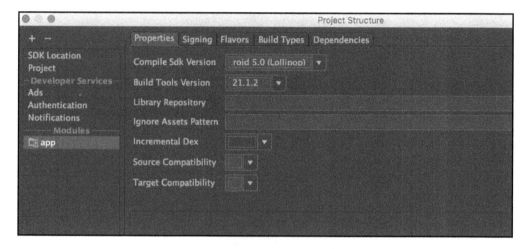

The preconfiguration of Automatic Signing Procedure

3. Next, click on the **Signing** tab and then click on add (+) to add a key.
4. Select your key store file, enter a name for this signing configuration, and enter the required information:

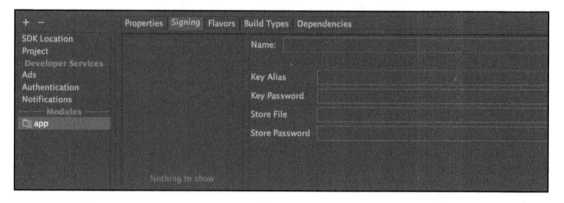

The preconfiguration of Automatic Signing Procedure

5. Under the **Build Types** tab, click on the **release** build. In the options list in Signing Config, select the signing configuration you just created.
6. Next, click on **OK**, and the setup is complete.

Now, every time you build your release build type using Android Studio, the IDE will sign the APK automatically, bypassing all the steps we did in the preceding Generating Signed APK section. This signing will happen based on the signing configuration you specified. You can find the signed APKs in the **build** | **outputs** | **apk** folder inside your project directory for the module you are building the signed APK for.

In the next segment, we will discuss how to upload the app for Beta Testing, wherein we will discuss how to set Alpha and Beta testers for the App.

Android Instant Apps

Sometimes, users need to experience the app before actually installing it on their device. That not only saves space and time but also makes users check out the app before they find it worthy of being installed on their device. With the same intention in mind, Google's Android team launched Android Instant Apps. This option can be seen under **Release Management** | **Android Instant Apps**, in the Google Play Developer Console:

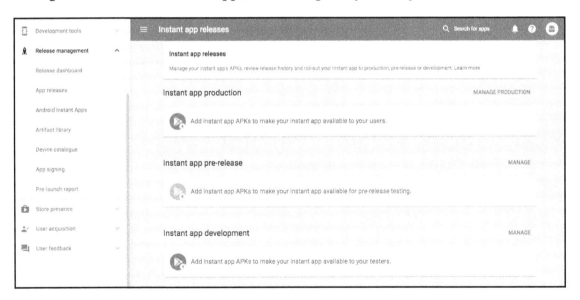

The support for Android Instant Apps begins from Android v6.0 (API Level 23) through Android O. This feature is available across more than 40 countries. The Android team is also looking to expand the support to Android v5.0 (API level 21) devices too.

As an app developer, you can add APKs for production release, pre-release testing or the managing development process during testing:

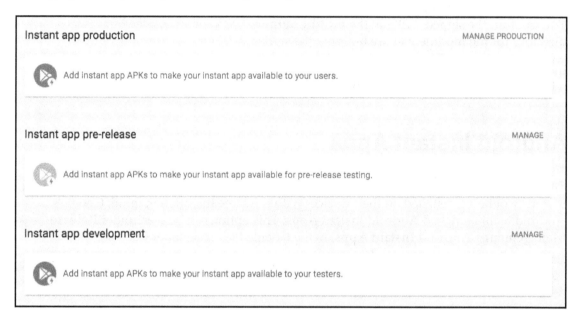

Android Instant Apps in Google Play Development Console

Alpha and Beta testing the App

The Google Play Developer Console will allow users to test the app, by giving them an opportunity to fix any technical glitches or user experience issues before the app goes live to a larger set of users. This approach sets a tone in releasing the right version to the users. One point to be noted here is that feedback from the test users does not affect your app's public rating.

Here are some key tips to keep in mind while engaging users to test:

1. Ensuring that the users join your tests requires that they have a Google account (@gmail.com) or G Suite account to join. To enable this, you will have to navigate to **Google Play Developer Console**, select the app you want in the left panel, select **Release Management | App Releases**. Here, you can select either the Alpha release or Beta release, depending on the step of testing you wish to proceed with. In either of the two cases, you can have Open Testing, Closed Group Testing, or Testing using Google Groups or Google+ communities. The following screenshot shows an example of Beta Testing. Consider Closed Testing if you want to run a test with a smaller group, whereas Open Testing should be considered if you want to run a test with a large group and surface your app's beta version on the Play Store. Under Closed Testing, the app developer can create a set of user's lists based on emails. Google Play testing can also be built around a Google+ community or Groups, which set a central place where you and your team can interact with your testers. The URL then can be shared with the testers, where they can click on **Become a Tester** option. This will allow them to install the app on their Android device:

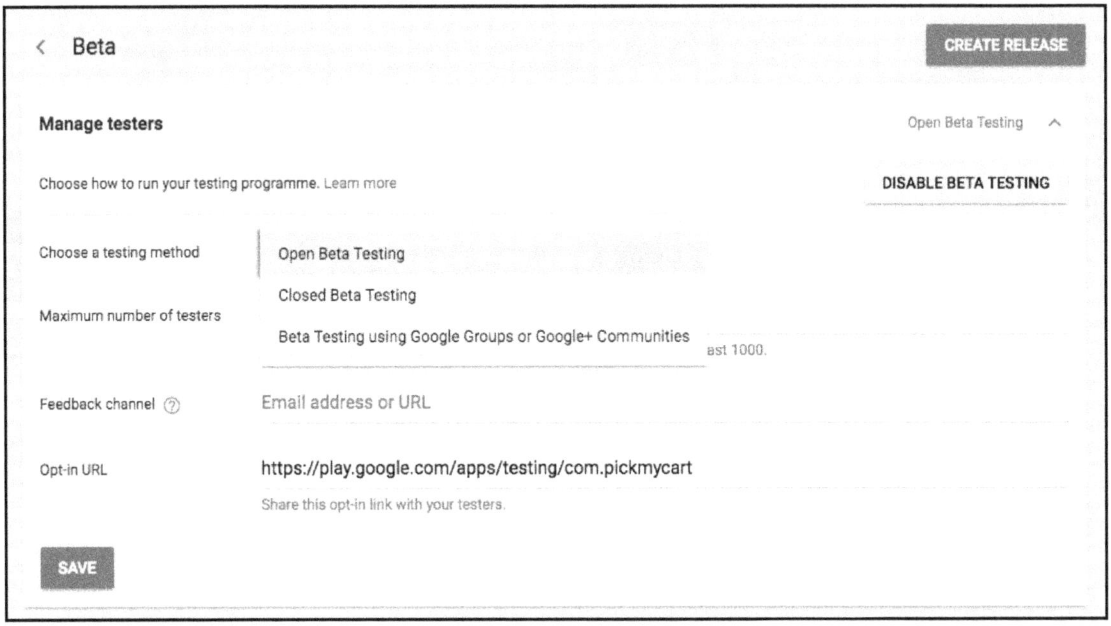

Beta testing

2. Keep an eye on the APK versions in testing. For an APK to be available to alpha testers, it must have a higher version number than your beta or production version, whereas in Beta testing, the APK must have a higher version number than your production version.

3. Ensure that you set up the Pricing And Distribution option for the app properly. Any changes to this section can affect your app's current and future production and its alpha and beta versions. To set this up, navigate to the **Store Presence** | **Pricing and Distribution** option. The following screenshot shows some of the setting options available. Under manage countries, users can select the countries where the app can be made available for download:

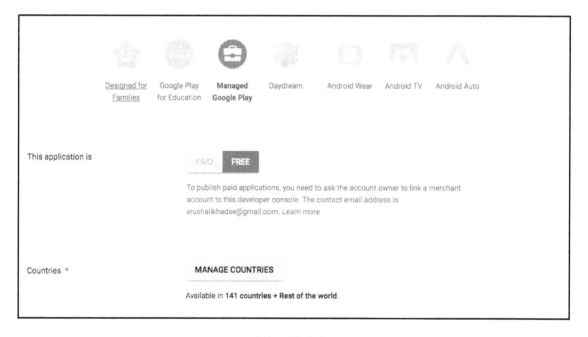

Pricing and distribution

4. One of the most useful features that this panel offers is how the App developers can limit distribution to specific operators within a country:

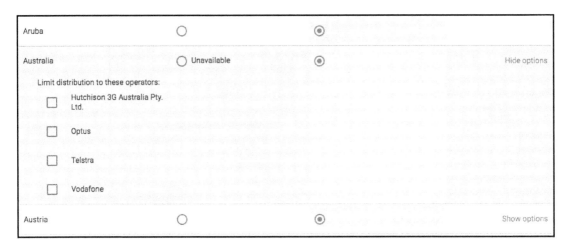

Carrier-based availability for the app

5. You can run a closed alpha and an open beta test on your app concurrently. However, one thing to be noted is that if you run an open alpha test, you can't use the open or closed beta track.

6. Choose to opt in for **Pre-Launch reports**. This is one of the best features Google allows in the Play Developer console. After you upload and publish an alpha or beta APK, the test devices will automatically launch and crawl your app for several minutes. This crawl will perform several basic actions every few seconds on your apps, such as typing, tapping, and swiping. Reports of the **pre-launch** will be available in the **Pre-launch** section of your Play Console. Using this feature, the developer can see screenshots from devices that use different Android versions, languages, and screen resolutions. This will help them to understand how the app looks on different devices. This report also helps to identify security issues found after scanning your app's APK file for a set of known vulnerabilities:

Pre-launch report

Would you like pre-launch testing to be performed on all your alpha & beta apps? Learn more

○ **Yes, activate pre-launch report testing**
⦿ **No**

Opt-in for the prelaunch report

Preparing App Store Listing

App Store Listing allows users to understand the kind and details of the app you have developed. Flaunting the title, descriptions, and images, this page is one of the most crucial one to tempt a user to download your app on their device:

Play Store Listing

Some of the most basic options include **Title**, **Short Description**, **Full Descriptions** and Graphic Assets for each of **Phones**, **Tablets**, **Wearables**, and **Android TV**:

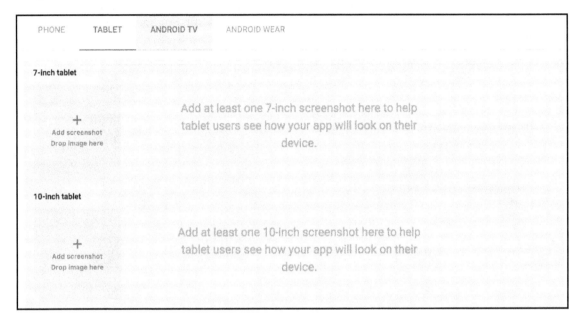

Graphical assets for the app

The developer can also select the application type and category based on the theme of the app. Google plays a crucial role in streamlining the content ratings for Apps and games on Google Play Store. Using the content rating system, one can communicate familiar and locally relevant content ratings to your users. This improves app engagements by targeting the right audience for your app's content:

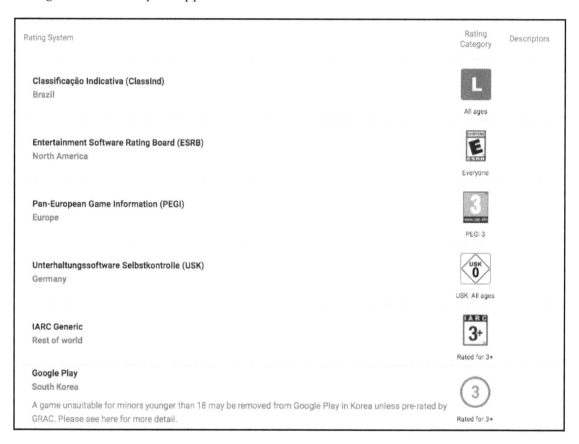

Rating System	Rating Category	Descriptors
Classificação Indicativa (ClassInd) Brazil	L All ages	
Entertainment Software Rating Board (ESRB) North America	E Everyone	
Pan-European Game Information (PEGI) Europe	3 PEGI 3	
Unterhaltungssoftware Selbstkontrolle (USK) Germany	USK 0 USK: All ages	
IARC Generic Rest of world	3+ Rated for 3+	
Google Play South Korea A game unsuitable for minors younger than 18 may be removed from Google Play in Korea unless pre-rated by GRAC. Please see here for more detail.	3 Rated for 3+	

Content rating for the app

Google also allows users to *Experiment* with your store listing. This is nothing but a feature to run an A/B test on your app's store listing page:

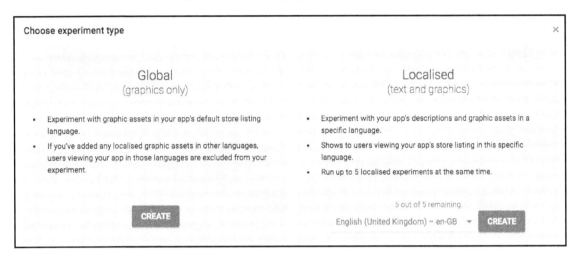

Google Play Store Experiments

You can either run global or localized Tests:

1. **Global Experiments**: You can experiment with graphics in your app's default store listing language. This enables developers to experiment with variants of their app's icons, features graphics, screenshots, and promo videos. If your app's store listing is only available in one language, this experiment page will be shown to all the users. However, in the case where the developers have added any localized graphic assets in a specific language and the app's default language is, say, English, the user's viewing in any other language will be excluded from the experiments.

2. **Localized**: Primarily intended for experimenting with text and graphics.Using this experiment option, you can experiment with your app's icons, feature graphics, screenshots, promotional videos, and/or your app's descriptions in up to five languages. In case the store listing is only available in one language, the default language will be the obvious choice.

Device Catalog

Device Catalog is one of the best features available in Google Play Developer Console. Once you upload at least one APK, this section allows you to view the catalog of available devices and review which of the available devices in the market are compatible with your app. These statistics allow you to prevent any app crashes that might occur on specific devices:

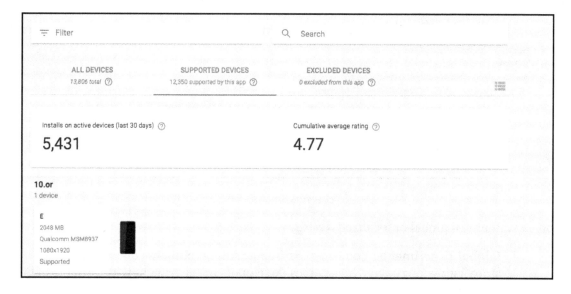

The device catalog

To understand the lists of included and excluded devices, perform the following steps:

1. Sign in to your Play Console and select the app.
2. On the left side of the page menu, click on **Release management** | **Device catalog**.
3. Select the **All**, **Supported**, and **Excluded** tabs.

To provide amazing experience to the end users, it is important that app developers review this section clearly to understand the supported and excluded devices.

App signing

Google has introduced a service called Google Play App Signing, which enabled developers to store their app signing keys on Google's server. This helps to prevent the risk of keys getting lost or maliciously destroyed or multiple apps using the same keys, as sometimes happens.

Once you hand over the keys to Google, it will help you keep them the same with a trust. Google will then sign your apps with your key on your behalf. Google ensures that your key gets encrypted using a tool before its transmission to their secure key handling server. This step takes place when you sign them with your new **Upload Key** and push them to play.

Note that once you agree to opt in for App Signing, it is a permanent change. You cannot withdraw or remove your keys from their cloud servers. It means that you would have to rerelease the app again separately if you want to opt out of this service.

Android Vitals

Poor app performance can badly impact how a user communicates with your app. Most of the one star-rated apps on Google Play suffer a lot of stability issues. If developers can take care of this aspect, not only will it improve the discoverability of the app but it can also help users to engage better with your app. Google launched a new section in the Google Play Developer Console that helps developers to understand their app's stability, battery usage, and render time on real devices.

Stability of the app depends on the following two factors:

Application Not Responding (**ANR**): ANR is one of the most annoying irritants that can easily frustrate any user. ANR occurs when a UI thread of an Android app is blocked for too long. If the app is running in the foreground, the system displays a dialog to the user with an option for the user to force quit the app. The ANR occurs mainly when one of the following conditions occurs:

- While your activity is in the foreground, your app fails to respond to an input event or `BroadcastReceiver` (such as key press or screen touch events) within the time frame of 5 seconds
- While you do not have an activity in the foreground, your `BroadcastReceiver` hasn't completed the execution within the stipulated amount of time

Handling ANRs are important, especially since one cares about retentions and bad reviews. Android Vitals has a provision to help developers to monitor when ANRs occur and report occurrences of the same.

Crash Rate: It is the best to tackle crashes before your app goes live to the masses. The best way to ensure stability is to run Pre-Launch reports on your app, which will test your alpha or beta apps on the physical devices so that you can identify and fix the issues before the app is launched. We will discuss pre-launch reports later in this chapter.

Android Vitals has a provision to show you the percentage of users experiencing crashes in your app. Statistically, it will show you the percentage of daily sessions during which your users experienced at least one crash on your app. A session here refers to a day during which your app was used.

When an app crashes, Android System terminates the app's process and displays a dialog to let the user know about this stoppage, as follows:

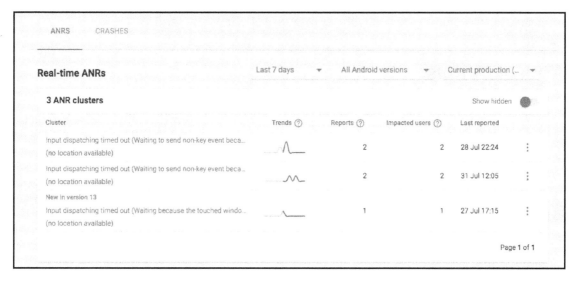

Real-time ANRs

Crashes are often caused due to several reasons such as unhandled exceptions, resource exhaustion, and other unexpected states. It is also important to know that the app need not be in the foreground for the crash to occur. Any app component, even components such as broadcast receivers or content providers that are running in the background, can stimulate an app crash. Tackling the crashes requires meticulous handling and one of the most important steps is to understand the root cause for this case. The following are some of the tips that can help you to understand crashes better:

- Reading and understanding the stack traces
- Creating a *crash-environment* to reproduce the same crash occurrence
- Understanding the Memory Errors and Network Exceptions, which are critical

To help developers understand the quality of the app, Android Vitals displays information that provides great insights on crash analytics. On this screen, you can filter as per the duration: last 24 hours, last 7 days, last 24 days, last 30 days, and last 60 days. You can also filter as per different Android Versions and the production versions:

Crash overview

Clicking on each of these clusters will allow you to see respective analytics of the crash. It shows the crash occurrence details for the clicked cluster along with the numbers, such as total reported occurrences, reports of crashes this week, number of unique users who experienced a crash from this particular cluster, and the last reported crash:

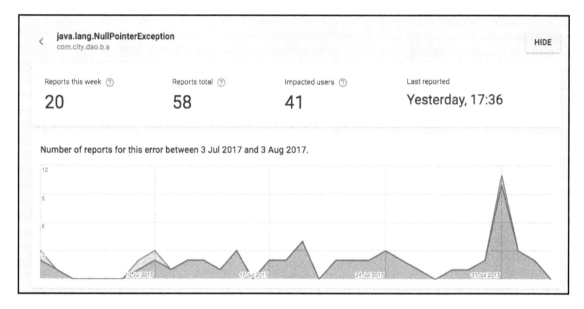

Cluster overview

This dashboard also provides information for this cluster on the app version, the Android app version, and the devices. You can also see the entire stack trace of the total number of crashes for this particular cluster, for each device:

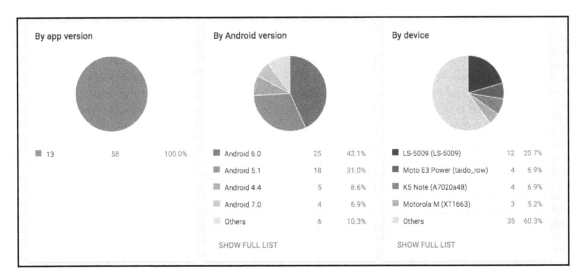

By app version			By Android version			By device		
▣ 13	58	100.0%	▪ Android 6.0	25	43.1%	▪ LS-5009 (LS-5009)	12	20.7%
			▪ Android 5.1	18	31.0%	▪ Moto E3 Power (taido_row)	4	6.9%
			▪ Android 4.4	5	8.6%	▪ K5 Note (A7020a48)	4	6.9%
			▪ Android 7.0	4	6.9%	▪ Motorola M (XT1663)	3	5.2%
			▪ Others	6	10.3%	▪ Others	35	60.3%
			SHOW FULL LIST			SHOW FULL LIST		

Analytics by the app version, OS version, and device

Battery is dear to the user, and most of the app developers do not unnecessarily keep device radio and CPU on, which can impact the battery performance. Android Vitals allows you to identify two major causes of the battery drain:

- **Excessive Wakeups:** Wakeups occur when alarms produce time-based activities, which prevent an idle device from sleeping. Android Vitals allows you to understand whether such occurrences are seen. It maps the percentage of battery sessions during which the user experiences more than 10 wakeups per hour. This data is collected only when the device is not charging and a session is calculated between two full charges of a device. Fixing the problem is not as tedious as it looks. Earlier versions of Android Platform had the `AlarmManager`, but the implementation of `JobScheduler` or Firebase `JobDispatcher` has overshadowed `AlarmManager` over time. Avoid using `AlarmManager` to schedule background tasks, especially the tasks that involve repeating or network background tasks. One of the key advantages of using `JobScheduler` or Firebase `JobDispatcher` is batching. Using batching, you can run simultaneous jobs so that the battery consumption is reduced. This implementation can also be triggered based on criteria, such as running the jobs under specific conditions such as Wi-Fi availability or the charge state of the device. These tasks can also be maintained in a persistent state; that is, jobs that are marked persistent will continue to run even after the device is rebooted.

- **Stuck Partial Wake Locks:** Wake Locks occur when an app has your system working so hard that it won't allow it to sleep. In Android Vitals, you can see the percentage of battery sessions during which users witnessed at least one wake lock of more than 1 hour. Like in the case of Wake Ups, this data is also based on the period between two full charges of a device. Data is collected only when the device is off the charger and the screen is off. One thing that needs to be noted is that some apps do require long wake locks, such as in the case of streaming service apps.

The speed at which your app renders on the screen can largely contribute to the experience of using the app. It not only can make a user engaged with the app, but if not rightly rendered, it can stimulate bad reviews on the app store. Android Vitals provides information on two of the key aspects of performance rendering:

- **Slow Rendering:** To ensure that the app is smooth, your app should render frames in under 16 ms to achieve 60 FPS (frame per second). The UI rendering is a process of generating a frame from your app and publishing it on the screen. A slow UI rendering can force the system to skip frames, and this will make users to witness stuttering in your app, known as jank.
- **Frozen Frames:** Frozen Frames can make your app appear to be stuck or unresponsive to user inputs for a full second, even when the frame is undergoing rendering. Theoretically, frozen frames are the UI frames that take longer than 700 ms to render. Sometimes, an app can take a longer duration, especially when starting or transitioning to a different screen, because your app must inflate views, lay out the screen, and trigger the initial draw from scratch.

Android Vitals automatically monitors the app for jank and displays the information that can help developers improve app quality. Under Slow Rendering analytics, the section displays the percentage of daily sessions during which users experienced more than 50 percent of frames with a render time higher than 16 ms. On the other hand, Android Vitals displays Frozen Frames as the percentage of daily sessions during which users found more than 01 percent of frames with a render time higher than 700 ms.

If you use ProGuard to optimize and obfuscate your APK files, Android Vitals allows you to upload the app's ProGuard deobfuscation file to deobfuscate future stack traces for any specific APK version. Under the **Android Vitals** | **Deobfuscation** Files option in Google Play Developer Console, you can upload the ProGuard deobfuscation files for each of the versions, as follows; these mapping files may be used to share a detailed crash and analytics data:

Uploaded	Version	Mapping uploaded on	
⊘	**13** (1.1)	–	UPLOAD
⊘	**12** (1.1)	–	UPLOAD
⊘	**11** (1.0.2)	–	UPLOAD
⊘	**10** (1.0.1)	–	UPLOAD
⊘	**9** (1.0)	–	UPLOAD
⊘	**8** (1.0)	–	UPLOAD
⊘	**7** (1.0)	–	UPLOAD
⊘	**6** (1.0)	–	UPLOAD
⊘	**5** (1.0)	–	UPLOAD

Uploading deobfuscation files in Android Vitals

User Feedback and Analytics

Valuing customer opinion is one of the essential ways to understand how well your app has been received. Google has recently updated the console to help app developers to understand the ratings and reviews from the app users. The dashboard gives developers clear indicators of the total ratings and the average ratings of their app. It also shows the total ratings with the reviews for a better understanding on how many users have left a review:

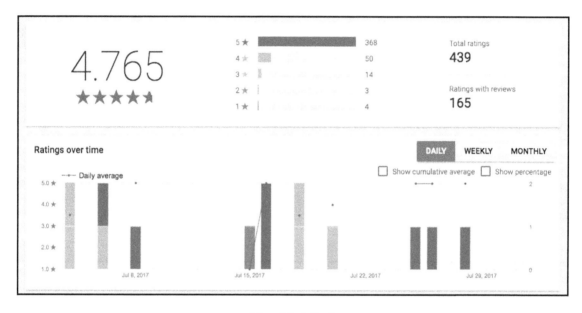

Rating analytics dashboard

The reviews help to understand the way users use keywords. These keywords play an important role in App Store Optimization.

The overview dashboard also shows rating-based filters, as shown in the following image; the user can sort the options based on ratings and periods, for example, Last Day, Last Week, and Last Month:

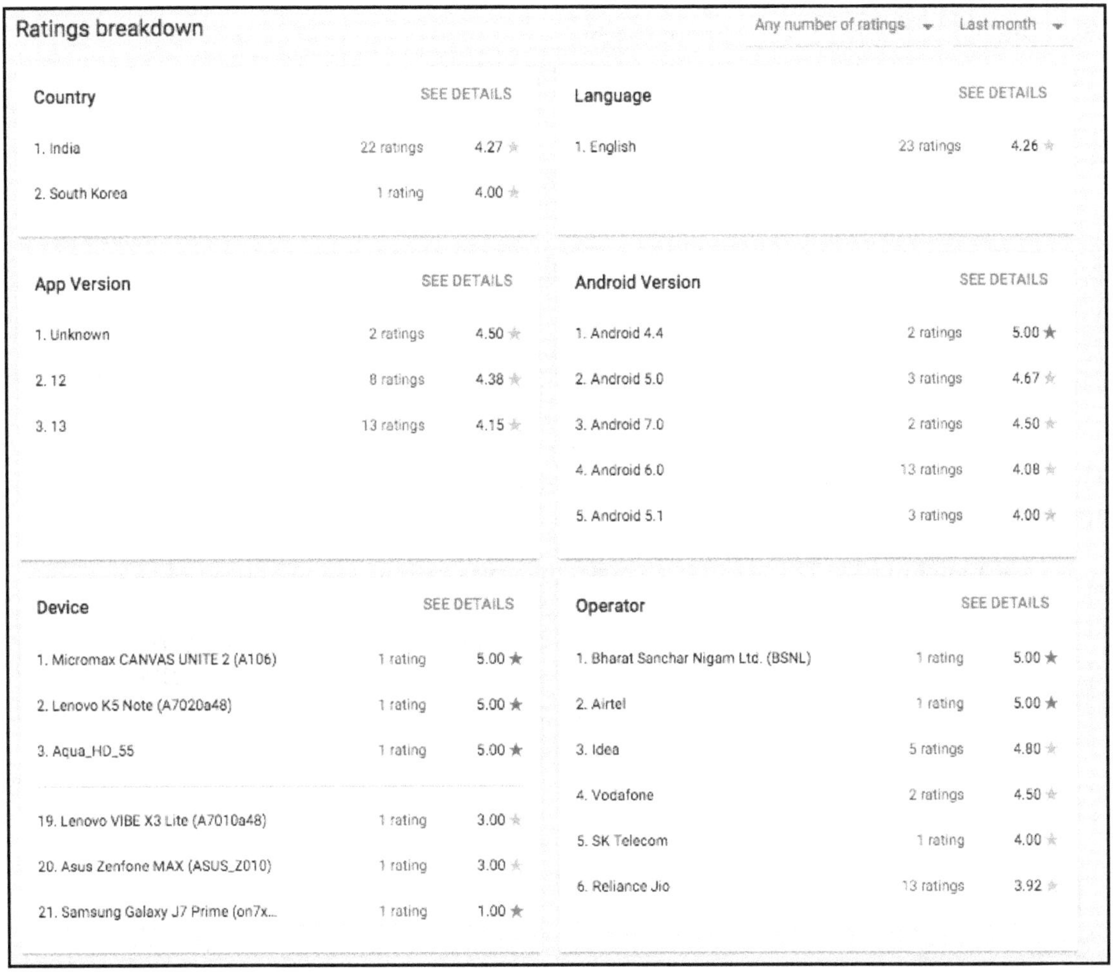

Ratings breakdown			Any number of ratings ▾	Last month ▾

Country		SEE DETAILS	Language		SEE DETAILS
1. India	22 ratings	4.27 ★	1. English	23 ratings	4.26 ★
2. South Korea	1 rating	4.00 ★			

App Version		SEE DETAILS	Android Version		SEE DETAILS
1. Unknown	2 ratings	4.50 ★	1. Android 4.4	2 ratings	5.00 ★
2. 12	8 ratings	4.38 ★	2. Android 5.0	3 ratings	4.67 ★
3. 13	13 ratings	4.15 ★	3. Android 7.0	2 ratings	4.50 ★
			4. Android 6.0	13 ratings	4.08 ★
			5. Android 5.1	3 ratings	4.00 ★

Device		SEE DETAILS	Operator		SEE DETAILS
1. Micromax CANVAS UNITE 2 (A106)	1 rating	5.00 ★	1. Bharat Sanchar Nigam Ltd. (BSNL)	1 rating	5.00 ★
2. Lenovo K5 Note (A7020a48)	1 rating	5.00 ★	2. Airtel	1 rating	5.00 ★
3. Aqua_HD_55	1 rating	5.00 ★	3. Idea	5 ratings	4.80 ★
			4. Vodafone	2 ratings	4.50 ★
19. Lenovo VIBE X3 Lite (A7010a48)	1 rating	3.00 ★	5. SK Telecom	1 rating	4.00 ★
20. Asus Zenfone MAX (ASUS_Z010)	1 rating	3.00 ★	6. Reliance Jio	13 ratings	3.92 ★
21. Samsung Galaxy J7 Prime (on7x...	1 rating	1.00 ★			

A breakdown of the rating

In the **Review Analysis** section under User Feedback, you can see how users review your application in relation to a specific category. This data is exclusive to app developers and not visible to the users. The Updated rating, as shown in the following screenshot, shows the way your app's ratings and reviews were updated, including the effect your replies had on those updates:

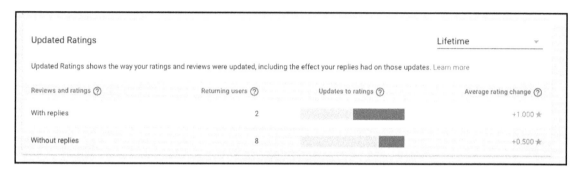

Updated rating analytics

There are two reports-Benchmarks and Topics-that analyze how each topics impact the app's overall rating.

- **Benchmarks:** This section displays the app's ratings for a fixed set of topics and compares these ratings with apps in a similar category. For example, if the app is of the News category type, then this benchmark will display ratings based on similar apps in the News & Magazines category. This analysis is available for reviews written in English:

Benchmarks display

This section defines certain data points to the review analytics. The following table explains each of the points in detail:

Data points	Value
Common Topics: A fixed set of topics relevant to most apps in the same Google Play category	• Design: Reviews that mention the app's visuals (for example, looks nice, good graphics, and so on) • Profile: Reviews that quote the app's sign-up experience (for example, signup, login, can't logout, can't login, and so on) • Resource usage: Reviews that specify the app's impact on hardware consumption (for example, battery, memory, data, and so on) • Speed: Reviews that mention the app speed (for example, slow, fast, and so on) • Stability: Reviews that mention app failures (for example, crashes, bugs, freezing, and so on) • Uninstalls: Reviews that reason why uninstallation has taken place (for example, uninstall, uninstalling, uninstalled, and so on) • Update: Reviews that mention quotes about the latest app version (for example, version, update, and so on) • Usability: Reviews that mention the user's experience while using the app (for example, user friendly, hard to navigate, and so on)
Average Rating	The most negative reviews will be marked in a red color with a rating of 1. On the other hand, be positive reviews with a rating of 5 will be green.

Number of reviews	The number of reviews associated with that topic. The line chart displays the change in volume over the length of time selected.
Effect on rating	Red bars bring down your rating, and green bars indicate improvement in your rating. The width of the colored bar shows how much that topic impacts your overall rating.

Additionally, the statistics also show data about your app in the Peer comparison mode against some of the other apps in the same category. The following table explains both the categories:

Type	Description
Rating versus Peers	Points at the ratings compared to other apps in the same category. For example, if your score for your app Speed is 2.3 against the benchmark difference of +1.0, the other apps will be at 3.3.
Number versus Peers	How the number of reviews per topic compares to apps that are on the Google Play store in the same category. For example, if your app has 2,000 reviews for stability with a volume difference of 0.5x, the similar apps in the same category will show average review volume as 4,000.

- **Topics**: This sections details your app's ratings for a set of dynamic words mentioned in the app's review. It is supported for reviews written in **English**, **Spanish**, and **Japanese**. Clicking on any of these translated topics leads to the Reviews section with that tag highlighted:

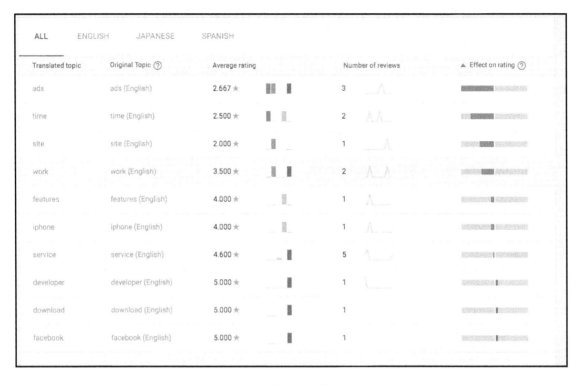

A review topic analysis

The *Review Analysis* section shows a list of all the reviews that have been published by the users using your app. The Dashboard overview provides the average rating of the app, and the section also has an option to filter the reviews based on the options, as follows:

A filter of reviews

One of the most interesting features of this filter is the **ADD DEVICE FILTER** option, which allows app developers to see the reviews based on users specific to a particular device. For example, if you wish to see reviews given by users using the Moto X phone, simply click on **ADD DEVICE FILTER**, search for the phone, and save the filter to show up the results.

The dashboard also allows you to reply to each of these comments and share the reviews. Each comment by the user is complemented with options that help developers understand the nature of the device and its system configurations. Simply click on the **MORE** option to get a detailed preview of the configuration:

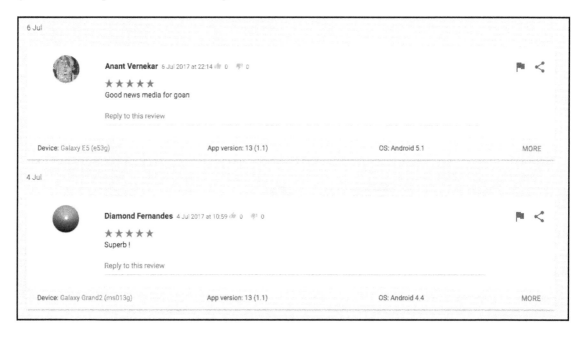

Review and replies

A lot of app users tend to change their rating and update the reviews based on how their problem is attended. For example, let's consider that your app had sign-up issues and you have received a 1 star rating. After updating your app, if the user is satisfied and the issue is fixed, they might want to change the ratings and reviews. The entire history trail of how the users have updated the ratings and the reviews can be seen in this section.

Google Play Developer Console makes it simple to understand the updated comments, with a small tag marking **UPDATED** in the left section of each updated comment to make the app developer notice the comment. The orange colored marking shows the updated comments, whereas the dashed lines show the scrapped lines from the user's previous comments.

In the Beta Feedback section, users can privately send app developers message, based on the testing done on the Alpha and Beta versions of the app. This is applicable when you run an open alpha or beta testing program for your app.

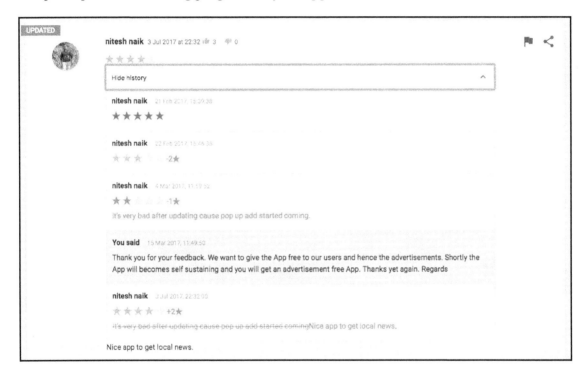

Review and rating changelog

Summary

At the start of the chapter, we discussed how to generate a signed APK. Once the signed APK was generated, we discussed how to prepare this APK for alpha/beta testing options on the Google Play Listing. In the final section, we glanced through some of the options available on the Google Play Store Listing for an app, where we highlighted the basic options along with Store experiment features, which allow users to experiment with the store listing.

16
Understanding App Store Analytics for Optimization

When you are ready with your app listing, one of the most essential components that plays an important role in the success of the app is the visibility of the app, among other players in the similar domain of app. Google Play Search is key for users to find relevant and popular apps for their Android device. For this very fact, it is important to constantly improve your app store listing and perform optimization steps to help your app be discovered by users on Google Play.

App Store Optimization (**ASO**) is a continuous process of improving the characteristics of the app for creating visibility for the app and stimulating more downloads from app stores. To achieve this, app developers need to focus on several factors, such as app name, keywords, descriptions, graphical assets, and promotional video.

There are a couple of myths surrounding ASO, and one of the most common ones is performing ASO just once. Some of the people think that ASO can be done just once and then, forgotten about. Remember that every day, there are many apps that get published on the app store, and it is important to monitor the keywords' ranking regularly. We highly recommend keeping a long-term marketing strategy that must be in line with continuously monitoring keywords over the lifetime of your app.

Now that we have spoken about keywords in the first myth, the second myth is just about it--over dependence on keywords. There's no doubt that keywords are essential while searching the app, but you also need to make the app visually appealing so that it tempts users to download it. The visual cue can impact the user's interest in downloading the app, especially if the app has a beautiful app icon and compelling screenshots. Sometimes, these elements can help convince users to choose your app over your competitors', irrespective of how popular the other app is.

One fact that can't be denied is that most apps are downloaded via organic downloads. Though many of the app developers also choose paid marketing to get downloads, ASO still holds the key to tempting user's' download interest. ASO is also a very cost-effective way of getting more downloads.

Let's discuss some of the key ways to improve the ASO of an app.

Keep an eye on Google Play policies

Before starting to talk about ASO, it is important to know who's the boss. Google has certain guidelines for apps and games that get published on Play Store. It is important to know the same, to allow users to download legitimate apps from the store, which are under the policy terms of Google Play. The details of the policy can be read at `https://play.google.com/about/developer-content-policy/`.

Get your app title right

Google Play Store allows the app name to be up to 30 characters. The algorithm understands the keywords in the title of the app in a better way than from any other source. This is the very reason you have to be very selective in choosing your keywords. The question to ask yourself is *Does my app hint what the app could be doing?* Using a keyword in the app title can be another way, but it depends, on a case-to-case basis. Take a look at keyword density patterns to understand what keywords will go with the title of the app.

For example, let's take the case of the game **Candy Crush Saga**; the name is good enough to hint what the game could be doing:

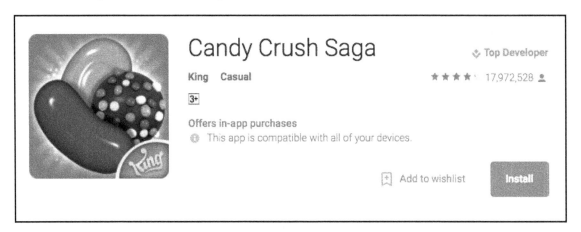

Title hinting the app's theme

Effectively using keywords in description

Most of the searched keywords are pulled from the description of the app, and Google allows up to 4,000 characters for the description of the app. Google does not permit apps to have improper, misleading, irrelevant, or excessive metadata in the app. The same applies for titles, icons, screenshots, and promotional images. Google does not allow users to even post testimonials on the app's description.

Having settled the mentioned points, also ensure that the description reads in mobile-friendly mode. This doesn't just allow users to read, but also allows better formatting presence. Try to use more effective keywords in the description. Also, based on your competitive keywords, try to change the description more often to match market demands on how people search for the app in your category.

When given the privilege of 400 characters, the chances of users reading all of it is rare. We highly recommend presenting the first three lines of your app description in the most appealing manner. This doesn't just catch the attention of users but also tempts them to download.

The Google Play app description also allows formatting of text. As in the following case, **Candy Crush Saga** description uses bullet points and paragraphs to format the content well. This content is also mobile friendly for the users:

Take on this deliciously sweet Saga alone or play with friends to see who can get the top score!

Candy Crush Saga is completely free to play but some optional
in-game items will require payment.

By downloading this game you are agreeing to our terms of service; http://about.king.com/consumer-terms/terms

Candy Crush Saga features:
• Tasty ways to play: Target Score, Timed Levels, Drop Down Mode and Order Mode
• Collect sugar drops to progress along the Sugar Track for super sweet surprises!
• Spin the Daily Booster Wheel for a delicious prize
• Pass level 50 to unlock Dreamworld and escape reality with Odus the Owl
• Unwrap delicious environments and meet the sweetest characters
• Tasty Candies, wrapped and striped Special Candies, Color Bombs and various other magical boosters to help with challenging levels
• Hundreds of the best levels in the Candy Kingdom with more added every 2 weeks for your entertainment
• Leaderboards to watch your friends and competitors!
• It's easy to sync the game between devices and unlock full game features when connected to the Internet

Formatting description more effectively for readability

You can also test out using long trail keywords in the descriptions. Many of the app developers follow single word characters without use of long trails, which can be effective and less widely used, hence producing a competitive edge.

Does your icon reflect the app theme?

App icons are the most impactful element of the app. Though it is simple to put down, it's equally difficult to build an icon that speaks all about an app. The best way you can come to a conclusion is by either building an app like a branded icon if you have an established brand, or by elaborating on what the app does:

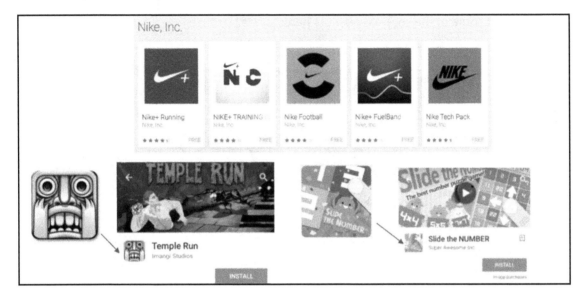

Effective App Icons

In the preceding figure, you can see several examples from Nike. Since the brand is known worldwide, it uses the *Nike* symbol in almost all the apps they have on the Google Store. This allows them to put a relation in the user's mind that these are Nike apps. On the other hand, take a look at the icon of **Temple Run**. The app is not just clear on the desktop view but also, when scaled down on mobile, retains its resolution. However, in the case of **Slide the NUMBER**, the app icons shrinks and it's hard to understand what the app icon is about. One thing we would like to recommend is to not be afraid to experiment with variations of graphical assets after the first version.

Are your app screenshots nailing it?

The most obvious choice for many app developers is putting up the same screenshots of how the app looks. This may not be a great strategy. Screenshots are a great way to make your app appealing to prospective users. Like they say, pictures speak a thousand words; have a great blend of app screenshots. Take a close look at how the screenshots look on the mobile app as eventually, many users will search the app via the mobile Google Play app. Take a look at some of the cool screenshots here:

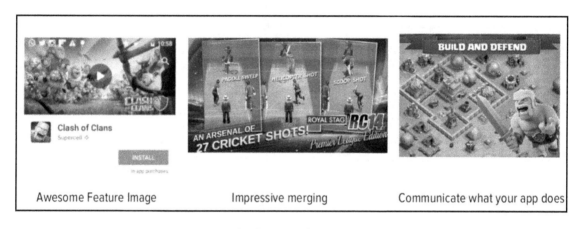

Appealing screenshots for your app

If you are still tempted to use app screenshots, there are some techniques you can use to present it with awesomeness, such as the following example, wherein the app flaunts the key features of the app along with the screenshots, but in a well-presented manner. The app developers highlight the key features in the bright-bold manner to catch attention and use the keywords that they can relate to photo capture apps:

Using the app screenshots

Another interesting way to show off the screenshots is using emotional connections. Nothing connects with users better than emotional bonding. Use the emotional bond to tempt users to install the app. Some apps even share the awards that the app has been rewarded with.

Both the preceding cases can be best explained by the following app screenshot:

Emotion as a weapon of tempting

Some of the most common errors made by the app developers are underestimating the value of the screenshots, as in the following case, wherein even though the app screenshots are great, there is a repetition of the screenshot:

Short of images? Do not repeat

Say a strict no to the following kind of screenshots that are pure cases of being heartless. No matter how many app features you may have, if the screenshots are not appealing, there is a lesser chance for it to be downloaded. Also, avoid screenshots with text-heavy content, as shown:

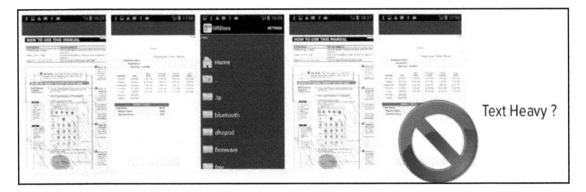

Avoid text-heavy screenshots

Here are some of the best practices you can keep in mind when you prepare the store listing for your app:

1. Have at least 5-6 screenshots of the app. Make the first three screenshots the most appealing ones as they are the ones that will be glanced at most often.
2. Ensure that individual screenshots communicate one benefit each of your app. This keeps users to check the screenshots, rather than spending time reading the description.
3. Keep screenshots clean, bright, and easy to read. Use the best of resolutions.

Use emphasis, magnification, or pointers to specific areas in the screenshot to show off the key aspects of the app.

Video can be a crowd puller

Though not many apps use the feature, it is an essential feature in the kitty. If your app has multiple features that can't be shown just by screenshots, videos can be handy. The first thing to remember is to keep videos as short as possible. Embed lovely music that just catches user's' attention. If you are using voiceover, ensure that it is clear to understand:

Context Video   Feature Video

Promotional videos in app listings

In the case of games, many choose to have multiple videos to show features of the app. If you still wish to create a longer video, aim at telling a story to the user. This can be an effective way to create visual impact.

Responding to reviews

Reviews is one of the best ways to know how people search for the app. Some of the keywords in the comment can hint at how people speak about your brand in the public. Check out mediums such as Twitter and Facebook to know how they use your app name and what context are they speaking about. Use the keywords of the app in comments wherever applicable.

There's no that doubt positive ratings and reviews can encourage customers to download or purchase your app. However, also ensure that you are responding to negative comments. By delivering great responses, you can turn up your rating as well.

There are several types of people who post their reviews and ratings. Ensure that you handle each case well. For example, in the case of people who talk highly technically about the app, avoid responding in depth; keep the communication crisp and get in touch with them offline by asking them their email.

One of the most common mistakes people make is buying paid reviews and rating services from several sites. Avoid this to ensure legitimate reviews on your app; there's nothing more special than actual users reviewing your app. It doesn't just allow you to receive feedback, but also allows you to learn from the criticisms posted.

Keep a close eye on the reviews and rating section analytics, which provide you with an amazing analysis on how the ratings have been given:

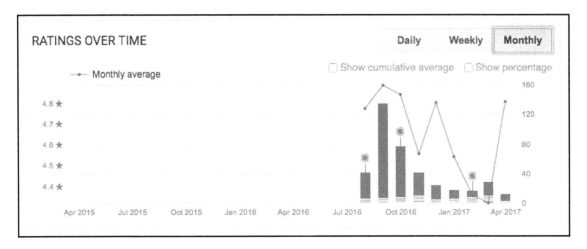

Review analysis

Are you LOCALizing?

Localization is the process of translating your app, which enables users to understand the context of the app across the specific region. For example, if your app is targeted to be used in Germany, having support for this locale can be an added boon. If you are launching the app, you may not think of going international right away. You can use experiments to understand what kind of users are accessing the app and from which countries; based on that, you can tweak your app pages.

You can just localize the elements of your app that appear on the app stores. This includes app descriptions, keywords, and screenshots.

There was an interesting case shared by Google on how localization of one of the Indian Maker **Zombie Ragdoll**, as illustrated, increased the app installations:

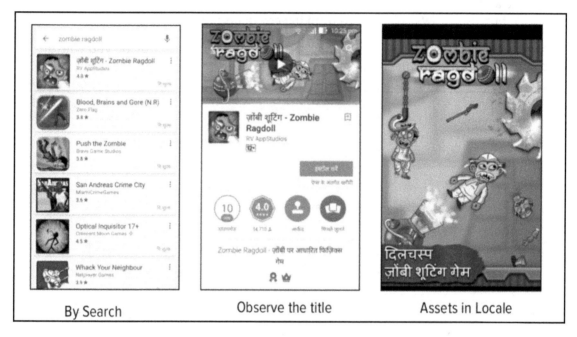

By Search   Observe the title   Assets in Locale

Local support in Zombie Ragdoll

The app makers understood that 80% of installs came from non-English language users, which tempted them to use local support in the app. The preceding screenshot makes this case clear.

Summary

The chapter started with helping users understand why ASO is important, followed by some of the tips that developers can leverage for improving the ASO. One thing to remember is that conditions in the App Store change constantly, so it is important for the app makers to adhere to them to stay on top of the changes and the growing *mobile ecosystem*.

Index